What Doesn't Kill Us
Brandy Liên Worrall
Rabbit Fool Press
Vancouver

"War does not determine who is right—only who is left."

- Bertrand Russell

Part One

Trade

Things are not fun right now. In fact, they kinda suck. However, things that suck usually turn out funny later—much later.

Take, for example, the time I was home from college for summer vacation. I was out with my best friend Lisa writing poetry at the local truck stop. A few background details: Lisa and I were dorks in high school; our hometown, Mifflintown, has more churches than restaurants and more cattle than people; and there was not much else to do other than compose angst-filled poetry about how much we loathed being forced to reside there.

I came home from the truck stop diner at midnight, satisfied with my witty sonnet about some dickwad from our graduating class fucking his John Deere tractor. As soon as I walked through the door, there was my cute little Vietnamese mother sitting in the dark, waiting for me. She jumped up out of her chair, pointed a crooked arthritic finger at me, and said, "Where were you, ha?! You go out and be a whore?"

"Um, no. Lisa and I were writing poetry at Stop 35."

"Yeah, that's right! You be whore!"

Did she mean that poetry is the equivalent of whoring, or was she just completely ignoring what I said and just agreeing with herself that undoubtedly, I was out whoring? I wasn't sure.

"Mom, first of all, there's no way I would have sex with anyone in this shithole town, no matter how much money they gave me. Second, seriously, we were writing poetry."

"You write till midnight, ha? Whore!"

She yelled some more. She tried slapping me, but I

caught her hand midair and backed away and went into my bedroom and locked the door. I heard my dad bellow in his slow rural twang, "Goddamn it, Liên, go the hell ta bed!"

Then, the next day. I called my older sister, crying, thinking about how Mom might try to murder me in some sort of honour killing for whoring. Sis calmed me down ("That's Mom. You know how she is."), and I went on with my life, not acknowledging my mother's existence, she not acknowledging mine. One day went by. Two. Two and a half. Dad broke the silence.

"Brandy, apologize to your mother."

"What? I'm not apologizing to her, Dad! She called me a whore. You know I was just hanging out with Lisa, writing poetry!"

"I know that, but she was just worried sick about where you were."

"And that's her way of showing it? By calling me a whore?"

Enter the mother. She breathes fire. Sit still. Hold your tongue. It'll be over soon. Just think happy thoughts while your face becomes damp from her spit and fury. Think about crowd-surfing at concerts, the biggest bong in the world, and a car full of Reese's peanut butter cups. Think about anything other than how you hope you don't inherit this insanity someday.

Years later, Lisa and I still laugh about it. Sometimes it comes up in therapy, and I work through it. But god, isn't it hysterical, that story? Can you believe that really happened? I can't either! Me, being called a whore for writing poetry! And there's more! But I don't think you could handle how hilarious it is.

Too bad though, I lost that sonnet about that dickwad fucking his tractor. I remember it being a good one.

My parents come to live with me and my family in my times of need, but I always question if I really, *really* need them to come. Sure, it is an epic odyssey to get from Amish-country Pennsylvania to Vancouver. One needs to cross three time zones, a border, and eras of social progress and urbanization. My Pennsylvania Dutch grandparents can hardly fathom such a trip. During one visit to my hometown, I sat down with my grandma after a ginormous Worrall family dinner and chatted with her. Mammy always asks me about my life in the big city, since she never really leaves our village in the valley, Arch Rock.

"You're not afraid to get on them big planes?"

"Not at all, Mammy. It's more likely you'll be in a car accident than a plane crash."

"Oh, Brandy, I could never do something like that, go so high up in the air. You're my brave little girl," she said, taking a bite of her devilled egg.

Mammy's fear and awe of flying shows you how much my family resists change and exploration. Which is why whenever I supposedly need my parents to fly out to Vancouver, the rest of the Worrall clan thinks it's like they're coming to rescue me from the hard city life, which they know exists because they watch *NBC Nightly News with Brian Williams* (though they usually refer to him as That Youngish Man That Replaced Tom Brokaw).

I do need my parents sometimes, but here's the dilemma: my mom drives me fucking crazy. I know what you're thinking—everyone's mom drives her children crazy. No, you don't understand. My mom is exceptionally good at what she does. And honestly, no grown woman should suffer living under the same roof as her mother, especially if her mother is a CAM—Crazy Asian Mother. My dad, he's okay, but he can be a handful sometimes. He was diagnosed with post-traumatic stress disorder from his tour of duty in the Vietnam War and sometimes takes his drinking and drugging to new heights. Right now, he kind of just slouches in whatever comfy chair he can fall into and dozes, thanks to the prescription drugs he gets every month from the VA. Anyway, when I pick them up at the airport, or even before that, like when my husband Charles says we need to go on a trip and maybe my parents could come out and watch the kids, and so can I ask them and make the arrangements, I think, *do I really have to?*

But I do. Because I feel bad. Seriously. I talk to my parents on the phone every week, and every time, my mother says sadly and hopefully, "You come home soon, ha? Or you need me come?"

I, remembering my last vow never to spend more than two weeks with them ever again, say, "No, Mom, I don't need you to come."

When she says, "Okay, you no need mommy," I feel both guilty and defiant.

When the opportunity arises for them to visit us, I struggle all over again. They want to come, a lot. My mom often thinks about how she left behind loved ones in Vietnam when she married my dad and made a life in Pennsylvania with his family, about how she never got to see some of her family again because they died before she could go back to Vietnam. I think about that, and I feel bad. I don't want my mother to miss out on this part of her life and family, like she had to with her family in Vietnam. The only distance that's too great is the one that causes a lifetime of regret.

I relent. I ask them to come. They are more than happy to do so. They get to see their grandkids, my mom gets to hang with her Vietnamese homies in my East Vancouver hood (there ain't that many Viets besides my mom in Mifflintown, like none), and my dad gets to buy sweet BC weed from my next-door neighbour.

But hey, what about that defiance I was talking about? The defiance that shouts, "You don't need your mom to come! You don't need her crazy-making in this house! You're fine. You are a capable mother on your own, and you don't need to go travelling or whatever reason it is this time!" Well, never mind that. It'll all be okay this time. Just watch.

I walk into my son's room. Mom has plopped my two-year-old in front of the TV and is feeding him hotdogs. Why is she doing that?

"Mom, you shouldn't feed Mylo. He can feed himself now. Why don't you put him in his high chair in the kitchen?"

Staring right at Mylo, she says, "That not your mother. That Brandy." Holding Mylo's attention, she points to herself and says, "I your mother."

What. The. Fuck.

"Mom, don't say that. I don't like it."

She looks at me, laughs, and repeats, "I your mother, Mylo." She rubs a speck of ketchup from his chubby cheek. Mylo squirms.

"Mom, please stop saying that." My face is getting hot and tingly.

"Oh, he no understand anyway. I joking."

"It's not funny. Don't say it again."

As I walk out of the room, I hear her say loudly to my son, even though she's really saying it to me, "Your mother no like what I say. Okay, I no say no more."

I stomp downstairs to find my dad sitting in the leather recliner, watching an episode of *Law & Order*. I plunk down on the couch and sulk.

"What did your mother do now?" Dad asks. He folds his hands across his soft belly and turns his attention away from the television.

"She's telling Mylo that I'm not his mother and that she is."

Dad shakes his head. "I'll talk to her after this show is over."

"What's the point, Dad? It's not like she listens. I don't really want to go to Asia with Charles. What'll she say to the kids when I'm gone for a couple of weeks?"

"She won't say nothing. Go have a good time." He turns back to the TV.

Dad and Sis are shitty at trying to make me forget Mom's nuttiness. She won't say anything? When has she not said anything?

Meditate. Just breathe. Lie down on the couch and listen to the whir of the ceiling fan and try not to imagine a freak accident where it falls and decapitates your mother. That would be bad. But at least she'd be quiet. No, she wouldn't be quiet. That dismembered head is going to yap and criticize and say wildly inappropriate things to you until your universe explodes out of frustration. This meditation isn't working. Just close your eyes. Maybe you'll be magically be blessed with deafness.

Mom appears out of nowhere and stands over me.

"What you doing, ha?! Just lay on couch, sleeping? Why you no make your husband supper?" The shrieking reaches into the depths of my soul.

"Mom, I'm just lying here for a second. I'm exhausted. I've been doing homework all day for school. Please let me rest." Mom doesn't understand that doing homework doesn't mean doing simple math but rather writing a twenty-page personal essay for the nonfiction workshop, a short story for the fiction workshop, and a poetry portfolio for the poetry workshop in my MFA program.

"You better go cook for your husband, or he leave you. Why you have pimple all over your face? You no want be ugly like that. Charles no like that, he like pretty young woman."

"Charles isn't coming home for at least another hour, probably more, so why would I make him dinner now? And if he wants to leave me for my acne, he's welcome to do so because that's a lame excuse for leaving someone."

"You better no talk like that to him. Why you no talk nice, like sweet?"

"Why don't you?"

"I your mother. I no talk nice to you. I talk right."

Before my head kablooms into a billion microscopic pieces, Mylo waddles into the room. He comes over to me and hoists himself on the couch and wriggles on top of me to snuggle. He's a hefty little guy, but his weight and warmth comfort me, like a thick, soft blanket. I rub his back. He grabs the squishy skin of my right elbow and squeezes and rubs it between his fingers. My elbow is his blankie. He can rub my elbow and suck on his bottom lip for hours.

Dad interrupts Mom. "Liên, be quiet! I'm trying to watch my show."

She humphs and skulks into the guest room. She shuts the door, and I can hear her Vietnamese Buddhist music and chants. It's her way of re-centring and telling herself that she's above us all.

Mylo turns his head on my chest. I feel soreness where he has positioned his head, and I move him a few inches so

I can feel what that soreness is. There's a little ropey bump, about the size of a marble, on my boob. I push on it. It hurts. I could see the doctor before going to Asia, I guess.

Oh fuck me. The stress. The headache. Asia, school, work, kids, my crazy-ass mother. Dad snores. He's out. I'd like to take some of his drugs. Lucky him, the U.S. government recognizes that he lives with a lunatic and gives him medicine to cope. Actually, if they really understood the situation as such, maybe they'd give him even more.

It's a week before I leave for Asia with Charles on his summer exchange class. My husband is a university professor, and for a month he's teaching a class of undergraduate students about the history of migration. Me, I'm just going to eat loads of food and drink oodles of beer and watch people and write, but not in a sleazy ex-pat kind of way. I might engage in more beer-drinking than usual, however, just so I can stop obsessing about how Mom is trying to poison my kids against me and kidnap them and raise them in rural Pennsylvania. You might think that she'd get stopped by Homeland Security before that would happen, but Mom uses Jedi Buddhist mind tricks to get her way when encountering border agents in any country. One time, she smuggled a suitcase full of ripe mangoes from Vietnam. The customs dude at O'Hare knew she had them (I could smell them as soon as I heaved her luggage off the belt at Harrisburg Airport), but he let her go anyway, despite the strict regulations against bringing in fruit from another country. She'd be a perfect drug mule, except that she hates drugs because ingesting them is a sin that would cause her to be reincarnated as an ant, or something like that. It's true. She showed it to me in one of her Buddhist books. Except that my Vietnamese literacy has become shitty over the years since I started studying it, so I couldn't actually read it to verify this. She hates it when I speak Vietnamese because I was taught the northern dialect, and she speaks the southern dialect, so when I talk to her in Vietnamese, it pisses her off. According to her, "You talk like communist, all gargle." Every time I think of speaking Vietnamese, I have the urge to gargle Listerine too.

Before I get to my own personal beer-drinking contest in Southeast Asia, I decide to see the doctor about that lump on my tit. I'm pretty sure it's harmless, like a really large boil or bump from Mylo's massive head resting on my chest, but it's been drilled into women to check out any sort of odd thing we find on our boobs.

"Hey, Mom, I'm going to the doctor. Can you get Chloe from preschool?"

"Why you go to doctor? What wrong with you?"

"Nothing. I just have this thing on my boob."

"What thing?"

"Nothing, Mom. Just this thing."

I pull down the neck of my shirt so she can check it out. She puts two fingers on the lump and gently pushes on it.

She furrows her brows and says, "You better go have them take it out."

"They have to see what it is first. They just don't cut shit out of you like that."

"Yeah, okay, go see doctor. Mommy get Chloe at school."

There's softness in her tone. My heart fills with warmth and sadness because I haven't heard that kind of tone much in my life. She herself has never been accustomed to sticky gooey feelings from family. Her mother was physically abusive with her, but Mom never saw it like that. She felt she deserved the abuse and that, in fact, it had made her a better person. Knowing that, I was surprised by her sudden gentle concern.

"But you be back soon. No run round! Charles come home, he get hungry."

Just like that, the warmth is gone.

When I leave the house, I release a deep sigh. I've noticed that I always do that when I close the front door and start down the sidewalk.

I'm all sweaty when I arrive at the doctor's office. I decided to get some exercise and walked the five kilometres to the appointment. The waiting room is packed, and the doctor is running behind schedule. Finally, the nurse calls my name, and I follow her into an exam room.

"What brings you in today?"

"I found this lump on my right breast."

Without glancing up from her chart, she tells me that Dr. Mansur will be right in. A few minutes later, he breezes into the room.

"You say you have a lump in your breast. And you're... thirty-one years old, is that correct?"

"Yes."

"When did you detect this lump?"

"Two weeks ago."

"When was your last period?"

"A week before I found the lump."

"Do you have a history of breast cancer in your family?"

"I had a great half-aunt who died of breast cancer, but other than her, no."

"I'm sure it's nothing. You're too young to have cancer, so you shouldn't worry about that. Probably hormonal. Let's have a quick look." He puts my chart on his desk.

I lift up my shirt, unhook my bra, and indicate to Dr. Mansur where the lump is. He squints at it, lightly touches it, and scribbles on my chart "benign appearance."

"Nothing to worry about. Just keep an eye on it. If it gets bigger, come back."

I shrug. "Okay, thanks."

I walk home, head aching. As I push open the door, I can smell rice cooking. Mom's making dinner. She's trying to make up for all that she thinks I cannot be.

"Okay, Brandy, I have to tell you something. Chloe said that her mama ran away. I told her that no, you didn't run away, that you would be back soon, that you and her daddy are just working." I'm on the phone with my mother-in-law, and she's cautiously reporting the highlights in the kids' lives over the last week. One more week before I return to Vancouver. I had thought that all had been well on the home front, that Mom had been "normal" (like normal people normal, not CAM normal) until she and Dad went back to Pennsylvania last week and my in-laws took over childcare. Why would I be so foolish as to think that?

"Ma-Ma, I think my mom probably said something to Chloe like that. I don't know why she says those things."

"It's okay, Brandy, I tell them that you are returning soon, and Chloe is not saying it anymore. She'll be fine. She misses you very much."

"Can I talk to her?"

"Yes, hold on one moment, please." I can hear Ma-Ma go into Chloe's bedroom and coo with her Chinese accent, "Ca-lo-ee, your mother would like to talk to you." I hear the phone drop and then be picked up by clumsy fingers.

"Hi, Mama!" Hearing her tiny voice brings me to tears.

"Hi, Baby Girl! How are you?"

"Good, Mama! I'm playing. Mylo is taking a nap. You and Daddy coming home soon?"

"Yes, I can't wait to come home and tell you all about Asia. I got you and Mylo some really fun toys. Be good for Nai-Nai and Yeh-Yeh, okay?"

"Okay, Mama! Bye!" Chloe hands the phone back to my mother-in-law.

"Brandy? You see—she is fine. Not to worry. Just have a good time, okay?"

I hang up the phone, emotionally exhausted after only a five-minute phone call home. What was my mother thinking, telling my kids that I ran away? Thanks to the universe that my mother-in-law isn't insane. Baby Jesus Christ.

This is my second trip to Asia, and no, I've never been to Vietnam. People are always surprised when I tell them that. They assume that I naturally would've visited my motherland by now. But the first couple of trips Mom made since she left in 1971, she took only my sister. I guess she figured I had no interest, or it would be too much work for her to tote around her American mixed daughter. So I stayed home with Dad. We lived separate lives in the same house, in peace and quiet. Dad took the opportunity to drink and drug to his heart's content, and I relished temporary serenity.

When Sis and Mom returned, Vietnam seemed to me like some nightmarish ancestral destination. My sister and mother's faces were bruised from the cosmetic surgery they got there. My mom's face was stretched tight and swollen from a facelift. The skin around her hairline and jaw was yellow from healing.

It's common for overseas Vietnamese women to return to Vietnam for cosmetic surgery procedures that make them look, ironically, more Western, like getting double eyelids or narrower noses. I always thought my mom and sister had been beautiful already.

Sis was bone thin, which was saying a lot because she had already been skinny. After returning from the first trip, my sister said, "I'm never going back there again," though she would make a second trip a few years later.

Later, when my sister and I were in her apartment, she told me about her trip.

"It was horrible, that's all," Sis said with a blank stare. "Imagine being there, not being able to speak Vietnamese and having Mom in total control."

Sis left Vietnam with my mom and dad when she was seven years old. With my sister's father nowhere to be found, my dad had officially adopted her, and when they came to Pennsylvania, he didn't want Mom and Sis to speak Vietnamese anymore, only English. Sis also didn't want to speak Vietnamese, so that Dad could understand at least half of the conversation between her and Mom, especially when Mom was being more crazed than usual. She eventually lost the ability to speak Vietnamese, but she could still comprehend what was being said.

"Because no one thought I understood Vietnamese, the family kept saying horrible things about me, but I understood everything," Sis continued. "They're terrible people, especially Uncle. He just wants Mom's money."

Imagine being in a different country where you can't speak the language and your only guide is a raving lunatic who translates everything for you, and likewise translates what you say back to the natives. If there is a hell, that'd be mine.

Sis also told me about family whom she'd hope to visit but wasn't allowed to: her biological father's family, especially her grandmother and aunt. But for some reason, our mother's family forbade her from going. When she described her hopes to me, I felt like something had been lost for her, but I didn't know exactly what. It was just something I couldn't really speak to or about. A bone-deep loss that could break your soul into scattered fragments that don't fit together the same way ever again.

As I sit in this ancestral home-turned-hotel in Malacca, I watch these strange birds—they're strange to me anyway—nest in the corners of the courtyard ceiling. They've gathered straw and mud, and their droppings dry up behind a bench below them. It's peaceful here, and I can collect my thoughts in my journal. My kids know I will come back to them.

The exchange class is wrapping up, and all the students are going home today. Charles and I are headed back to Singapore for a few days on our own before we return to Vancouver. I want to go home now. I miss the kids so much. And sorry, but for all the bragging about how clean Singapore is, it's not tree-hugging, pristine, polite, cool-climate Vancouver.

Charles and I are at that self-help, couples-therapy point in our marriage. We don't talk much, and the sex is *meh*. Frankly, it's abysmal. I try to not obsess about it, but c'mon, I'm only thirty-one years old. It's not like I don't want to get laid. Quite the contrary. I've had an astonishing number of brazen adventures back in the day. Not that I'm saying that I need to go relive that, but I need something. Anything.

This alone time is good. Then again, we've had alone time during this whole trip. Charles has always been too tired or wrapped up in the course he's teaching to pay much attention to our relationship. Maybe now is the time.

We're at an underground food court that's beneath three stories of nightclubs and bars. The food is good and cheap, but the patronage is unsettling. I never imagined that I would possess a gawking naïveté when it comes to sleazy old white guys walking hand-in-hand with young, petite Asian women, but yeah, I got it. As I'm trying to focus on my steaming bowl of chicken *laksa*, my eyes are drawn to this one wrinkly, ruddy-faced dude and his heavily made-up lady friend in a skirt so short I'm not sure why she bothers. She turns her head my way, and before I look away, I can see that she is a he.

I lean over to Charles and try to be subtle in pointing out the couple. "Do you think that old dude knows he's with a transsexual?"

"Where?"

"Over there." I blink my eyes and purse my lips in that direction.

"I don't see what you're talking about."

"Seriously, Charles, do you not see that old white guy in the Hawaiian shirt with a lady-like person who could be his granddaughter, except that she has an Adam's freakin' apple and angular jaw, which would make her his grandson?"

Charles finally squints his eyes in their direction and says loudly, "Oh, them! Yeah, I see now."

I roll my eyes at him.

"Maybe that's what he likes," is his final verdict before digging into his ginger chicken with fried rice.

I feel like prodding. "Don't you think it's weird seeing all these old dudes with sex workers?"

He shrugs. "I guess."

Then I say what I've been thinking. "Maybe they're not sex workers. Maybe they're married."

He swallows his rice before saying, "You honestly think that?"

"Yeah, well, what about my mom and dad? They're legit, and he's a white guy and she's Vietnamese." Like I have to remind him what my parents are.

"What about when they met? You think they were legit back then?"

"I don't know. But that was during a war. There's no war here."

I know, war or no war, there's always the sex tourism industry in Asia. It's just kind of weird and hard to see it right in front of me. The rare virginal sensibility in me—that I actually didn't know I had—comes out as a defense against the truth. I don't feel like eating anymore.

"Wanna go check out the nightclubs upstairs?" I ask. I'm guessing that the customers down here are spilling out from the clubs above us. Hunger is probably common after engaging in paid sex.

I want to see what the sex worker thing is about first-hand to get over my innocence and denial, but do I really want to pay for a sex worker? What would we do with her, or him-her?

Charles raises his eyebrow. "If you want to, sure," he says.

We finish our food and head to the clubs. A disco ball casts shimmers on the dark walls. The bartender looks bored. Everyone, either worker or patron, stands drunk and listless. The music is giving me a headache. This is fucking depressing.

"This looks lame. Let's go back to the hotel," I mutter.

"Good call," he says.

As we walk back to the hotel, I notice more and more sex workers eyeing us. I become paranoid. Do they think I'm one of them? Do they want to get with Charles? I thought we were staying at one of the fancier hotels in Singapore, but maybe that's an indication of one's intentions as a tourist here. The more money you have to spend, the more you'll spend it on sex?

We return to the room. I try to take my mind off this whole prostitution trade, or maybe channel that energy for my own purposes. I hug Charles, sinking my body into his. He smiles and then sighs.

"I'm really tired, and I have a bunch of email I've put off," he tells me.

Fuck me. No, really, fuck me. But fuck me, you suck, you fucking fucker.

"Okay," I say. "I'm tired too. I'm going to sleep."

I lie down on the bed. Charles settles at the desk and opens his laptop. I think about what it was like when we first got together, when I was a graduate student in California, and I was his teaching assistant, and how I had this major schoolgirl crush on him. He was the young, charismatic professor. I didn't think my crush would turn into anything. But it did. Now, seven years and two kids later, this is where we are.

I close my eyes, and I can hear my mother telling me to be his servant, his slave, to give him what he wants, anything at all, whether it be food, sex, or even another woman, just so he won't leave me. How many times has she told me to be careful because he's always around young girls he teaches—girls who will always be younger and prettier than I am? I laugh at her, but her words stay with me.

I want to go home. I want to go back to my kids and tell them I'll never leave them again. They are my constant. With them, there's no abandonment.

PART TWO

Core

http://brandybug22.livejournal.com/
July 7, 2007, 11:47 PM
Edward, RIP

My brother-in-law passed away this afternoon. He was forty years old. He was diagnosed with stage IV lung cancer three years and five days ago. He leaves behind a wife and two daughters. Edward was amazing in all that he had accomplished in his short life, and in many ways, he and Charles are a lot alike. I watch Charles, and I wonder what's going on in his mind. Right now, the hardest thing is to look at pictures of Charles and Edward when they were little boys, playing together. And then I think of Charles's parents. I'm sad knowing how they weren't able to say goodbye to their son before he passed away. They were planning on going to be with him the past couple days, but they just didn't get there soon enough. I suppose it must be common to think this, but it seems like it happened so fast. I mean, sure, he hadn't been doing well for the past few months, but all of a sudden—he's gone. We didn't know we wouldn't have a few more days to get there, to be by his side. Now it's too late. I just hope that Edward was at peace when the moment came. I hope he's at peace now. I love you, Edward—we all do. May your spirit live on.

Current mood: sad :(

About ten hours ago, I was playing with the kids when Charles's dad called to say that Edward wasn't breathing. Maybe it was the calm in Ba-Ba's voice, or maybe it was the fact that we'd spent three years with Edward's close calls that have always ended in him pulling through—whatever it was, it didn't strike me that *that* would be the moment. After all, this was Edward we were talking about—my brother-in-law who despite having terminal cancer had taken on numerous international architectural projects while undergoing aggressive chemotherapy and radiation. Edward had toured the world giving lectures and presentations. He'd been active with his beach and ice hockey leagues. Edward had made it clear to everyone that he wasn't ready to die, even up til a few months ago, when he came to Vancouver to give a presentation to one of the most prestigious architectural organizations in the world. His cancer had metastasized to his brain, but he stood up and delivered his speech, which ended in a standing ovation. He collapsed in his wheelchair afterward, but he did it.

There was a price to Edward's defiance and independence. He didn't want the family to hover around him as he was dying, even up to his final breath. Since his diagnosis, he fought his parents' natural inclination to help take care of him. We could tell how much his resistance broke their hearts, especially Ma-Ma's, but we tried to respect his wishes. A couple of times, I emailed Edward and his wife Cindy, asking them to put themselves in Ma-Ma's shoes, asking them if they could imagine a time when, god forbid, one of their children were to fall ill and how they might want to be there in whatever way was allowed. But Edward and Cindy wanted to deal with cancer on their own, thus that was how it had been.

During this last week, Cindy told us that the time was near, that Edward was close to the end. We started making arrangements to go to Los Angeles to be with them. But there was confusion. Was it really the time now? First, Cindy said to come, then she wasn't as sure. We waited.

This afternoon, when Ba-Ba called to tell me that Edward had died, I didn't believe him. Didn't I just see Edward play hockey a few months ago? I told Ba-Ba that I would call Charles to let him know, and I hung up, in that daze that you get when someone has just died and his life flashes before your eyes.

I called Charles, who was out giving a lecture tour on Chinatown. He said he'd come home right away. I spent some time watching the kids, letting the tears fall as they played. Edward wouldn't get to see his daughters grow up. The girls were already exhibiting some likeness to him—Alison with her drive and creativity, Lindsay with her showiness. What parts of me would Chloe and Mylo carry on and make their own if something were to happen to me?

A few hours ago, Ba-Ba, Ma-Ma, and Charles's sister Liz flew to Los Angeles. Charles and I can't go yet because I have a core biopsy on Monday morning. Really, it's the last thing on my mind, and I know it's not serious. I went back to the doctor last month because that lump on my boob got bigger. Dr. Mansur wasn't there, but there was a female locum. She didn't think much of the lump either, but just to see what it could be, she ordered an ultrasound and told me it was likely a benign cyst that would end up being drained.

I did the ultrasound two days ago, and the radiologist said that the lump looked interesting. She sent me to the room across the hall to get a mammogram—and then another mammogram. It was weird to be sitting in a room full of old women dressed in hospital gowns from the waist-up, a lot of whom were looking at me funny, as if they were pitying me for being young and being there. I tried not to freak out. After all, the doc didn't say, "That totally looks like cancer." She said, "That looks interesting." I usually like interesting things.

After the second mammogram, I waited for the doctor to come tell me when I should have the cyst drained. Instead, she told me to come in for a core biopsy first thing Monday morning, and she handed me instructions for how to prepare for the procedure. They want to make sure what it is before it's drained.

It's almost midnight. I'm trying to quell the cacophony in my head. Charles is downstairs working on his laptop. The kids are asleep. With Charles's parents and sister in LA, there's a stillness, a time for rest.

That core biopsy sucked ass. I'm so freakin' pissed that no one told me how much it would suck. It's kind of like how no one said shit about childbirth. When I gave birth to Chloe, I was amazed that nobody had told me about how I'd have to do extra work after she was out, delivering the placenta that was almost as big as she was, or how pushing feels like taking an impossible dump. These are key bits of info that every expectant mother should know! Or do folks figure that they won't disclose that info because it would scare the living daylights out of whomever? Anyway, how come no one told me that this biopsy procedure is the technicians and doctor using a staple gun with a thick, giant needle attached, which shoots into my flesh to extract tissue? Sure, they froze the area beforehand, but one of the lumps was way down in a place where the freezing didn't go, and I fucking felt that shit. Oh yeah, and thanks for not telling me beforehand that I have three lumps instead of one that needed to be biopsied. . .and oh right, that there are lymph nodes in my armpit too that you had to use a needle for, digging that shit in my armpit and that fucking hurt like a bitch motherfucker. God! Ranting is more effective than the ibuprofen they told me to take for the soreness. Soreness? That shit hurts! I got this bloody fucking gauze taped to my boob, and I have this baggie full of ice melting all over my shirt. This blows.

Charles is at a meeting, and the kids are taking a nap. They have no clue about my boo-boo. Right now, no one does. Only me.

I have a new blog. I've really been into the blogging thing the past two years, creating blogs for everything that I could think of: my poetry, my short stories, my foodie adventures, my book reviews, my life in general in the ever-eloquent genre of rant. Add to that repertoire, a blog for my cancer.

How will this persona reflect the others? How will this voice speak more loudly than the rest? Or how will it exist more quietly?

I'm also sending out an email to hundreds of our closest friends and colleagues, announcing the reason why I might be MIA from dinner parties and conferences, or why I might decline involvement in the next exciting academic/activist/artist project in the next few months. In other words, you'll see less of me in real life and more of me on your computer screen, where the dying doesn't look as bad close-up.

How melodramatic, Brandy. I'm not dying. I'm not.

The blog is also there to remind me that I have cancer because when I wake up, I forget, or I think the whole cancer thing is a dream. Then I go to the bathroom, look in the mirror, and suddenly, I remember. I touch my breast to make sure, and yeah, the tumour is still there. Diagnosis: disbelief.

Three days after my biopsy, I got a call from the doctor's receptionist to come in immediately to discuss the results. I was surprised that they came back so soon because I was told that it would take at least a week to get them. When Charles came home from a meeting, we took the kids to his parents' house and went to the doctor's office. Of course, Dr. Mansur wasn't there. Or maybe he was there, but he was too chickenshit to give me the news.

We went into the exam room and waited. A young female doctor came in, and right away she looked nervous and scared. She blurted out that I have breast cancer.

This is the first cancer diagnosis she's ever had to give, I thought.

I looked at Charles. Fuck. What did she say? What? Now she's saying she's sorry? Is she sorry that she had to do the shitty job of telling a thirty-one-year old woman with two kids under the age of four that she's got cancer? Oh, now she's covering up her feelings of shit with big words. *Invasive ductal locally advanced carcinoma blah blah blah.*

The pressure in my chest was too great, and the tears started coming. Of course, Young Miss Sorryass Doctor didn't come prepared with tissues. It hadn't occurred to her that her patient might start crying when she gave her the diagnosis. I wiped a long line of snot on my arm. She ran out of the room to find a box.

I don't remember how we got from the room to the street, but I entered my second wave of shock as I watched traffic on Pacific Boulevard and Davie Street. Some kids were playing soccer at David Lam Park. A woman jogged by me and rounded the corner. I ran a 10K twelve days ago, a Canada Day race. My time sucked because I had pain in my leg, which turned out to be a stress fracture. I finished the race anyway. Even though I have cancer. I have cancer. Cancer—it has me.

I stood transfixed at the corner of the intersection, not sure which direction I was facing. The water to my left. The mountains in front of me. Sky above. Standing at the divide between then—ten minutes ago, before my diagnosis—and now, all this weight bearing down on me, held in place by gravity. Where have I been placed? Do I cross this street?

The atmosphere suddenly became so foreign, everything with its vitality, unaware of or unconcerned with my diagnosis. I remembered how my mother said she got so sick during her first winter in Pennsylvania. She arrived at her new home during a snowstorm. Heavy icicles hung precariously off roofs, and thick flakes limited her sight so badly that she couldn't see ten feet in front of her. She told me of how she struggled, how she almost died the first few months there, how she wanted so badly to go home. She crossed the divide, and it was the hardest thing she'd ever done. That's when her new normal began.

I understand now, Mom, the divide. The harsh precipice between there and here, then and now.

When Charles and I got home, he called his parents and gave them the news. That moment was shittier than getting the diagnosis. Their first-born died of lung cancer five days ago, and they just got back from LA where they said goodbye to him. Now they are being told that their daughter-in-law has breast cancer? What the fuck.

Ma-Ma said that she and Ba-Ba would watch the kids for the rest of the day. It was my turn to call my parents.

In his sleepy twang Dad said, "Hello?"

"Hi Dad. Whatchu doing?" I was trying my best to keep my shit together.

"Nothin'. Your mother is watering her garden."

"Dad, I have something to tell you." My voice cracked.

"Uh-huh?" he asked.

I couldn't speak. Dad's tone took on one full of concern and worry. He suddenly sounded more awake.

"Brandy, what is it?"

I slid down to the cold kitchen floor, lodging myself into the corner between the sink and the stove. "Daddy, I have cancer." The uncontrollable sobbing started, and I felt like I was six years old.

"Brandy, now you listen to me. You've got to be strong."

The old dad I knew as a kid—the one who wasn't medicated and half-conscious—was talking, and that made me sob harder. Then I thought of the mom I had as a kid, the one who blamed me for every illness I got, including epilepsy. The mom who, upon hearing me cough in the middle of the night, stormed into my room with a bottle of Vicks Vaporub, dug out a glob with her index and middle fingers, and shoved what was supposed to be a topical ointment in my mouth and down my throat, angrily telling me that me not wearing socks around the house was why I was coughing, which woke her up in the middle of the night, which pissed her off like nothing else. That mom was still the same.

"Dad, please talk to Mom for me. I can't tell her about it right now."

"Just relax. Are you going to be okay?"

"Yes, Dad." Deep, deep breaths.

"Okay, I will talk to your mother, and you call us when you have more information. We will come out as soon as you want us to, okay? It's going to be fine."

I believed him. I had to.

I heard the screen door slam in their house. Mom, done watering her garden, shouted, "Hey, Lee! Where you?"

"Dad, I have to go."

"You call me later, Brandy. I love you."

"Love you too. Bye."

I held my head in my hands. Charles had taken to his laptop to research all that he could about my type of breast cancer, I assumed.

I got up off the floor and walked over to him. I stood before him, my face puffy from crying. He stood up. As we hugged, I looked out the window at the street below. He smoothed my hair. I kept looking at the streets and sidewalks, wondering about other people who are living their lives, wondering what they've got going on.

I released myself from Charles's embrace and walked downstairs to sit in the recliner that my dad likes to doze in so much. I kept thinking of a poem that I'd published five years ago, a poem that I wrote about my mother's mother, my *ba ngoai*, about how my introduction to my grandmother was the day she died. I was almost seven years old, and on that day I was fixated on collecting fallen leaves. When I came back into the house, I saw my parents in the kitchen, hugging each other. It was an entirely foreign sight to me. Mom was holding a really thin letter, and she was crying. Dad told me that they just found out that her mother died. Her ghost followed me in the sense that life could be snuffed out just like that, even before it's been realized. Here was a woman who was so close to me by blood, but I had never met her, I'd rarely heard talk about her, and then all of a sudden, she came rushing at me in the form of death, of passing on and beyond me.

I don't want to be gone, just like that, like Ba ngoai, I thought, my life as thin as that letter that had travelled so far to reach my mother's hands.

Dear Dr. Mansur:

We received your request for payment of $75 for photocopying our files and transferring them to our new family doctor. Please find enclosed payment for services.

We had been quite confident about your level of care since we began attending your practice. However, in the past year we've found that as your popularity as a doctor has increased, your attention to patients has been lacking. Your presence at the clinic has also been inconsistent, leaving our family in the care of random doctors. It was for these reasons that we began considering looking for other family practices.

But the real clincher was when I came in to see you in March for a lump that I'd discovered in my breast. You gave me a quick physical examination and told me not to worry about it, that it was nothing, and to come back if it got worse. It's true—why worry when the patient is a thirty-one-year-old woman with no family history of cancer? But I still worried, and the lump was tender, and at the very least, I wish it could have been examined more closely.

The lump didn't get worse in terms of size (as far as I could tell), but it became more painful, and in June I came into your office for a second consultation. You weren't there; instead, I saw Dr. Suzuki, who told me it was probably just a cyst, but she would order an ultrasound just to make sure, and that they would likely drain it.

As you might now know from looking at my chart, it turned out that it wasn't nothing at all—that in fact, I have stage III, locally advanced breast cancer, with three confirmed tumours in my right breast and two masses in my lymph nodes. My situation thus far is going to require a six-month chemotherapy trial, a mastectomy, and radiation.

I am not angry about your misdiagnosis, Dr. Mansur—only regretful that you didn't take the lump seriously and at least order at ultrasound, which is really not that hard a thing to do. I'm also regretful that I wasn't more proactive about my situation and insist on an ultrasound. I will always wonder what a difference three months could have made in my situation, but I also have to move on and heal. I just wanted to let you know about my situation so that in the future, if a young woman comes into your office with a lump in her breast, you take her more seriously. After all, you yourself—as well as other doctors—tell patients to check for lumps and other abnormalities in their breasts and to report anything that might be of concern. I did what I was told, and I was not taken seriously. In hindsight, this could have proven a crucial time to correctly diagnose the condition and start receiving treatment.

Unfortunately, it is the case that more and more young people are being affected by cancer. Five days before my diagnosis, my brother-in-law passed away from lung cancer, and he was only forty years old and a non-smoker.

Along with wishing you the best for your continued practice, I also hope that you will remember my case and take younger patients more seriously when they come in with concerns such as mine.

Sincerely,

Brandy L. Worrall

I signed the letter, folded it around my cheque, stuffed it in the envelope, and sealed and addressed it. Then I beat the shit out of my pillow because what I really wanted to write was how much of an ignorant motherfucker I thought he was and how ludicrous it was that I was giving him a $75 cheque for him making a huge-ass mistake that left me no choice but to switch doctors.

I've tried my best to remain calm and positive. When I met my oncologist for the first time, I was introduced to a new culture and language. Cancer-speak has a bunch of long words describing how bad cells take centre stage in the body they're inhabiting. The body is a battlefield, the war between the colonizer and the colonized. I have to learn the language of the colonizer. (Thank god for my postcolonial ethnic studies graduate degree, or I wouldn't be feeling as smart and self-satisfied as I do right now.)

Dr. Simpson is really nice, sympathetic, and sharp. She relayed a lot of the tough info in a deliberate and tender way, taking out her notepad and drawing a picture—which I'm sure she's drawn a hundred times before—of my tumours and how she wants to defeat them. There were even X's and O's and dotted lines. Charles and I took it all in, but the part that knocked the wind out of me was when she said the word "mastectomy." I mean, I joked on my blog about getting new boobs and all, but I didn't really think that I would have to amputate my tit. I thought I'd just have the lumps taken out or something. But no—chop, chop, and no more fun boobie time.

Dr. Simpson's plan to put me on a six-month chemo trial, rads, and then a mastectomy caused Charles and me to have concern that I'd have to live with the tumours for another nine months. But Dr. Simpson and her nurse reassured us that this is the best course of action, especially in preventing a recurrence. I signed the papers agreeing to be part of the clinical trial, my life as an experiment.

Dr. Simpson gave me a prescription for a wig, for my impending alopecia. Charles and I looked at it and laughed.

"Holy shit, I'm gonna lose my hair," I said and suddenly stopped laughing. I was beginning to feel completely manic about all this cancer bullshit.

"Yeah, you are," he said, glancing at my reddish-brown-black hair.

"That sucks. I should dye it some funky colour, yeah?"

"Whatever you want," he said, smiling.

The wheels started turning in my head. Whenever I've had a major life change in adulthood, I've gotten either a tattoo or a piercing or both. The height of my bod-mods was when I got my septum pierced before Chloe was born. Mom constantly berated me for looking like a bull. ("Why you want look like that for, ha? I pull you by nose and give you grass? So ugly!") But as I had children, I found that stretch marks and scarred holes began replacing piercings. First went the navel ring. Then grubby toddler hands pulled at my lip ring, so out of fear of my bottom lip being ripped out, I removed it. Next, I stopped wearing my nose rings. When Mylo came along, out came the septum ring. All that are left are my tongue ring and earrings. Now, however, was not the time for any of that. Instead, I decided to hold onto my wild side by dyeing my thick locks into a punky rainbow of joy.

I told Charles I wanted to have a pre-chemo party. Everyone could help me dye my hair, like a community art project. I announced the party on my cancer blog. I've started to have this weird disconnect with the blog, where I think I'm only writing to myself, but it turns out that hundreds of people are actually paying attention to it. It was shocking to see all the RSVP's and well wishes for a fun night.

A day before the party, one of my best friends from grad school showed up to help me bleach my hair. Jamie has been a big Hapa brother to me for the past eight years. Jamie is half-Filipino, half-White, so we understand each other's mixedness. We've worked together on mixed-race projects for years. He's also the closest friend to me from my life-before-Charles, distance-wise, since he lives in Seattle. I'm beyond grateful that he can hop in his car to drive two hours north to see me.

"Dang, girl, your hair is so thick. It's gonna take a few treatments to get all the colour out," Jamie said.

"Well, whatever we gotta do, right? Oh my god, that shit stinks like fermented pussy and rotten eggs!" The smell of the bleach took me back to when Sis would dye Mom's hair blue-black every six weeks, to cover up all the evidence of how old she really was. The acrid fumes also reminded me of the overpowering stench of ammonia that had been flooding my nose and throat months before my diagnosis.

Miraculously, my scalp did not itch or burn after Jamie applied three treatments in order to achieve our blank canvas. My hair white-ish, I started slinging back the wine, readying myself for a night of colour and near-debauchery. (Because I couldn't indulge in complete debauchery, being a mom and all.)

An assload of friends arrived, and I got mega-wasted in the process of my girlfriends putting purple, pink, blue, and yellow colour into my hair. I sat on the toilet facing the mirror, and they went to town.

Jenny draped a towel over my shoulders. Katie laid out a buffet of cheeses, sausages, and pickles that magically appeared out of her hobo handbag. Jamie kept handing me glasses of wine.

As Amy applied a line of deep purple, I shifted my eyes to the light above the sink, trying to avoid my reflection.

"Hey, Brandy, your hair is starting to look pretty hardcore!" I looked up into the mirror to see who the newcomer was. Michael was trying to get a glimpse through the crowd that I was surprised to see congregating at the door.

"Thanks! I think it's going to look hella dope!" I laughed, taking a sip from my wine. For a second, I stared at myself in the eyes. Then I looked away, hoping that no one caught me looking at myself.

Although everyone seemed in good spirits, I hoped that no one was feeling sad about what would inevitably happen to their work of art. Some of my friends brought their children up to watch, and they found themselves having to explain to them what cancer is. Meanwhile, my own kids were in the dark, too young to understand and in the care of friends who just wanted to make the night fun for them.

Charles remained downstairs the whole time, entertaining those who weren't as comfortable checking in on the dyeing process. I guess the dyeing made them think of me dying, and that was a hard thought to take, especially for the older folks.

With my rainbow head, I made my entrance downstairs. Everyone laughed and applauded as I brushed and swooped my hair from side to side. I noticed that my blouse was totally unbuttoned, exposing my bra, and I declared, "Well, y'all might as well take a good look while you can cause these puppies are coming off anyway!" I hoped that everyone else was wasted enough to find that as funny as I had. I fell into the beige leather recliner and accepted another glass of chardonnay. Everything became swirly and surreal.

When I woke up and looked in the mirror this morning, I touched my head, hung over and confused. It's still happening: I'm still waking up in shock at the thought of having cancer. I tried shaking the fog out of my head. At least my hair looked awesome.

I never thought I'd ever be sitting cross-legged in a Buddhist temple in Hawaii with a Zen master interrogating me about life and death and the cycle of suffering, but here I am. What would Mom, with her fervent Buddhist discipline, think of me now?

Roshi peers at me with a not-smile. I mean, it kinda looks like he's smiling, but he's not. He's just peaceful. . .but terrifying. He's doing an awesome job of freaking me out.

"You are now faced with death," Roshi says. Holy shit. He's freaking me out more than my oncologist did. He looks at me. He looks at Charles. He smiles, or not-smiles.

"I will prepare us some tea." Roshi gets up and turns to the door.

I squeak, "Okay." When he walks out of the room, I release a deep sigh.

It's weird and mystical how we ended up here. Charles and I came to Hawaii because he has a conference to attend, and I have friends to see. Three years ago, when I was preggers with Mylo, we were married here in a boat called The Love Boat, by a dude named Captain Kermit, just off Waikiki at sunset. Edward had just been diagnosed with lung cancer three years ago. There seems to be some sort of design to all this madness, this synchronicity, but I can't figure out what it is.

This time, as soon as we landed at the airport in Honolulu and collected our bags, we ran into two of our friends from Los Angeles, Ming and Angela. They were on their way out, and we were on our way in.

Ming was a colleague of mine from when I was an editor at an academic journal at UCLA. He is an amazing artist with an incredible history. He served as a bodyguard for Chiang Kai-Shek before coming to the U.S. to study film and art.

As for Angela, I had edited her collection of personal essays. Angela had been a very well respected lawyer who mediated for the Asian American community during the 1992 Los Angeles riots. A few years later, she gave up her practice to become an ordained Zen Buddhist priest. These two individuals have a magical aura around them under normal circumstances, but to run into them in an airport in Hawaii—that blew my mind.

"Ming!" I called out. His eyes widened with recognition, and he and Angela turned to embrace us.

"What are you doing here?" he asked.

"Charles has a conference, and we're kinda celebrating our third wedding anniversary too."

Angela touched my hair. "Why is your hair purple?"

A breath caught in my throat. I hadn't yet had to explain to anyone whom I've run into about my cancer diagnosis. When I told Angela and Ming about it and how I dyed my hair because I wanted to do something fun before it fell out from the chemo, Angela brought her hand to my breast, exactly where the largest tumour is, without me telling her which breast has the cancer.

"This was meant to be," she said. "Ming and I just spent a few days at this Buddhist retreat. You should go there. Roshi is usually very booked weeks in advance, but I will call him now and see if he can make time for you."

She flipped open her cell phone and made the call. She told Roshi about me. Then she turned and asked me if we could go to the dojo on Thursday. I nodded yes.

"Thank you, Roshi." She hung up the phone and looked at me. "You'll need to take out your jewellery and wear long sleeves and pants."

I didn't know what to expect, but this was all too unreal.

"Let me know how it goes, okay? You are strong. I know you will be fine," Angela said before giving me one last hug.

That's how Charles and I ended up here. Charles is demonstrating his Zen knowledge to Roshi, and I'm happy to let him talk. When Roshi turns his attention to me and grills me about why I'm attached to suffering, I want to crawl under the big rock outside the dojo.

Roshi returns with a tray of tea and cups.

My face hurts from trying not to cry, which is completely ridiculous because it's obvious to Roshi that I'm trying not to cry.

"Why are you attached to this suffering?" he repeats. "We all die. In the end there is nothing. Let me show you."

Roshi draws on a piece of paper: $0=\infty$. Whoa. I really wish I were stoned right about now. "Do you understand this?" he asks.

All I can muster is a blank stare. I hear cartoon crickets chirping.

"Why these attachments when in the end, they do not matter? Why should they matter now?"

"My mother taught me suffering her whole life. It surrounds my family," I say. I glance at Charles. He's staring into a corner, looking bored, or maybe uncomfortable, or no, he must be hungry. Or maybe he's thinking about Edward and how his suffering ended just as ours was taken to the next level.

"What good is that suffering going to do you now that you are ill?"

"It's all I know. I'm familiar with it."

"Do you like being in pain?"

"Of course not."

"I think you do," he says, staring into me with such conviction that he is really starting to annoy the fuck out of me.

"Why did you dye your hair purple?"

"Because I'm going to lose my hair, and I wanted to dye it before it falls out."

"It's going to fall out anyway. It is temporary. It will become nothing."

"I can remember how it was, though."

Roshi smiles. What does his smile mean? I am finding it hard to breathe.

"Let's walk." Roshi gets up, and Charles and I do the same. I peek at my cell phone. We've been here for three hours already? Time is a paradox in this place. It feels like we've been here forever, yet it also seems like it was just minutes ago that we drove up the curvy road through the mist and microclimates to get here.

Roshi leads us around the grounds. He shows us the ceramics that people created as a form of meditation. He tells me that normally I would come to the dojo to train on a frequent basis, but since I do not live here, I should be able to train by myself with a shakuhachi. Shaku-what?

Roshi hands me a thing that looks like a recorder made out of PVC piping. I stifle a laugh, remembering how much I sucked at playing the flute in elementary and junior high school.

"The shakuhachi is a form of training. Like all forms of training, it takes years to master, even though it appears deceptively easy. Try making a sound," Roshi says, handing me the instrument.

I put my mouth to the smooth curve, close my eyes, and blow. All that comes out is a pathetic sound of hot air.

Another Roshi dude walks into the room. Roshi tells him to help me out with the shakuhachi. He looks gentle and kind and way less scary than the first Roshi. Satisfied that I'm in good hands, Scary Roshi exits the dojo, probably to go float on a cloud or something. Fucker.

A squat White dude walks in and sits in the middle of the room, chanting sutras in a low voice that sounds like a bullfrog. This is starting to feel like some ethereal Japanese anime world into which I've been transplanted.

Roshi Number Two says, "Okay, now look into the mirror on that wall and focus on breathing from your belly."

I do as he says, or at least try to. It's hard to look at myself in the mirror and block out everyone. I'm feeling self-conscious and embarrassed, not to mention light-headed. I'm not sure I'm doing this breathing thing correctly. In fact, I believe I'm hyperventilating.

I keep blowing, but no sound is coming out. I look over at Charles, who is just sitting there staring at absolutely nothing. This must be killing him. I've never seen him do nothing. He's always facing a computer or a book or a newspaper. What is going on in his head? Is he thinking about Edward? I keep wondering if the stuff that Roshi's been saying has resonated with Charles, in terms of Edward's life and death.

Roshi Number Two interrupts my train of thought. "Focus. Close your eyes and visualize the air coming up from your belly with purpose, to make a sound."

I close my eyes and inwardly see a trail of air, and. . . "Toooooooooooo. . ." I manage to make a sound! I take a deep breath and try to make another one. "Toooooooooooooo. . ." Roshi Number Two smiles.

"Very nice. Keep looking at yourself in the mirror and then close your eyes. See what you can do. Relax. Breathe from your belly."

I focus on my breathing and nothing else. I soften my eyes as I look at my reflection. In this very brief instance I can accept my flaws and find them wonderful. I exhale, and a lovely hum emanates from the shakuhachi. My breath has purpose.

I make more notes, trying out different rhythms of breath. Sometimes I just blow empty hot air, but I become more consistent with creating notes.

Scary Roshi returns and asks Roshi Number Two how I am doing.

"Brandy is impressive. She has a rare quality for a beginner. She can play clear, strong notes with purpose."

Scary Roshi looks at me and says, "Show me."

I look back at him and say, "No."

Smiling, Scary Roshi walks away.

Charles is conferencing at the University of Hawaii, and I'm just chilling in the hotel room. Three years ago, when Charles came to Hawaii to attend a meeting for a huge grant he got, it was just another trip where I was gonna tag along. Days before we left for Honolulu, his divorce with his first wife was finalized, after a painful four-year process. We were finally able to get married, though it wasn't the first thing that popped into my mind when he got the papers. While we were working in our home office, he asked me if we should get married, since we were going to Hawaii and all. After that romantic proposal, we made arrangements online for our ceremony. I started getting excited and made a mixed CD of love songs. At six months pregnant with our second child, that was about as much excitement as I could manage.

When we exchanged vows on the Love Boat with Captain Kermit at sunset, I got pretty teary-eyed. All the hardships that had brought us to that moment came rushing at me. I was also sad because it was a bit anti-climactic. I'm embarrassed to say that I've always been a pretty stereotypical girly girl when it comes to imagining my wedding day, with all the frills that romance has in fairytales. Even though we were getting married in paradise, this wasn't how I'd always pictured it.

Charles, pragmatic as always, advised me not to change my surname to his. "You'll have to deal with all your credit cards, driver's license, passport, and all that. It'll be a pain in the ass." I felt hurt by his discouragement, but I did as he suggested. If he didn't care to have me take his family name, then why would I?

Now we are here, three years later. I still have my maiden name. I'm still suffering.

I *am* perpetuating some cycle of suffering. Of course, I can't help but think of Mom. She, Dad, and Sis passed through Hawaii after they got married in Vietnam, before settling in Pennsylvania. I remember seeing the picture of the three of them with some friends here. My sister looked miserable in her too-small clothes and the lei around her neck. She was only seven years old then. And Mom—did she think about the family she left behind as she got married and created a new family? What thoughts ran through Dad's head as he made his way home with a new wife and daughter? All of them, all my family, in their own ways, were attached to suffering—and uncertainty—just as I am now.

I close my eyes and listen to the hum of the air conditioner. I pretend that I bring the shakuhachi to my lips, and I blow. I breathe from my belly. I listen to the soft wisp of hot air leaving my lips.

PART THREE

Repurposing

http://cancerfuckingsucks.blogspot.com
Monday, August 6, 2007
Growing and Not Knowing
This sucker is growing fast. Last week, when I went in to see the trial nurse and oncologist, I told them how the pain has moved from the site where I first discovered the abnormality (on the left side of my right breast) to just near my armpit. The trial nurse straight up told me that the tumour is growing, not just faster but exponentially—which to me, just means even faster cause I mean, the sucker doubles and doubles and doubles some more. Then when I got another core biopsy done last week, I asked the technician to move the ultrasound thing over to my armpit to check out what was going on there. Instead of seeing the one lymph node I was expecting to see, I saw two—the bulging one that you can now feel by touch without having to look for it (before, the oncologist had to find it and push into my pit to locate it), and the smaller one beside it. I'm like—get this shit out of me now!

But you know, the consolation is that Chloe and Mylo have no clue. Everyday, I'm just Mama. Not Mama Who Has Cancer. They make the day go by quickly with all that's involved in raising an almost-four and almost-three year old. They want to snack, go outside, destroy spider webs (I discourage this, but what to do. . .), listen to seashells, make up stories about caterpillars eating ice cream and cookies and going into the cocoon and coming out as fat butterflies, count and point out colours of trees and mountains and houses and cars; they want to protest naps and baths, but when they nap and bathe, they're happier.

Chloe saw the big bloody strips of gauze on my biopsy site when I was changing clothes the other day, and she asked me if I had a boo-boo. I said yeah. She asked me if I was going to the doctor. I said I already went. She asked me how many doctors. I said two. She said, "Two doctors?" For some reason, it really intrigued her. Kids have such a sense of wonder. Then she wanted to paint her fingernails and toenails, which we did. Now, I'm really into painting nails.

As corny as this is, I'm trying to take my lessons from the kiddins.

Posted by Brandy Lotus Blossom at 10:33 AM

This waiting—I feel like it's going to kill me before the cancer does. I haven't started chemo yet, but it could be any day now that I get the call to go in. Funny how I'm so eager to be poisoned. I just had an image of me in Michael Jackson's "Thriller" video—a bald zombie with skin falling off in shreds.

Mom and Dad are coming to stay with us in a couple weeks. Mom is already being a lunatic when I talk to her on the phone.

"You wanna talk to your mother?" Dad asks in his happy-sad-sleepy way.

Um, not really.

"Sure," I tell him.

"Liên! Brandy's on the phone!" After Dad shouts in my

ear (forgetting to take the phone away from his mouth when he screams at Mom), I hear her pick up the phone.

"Hi! How you?"

"I'm fine, Mom."

"You start medicine yet?"

"Not yet. Soon."

"Why they take so long?"

"I don't know, Mom. I just have to wait my turn."

Her tone changes from fake-happy to angry in one second flat.

"You better not die."

"What? Mom! God, what are you talking about?"

"If you die, I don't know what I do."

"Mom, don't talk like that. I'm not going to die." I can't believe she's freaking out like this. I mean, yeah, I believe it, but still. . .

"I try protect you, you know. Now you sick. You can no be sick. You have husband and kids."

"Mom, seriously!"

I hear Dad yell, "Liên, knock it off!"

She screams back at Dad, "What, you no let me talk to my daughter?"

I hang up the phone. Am I nuts, having them come out here?

The phone rings. I stare at it like it's a grizzly bear that wants to snack on my left arm. "Hello?"

"Brandy, don't listen to your mother. She's just worried right now. You know that's just how she talks."

"Yeah, Dad, but I don't need that."

"I'll talk to her. I love you."

"I love you too, Dad. Bye."

I feel pukey, and I haven't even started chemo yet. That Roshi dude—giving me a lecture about suffering, telling me how I'm attached to it, almost chastising me, mocking me for wallowing. Fuck that. He's obviously never met my mother.

I don't know why, but my family likes to repurpose housing and recreation structures and such, giving them second and third lives. Mobile homes become two-story houses. My grandparents' chicken house, which used to be full of thousands of chickens raised for the Kosher chicken plant in town, turned into a pigpen, which later turned into a consignment shop. My parents' swimming pool became a holy site for full-body baptisms for Arch Rock Village's Methodist church congregation (Dad hung up two-by-fours that had "We are not responsible for injury or death" crudely painted on them, and Mom served pork, beef, and shrimp eggrolls at the baptisms), after which they filled it with dirt and cement and turned it into a goldfish pond and an extension of my mother's vegetable garden. And so it was that almost two years ago, I was sitting with Mom in her garage-turned-kitchen. Mom didn't like cooking in the house anymore because she said that it made her house stinky. She made Dad build a new carport for their vehicles, install running water, a gas stove, and a refrigerator in the garage, and furnish the non-cooking area with couches and loveseats they picked up from rich people's garbage in Harrisburg. It became the Mom Cave.

As Mom cooked hamburgers and French fries for everyone else who was in the house, I listened to her complain about Dad's inertia.

"Why he just sit like that, like he already dead? I no understand how he live like that. I cook for him, clean, wash clothes. He be dead if I no around." She ranted as she flipped burgers and fries with her chopsticks. Every few sentences, she'd slip into Vietnamese. That means she's so pissed, there's no English translation for it.

I've heard this litany countless times. It goes on and on and on without any sight of an end. So for once, I decided to switch it up.

"Mom, are you happy? Like, really, honestly happy?" I asked.

"What you mean happy? Yeah, I happy. Why I not be happy?" she snapped.

"I'm just wondering because you always complain about Dad. You don't seem happy. Don't you want to go on a trip to see friends or something? Why do you and Dad always just sit here in this house? You can go somewhere, anywhere."

She stopped flipping her food and turned to look at me, with an odd smile on her face. Her voice became shrill and cracked. "I no want go nowhere! Why I want go somewhere? I like my own bed, my own house. I no need go see friends! I have your Daddy. That all." She turned her attention back to the stove.

I stared at the saws and hammers and conical Vietnamese hats hanging on the grey brick walls, the stairs leading to the attic where the fake Christmas tree lived. Before the garage was here and it was just a big hole in the ground, we buried pet rabbits that died here, cause unknown. The air in there was stale but not because of Mom's cooking or lack of ventilation. It was downright stifling, even more so because I couldn't figure out how Mom—and Dad—could live like this. Yet they did, and they wanted to. That's how it was. Happiness-turned-resignation.

Started chemo four days ago. Über-tired but can't sleep, thanks to the steroids I'm taking to offset the side effects of the chemo. I want to puke, but there ain't nothing to puke since I'm not eating because everything tastes like rust. Arms, heavy and dead. Mega-acid reflux. Anxiety. Claustrophobia. Really stoned.

But not the good kind of stoned where you just want to sink into a beanbag and listen to some trippy tunes. Or the kind where you REALLY enjoy a Chinese buffet. Or the kind where you can mosey on down to the beach, dig your feet into the sand, and just go with the waves of the ocean, bro. No. This is the kind of stoned that you get when your nineteen-year-old niece gives you some skunk weed that has a bunch of seeds, and all that ends up happening is that you walk around forgetting shit and wondering why time is moving so slowly.

Charles and the kids cut my hair the first night I was on chemo. It's totally going to fall out soon (the nurse told me it will fall out in two weeks). I don't want to look like I have mange when it does. We had to do the cutting while I still have some semblance of an immune system. I can't run the risk of getting nicked in the head and then getting an infection when my body's defenses are being annihilated.

The kids were stoked to be allowed to use scissors on my hair. I daresay they thought this was better than a bag full of candy on Halloween.

"Mylo, be careful not to stab Mommy!" Charles said, wincing as Mylo brought the scissors closer to my forehead.

I laughed. "Steady hands, boy. Um, Daddy, why don't you come here and help him make the first cut?" I instructed Charles. Chloe stood by, about to burst. She couldn't wait to get her hands on those precious scissors and go to town.

"Mylo! Let me do it! Please!" Chloe begged.

"Just wait your turn, Chloe Bean. He's almost done," I said. I don't know if Mylo picked up on the vibe of everyone being nervous of him wielding a sharp object so close to my eyes or what, but he seemed satisfied with one cut and passed along the scissors to his sister. Or I should say, he began to pass along the scissors at the moment that she reached out and grabbed them from him.

"My turn!" Chloe shouted.

Kid fingers pulled chunks of hair away from my scalp. Snip. I briefly felt content with this family bonding haircutting thing before the chemo started to really kick in and make me close my eyes and breathe through the nausea. I didn't want to ruin this moment for everyone.

Now I got this fuzzy rainbow head. When I got off the bus today, this chick from across the street shouted, "Cool hair!" At first, because I'm so out of it, I didn't know she was talking to me. Then I was like, yeah, thanks! Then I got sad because I remembered the reason that I have "cool hair," and how I will have no hair soon. I do hope that I have a cool bald head, and not a flat head or a cone head, or some super offensive birthmark that will be revealed by all my alopecia glory.

Walking into the house, I thought of when Charles and I went to a counselling session at the Cancer Agency last week. He doesn't like therapy. He thinks he's smart enough to process emotions on his own. But I made him go. I'm worried about him. How is he doing with Edward's death and my diagnosis being so close together, so fresh? He keeps telling me that it's all about me, it's whatever I want to do, it's however I feel, but I keep telling him that no, it's about us, about him and me. When he tells me that it's all about me, I feel alone. He has it all together, and I'm just falling apart by myself.

My life has come to a sudden halt. I've taken a leave of absence from my Master's program for a year. But Charles keeps on going. My cancer is shitty timing for him. He's got this huge blockbuster conference in a couple of weeks, so he's at meetings and press conferences nonstop. A lot of the time, I'm proud that he's such an academic rockstar, but I admit, I'm jealous and resentful. I wish he would slow down and check in with me, take care of me, even though I don't need much taking care of right now. My parents will be here in a few days to take care of me, but I don't want them to. I'm thirty-one years old, not eight. I need my husband, not my mommy and daddy. In sickness and in health.

No, life hasn't come to a halt. Rather, it's being lived out in spite of me. I can see it in another space, as I lie here and watch, like counting sheep in the hopes of a sleep that will never come when you want it to. Existing in a chemo haze while all else lives in another, separate, safe realm.

Mom and Dad are here. Mom's launched full-scale into being the over-protective mother I knew as a kid growing up with epilepsy. Back then, she would rarely let me go to a friend's house, and she wouldn't allow me to participate in any sports. I wanted to take karate so I could defend myself against my bully, Mandy Kerstetter. But Mom was afraid I'd get kicked in the head and would die, so I had to resign to lying to people about my innate Oriental martial arts skills. Now, she is forbidding me to get out of bed. (I'm pretty sure she won't allow me to go to friends' houses or participate in sports, either.)

"You sick! You go back to bed! Mommy wash dishes," she says from the kitchen sink with her back toward me.

"Mom, please, I can manage to wash a spoon, a plate, and a cup without hurting myself. I promise." I stand in the kitchen, waiting for her to acquiesce.

"No! I do it," she says.

"Okay, Mom."

I shuffle out of the room and up the stairs. The belt on my robe gets caught under my slipper, and I trip on the landing, smashing my shin onto the edge of the step. *"Puta madre coño mierda!"* (I instinctively curse in Spanish after having lived with my Latina best friend, Tammy, during college for four years.) Mom rushes over.

"What you do? You need be careful! You better not hurt yourself."

She tries to take my hand to help me up, which totally pisses me off. I recoil my hand and glare at her.

"Mom, I'm fine! Let me be! I'm not dead yet!" I scream.

She looks hurt. Fucking what the fuck, Brandy? Did you have to say that?

"Yeah, okay, I know," she says. Mom goes back to the sink, even though there are no more dishes to wash.

I try to soften the blow. "Mom, I'm fine. Please stop worrying. If I get sick, I'll let you know." Being around my mom while taking steroids—not a good combo.

She keeps her back turned to me. I give up and plod up to my bedroom. The sun shining through the skylight is bright. I get the doohickey that I use to turn the shade on the skylight, and I block out the sun. I like my fog black.

I lie down on my bed, remove my glasses, and put a pillow over my head. All I can hear is my breathing. I try holding my breath, to see if I can make myself pass out. I feel as if I could actually will myself to die, so I stop. Now I'm anxious. I reach for the Ativan, but it's not where I thought I'd left it. It's probably in the bathroom, but I'm too flattened to get up. I listen to the whir of the ceiling fan. At first, it calms me. But now, I'm nauseous. I'm floating. I'm drowning. This back-and-forth is making it hard to breathe.

This morning, I had to go to the bathroom, but it was incredibly difficult to move. I got out of bed, and halfway there, about five steps out of bed, I had to sit on the floor. I lay down, shoved myself into the walk-in closet, and had a good, long cry. Mom and Dad took the kids to the park, and Charles was out doing his thing, so I didn't worry about anyone hearing me sob. Sadness and solitude coursed through my body, this ravaged terrain of which I've lost control. How can I possibly endure seven more rounds of this shit?

The other day, Charles and I had coffee with an oncologist he knew twenty years ago when he volunteered at the Cancer Agency. He thought it would be good to talk to her about my situation. Right away, Charles and this woman launched into a catch-up session, with her pretty much ignoring me and asking him questions about his career. Charles went on about all his achievements and projects, and I just became increasingly annoyed. Why am I here? I kept asking this question in my blitzed-out brain. How is this supposed to help us? Or is it just helping Charles? Does he think he's doing his part as my supportive husband by subjecting me to this woman, who obviously doesn't give a shit about whether or not I exist?

After an hour and a half, I couldn't take anymore of this nonsense. I'd had way too much caffeine, and still, I was ready to pass out on the floor.

"Charles, I think we should go now."

He stopped talking to Dr. Annoying-Ass-Woman and looked at me surprised, as if he'd forgotten I was there.

"Oh? Are you feeling okay?"

"No, I'm tired."

At this point, I guess Dr. Complete-Waste-of-My-Time thought she should say something, or express concern for my condition—or perhaps chastise me for interrupting the stimulating conversation between her and my husband.

"How's your treatment going?" she asked, smiling at me.

"It sucks." I looked at her with dead eyes.

"Oh, it's not that bad, is it? The treatments are better nowadays." She chuckled and looked at Charles.

Wait. A. Second. You—you are an oncologist? You have the sensitivity of a rock. And when was the last time you had chemo, lady? Oh, right. Never. You never went through it. Fuck you very much, bitch.

"I'm on a clinical trial. It's pretty bad." That was about all I had to say to her, Dr. Lameass-Good-for-Nothing. "Charles, I really want to go." What was wrong with these people? He seriously looked like he wanted to stay there to talk to her for about three more hours.

"Okay, well, it was nice reconnecting with you, [whatever her name was, I can't remember since I was so enraged]," he said. He rose and gave her an apologetic look. Me? I just walked away. Nothing was nice about those precious few hours I'd never get back.

When we got into the car, I exploded. "What the hell was the point of that?"

"Why are you so mad?"

"Why? I don't know. Maybe it's because you totally built up this meeting with this stupid woman, telling me that how good it will be, how much she'd be able to help us, how much we'd learn from her. But what happened? All that happened was that you dominated the conversation, and I just sat there. All that I learned was that she was pretty fucking lame and that my oncologist is way better."

He snickered. "You're not five years old. You could've opened your mouth."

"Yeah right, I could have. At what point was I supposed to stop you from talking about yourself? I don't think she wanted to hear about me anyway. Why did you make me go to that?"

He scoffed, "You're ridiculous. You talk a lot too."

"Bullshit, Charles. I just sat there and drank coffee after coffee. And I fucking hate coffee right now. Such a waste of time. Are you angry that this cancer crap is all about me? You have to make it about you, is that it? Well, I don't want it to be about me. I keep asking you how you feel, and you fucking tell me it doesn't matter. That's a load of shit."

He drove in silence. End of discussion.

When we got home, I saw Dad sitting in his usual spot in the recliner, watching *CSI*. Charles went upstairs. I took the Ativan out of my purse and popped two under my tongue. As soon as the pills dissolved, a calm came over me. I sat on the couch and watched Dad. He was snoring. I watched the rise and fall of his belly.

I remember going through Dad's stash of prescription drugs last year, amazed by all the pills. I wrote down all the names of the drugs, looked up what they were used for, and occasionally wrote down my observations of his moods and activity. Now, I'm taking a few of the same prescriptions that he's been taking for decades. But I don't want to become my dad. Or what I thought my dad was.

I'm thinking, though, that I hadn't understood my dad—not really. He did go through a lot of trauma during the war in Vietnam, saw things that no one else back home in Pennsylvania could ever imagine. He saw his friends get shot, blown up. He saw children die—all the blood and guts and brains that are never meant for anyone to see outside the body, in bright display. During rare times of lucidity, Dad would tell me about the horror. The horror—that was his alone. And now, this horror is mine.

Throughout my life, I've had what I've come to call my Vietnam War dreams—dreams that have a bright orange-red aura with the smell of singed skin. Always in the dreams, I'm hiding and running away from persecutors, cramming myself inside hollowed logs on the beach, looking up at a blood orange sky, struck with terror as I smell people burning alive and bombs exploding not too far from my hiding place. Why do I have these dreams? My parents rarely talk about Vietnam, and I have never been there. I've had these dreams before I even knew what the Vietnam War was really about—before I knew about Buddhist monks performing self-immolation, before I knew about Agent Orange killing off lush forests in order to expose the enemy, before I knew how people were viciously executed or how my mother's uncle threatened to murder her family in Vietnam because she married my dad and gave birth to me.

I'm having these dreams even more frequently now, but when I wake up, my chemo haze makes me think I'm still living the dream, or the nightmare, that it's not ending any time soon, that I'm going to be stuck in it, like in one of those movies where dreams are real and forever.

The chemical smell and taste biting the insides of my nose, mouth, and throat make me wonder if Mom and Dad had the same assault on their senses when they breathed in the Agent Orange that was so casually dropped from planes flying overhead. Dad said the soldiers were told that the planes were dropping pesticides to get rid of the rampant mosquito population. Soon after that, they were told it was Agent Orange, but that it was harmless, nothing to worry about. See those bright trees suddenly dropping dead? Nothing to worry about. Later: see those babies being born without limbs? Nothing to worry about. See those vets dying of prostate cancer in alarming numbers? Nothing to worry about. Stuff happens.

See me getting poisoned so I can get rid of this inexplicable cancer? Nothing to worry about.

I watch a line of dust on a blade of the ceiling fan. I imagine particles too small to be seen from here going up my nose and in my mouth. Probably harmless.

This is the Vietnam War happening all over again. I inherited this nightmare from my parents. I hope it stops with me. I don't want to pass this on to my son, to my daughter. It needs to stop.

Oh, Roshi, you ask me why I am attached to suffering? How do I not suffer?

I take out the Ziploc bag that contains my ponytail of purple, pink, teal, and blond hair. I wrote "August 13, 2007" on the bag—the date I started chemo. Some years from now, will Chloe remember how she went shopping for wigs with me, how she picked out purple and green ones for me to try on? Will she remember how she and Mylo cut my hair before I lost it all? Or will she inherit this nightmare from me, from generation to generation, dreams of what those before us have lived and feared?

I tuck my bag of rainbow hair back into the bookshelf by my bed. Someday I will give this to the kids—a talisman to save them from the chemicals, the dreams.

http://cancerfuckingsucks.blogspot.com
Friday, August 31, 2007
Pubes

Yes, they fall out! And don't even get all embarrassed from reading that cause some of you have asked me that question, so I know that even more of you are probably asking it in your heads.

My moustache—hasn't come out. I guess not all hair is victim to chemo. Damn!

My armpit and leg hairs—I haven't noticed that they are falling out, but they've remained stubbly since I last shaved over a week ago. I dare not shave now, because if I get cut, the chances of infection are pretty high.

Eyebrows and lashes—should fall out but haven't thus far.

I have thin patches of hair on my head, mostly where my brain stem is right above my neck. Overall, my head is just one big itchy noggin. I've been putting tea tree oil and gel on it to relieve the itchiness.

The hairs on my arms, fingers, and toes look unfazed. So much for me being like one of those creepy hairless cats, which I swear are the work of the devil.

Poor little Chloe is trying to understand the whole "Mama is sick" thing, and keeps telling me that her hair is falling out too. I'm not sure how to talk to a four-year-old about this stuff. The programs at the Cancer Agency for kids with parents who have cancer start at age six, nothing for littler ones. I'm just trying to keep Chloe involved in whatever I can, to expose it rather than hide it, and make her feel a part of the treatment and recovery, but I'm not sure if that's the right thing to do.

As for Mylo, he just keeps saying this and that hurts. It's even tougher to talk to him, and I have absolutely no clue about how to get him involved, as his primary interest is destroying things and beating the crap out of them. At least with Chloe, she's into the whole girly make-up/dress-up thing.

This week, I've been feeling okay, even though my white blood count is at its lowest. It's kind of a deceptive, dangerous state to be in. I feel okay, but I know that if I get the smallest injury, I have to be really careful. A couple days ago, my finger accidentally pushed lightly on the vein from which they took blood last week. I have routine blood work done to monitor my hypothyroidism every three to six months, and it always heals right up. But when my finger touched the spot—a week after the test—it hurt! Then yesterday, as I was lighting some candles, my finger touched the hot metal on the lighter for less than a second, and what normally would have been a practically non-existent burn hurt like hell and swelled up a little. So I had to put Neosporin and a Band-aid on it, even though I could barely see where it was burned.

It's difficult for my mind to understand that my body sucks right now cause I'm used to being so active and running around all over the place, not giving a rat's ass if I trip or fall or be clumsy and all that. I should rest up because my next treatment is on Wednesday.

Posted by Brandy Lotus Blossom at 7:56 AM

My days used to consist of journaling as soon as I woke up, figuring out what editing jobs or writing assignments were due in the next couple weeks, and then heading off to the university to go to one of my MFA workshops, where feedback would be flying around like paper money or falling like poisoned-tipped daggers. Or at least, that's what it feels like to the writer's ego. Ever since my days as an undergraduate at a liberal arts college in Boston, I'd wanted to write about my parents' pasts. I became fascinated with them—the holes, the gaps, unanswered questions, and the complex strength and survivorship my parents embodied. My stories about them were a way for me to connect to them, especially since I'd been trying to find a connection all my life.

Now my days are different. The stories are still there, but the energy to write them down, work through them—it's hibernating. The stories are cowering from all the chemicals in my body, all the chemicals taking over my mind. I go to this hospital or that doctor every single day. I lie in bed waiting to die but not wanting to. Sometimes I do want to die. Sometimes I'm not sure who I am anymore, or where I came from. I'm living in a half dimension.

My parents are here. They are trying to keep me alive. I'm part of their story. I am some part of themselves that has flown so far away, or perhaps the part that keeps coming back, unwanted.

Mom, Dad, Sis, you, you and you, everyone—look, I can tell you I'm fine! Really. Okay, so maybe I look like I'm a prisoner of war, but that's really not far off from the truth. Did you know that some of the chemicals in my chemo were also used in mustard gas in World War I? Yeah, I just found that out. Crazy. And here I thought chemical warfare only caused cancer, not cured it! This is what trips me out though: I feel like I've exchanged one chemical warfare for another. I read that children of veterans who had been exposed to Agent Orange have started showing signs of genetic damage. Then I thought, Holy shit, my mom was also exposed. Double dose of exposure. So here it is. Mustard gas curing the effects of Agent Orange! Karma chemical chameleon. Maybe that idea will make more sense when I'm not chemo-stoned anymore. Or maybe it won't.

So now that I'm officially, medically speaking, dying, I use the precious few remaining brain cells for thinking about how people had lived right before they died. You know, I have asked two of my friends—older ladies—how they survived this breast cancer gig, and that's cool when they give me their advice and encouragement. But I can't really go around asking anybody how they lived before they died because well, the only people I can ask, they're dead. So I have to remember, or try to remember and fill in the gaps of their lives at the end, just so my crazy chemo-stoned, roid-raging brain can quiet this little apocalypse.

The last time I saw Edward alive, it was less than two months before he passed away. He stood beside Charles. No, actually, he wasn't standing. He was hunched over and being supported by his wife and older daughter. I don't know if it was my way of detaching from the tragedy of the situation, but I just looked at Edward and felt that he wasn't Edward. Edward, as I had known him for seven years, had already moved on. Edward's shell wavered, his eyes empty, his mouth slightly open like a door that everyone always forgets to close in their too hectic lives. He had some response to people's questions about his level of comfort. When Ba-Ba asked if perhaps Edward needed to go back up to his hotel room and rest, Edward slowly nodded and grunted. I took that gesture to mean, "I am here, yes, barely, not really."

Now I am here, barely, kind of. I'm fading, but the part that's still here is trying to come to the surface. Maybe this is what drowning feels like. Or having someone put a pillow over your face. The blurry thinness between struggle and fight, between resignation and acceptance.

The sanctuary that my bathroom has become. It's the only place where I can hide and lock the door, forget that I have a family who needs me to live. I am here in my deep oval tub filled with hot water. I opened the skylight above the tub, so steam is rising thickly, like at one of those hot springs where old people go to soothe their arthritis. I put candles all around the deck; the lavender ones are my favourite. I listen to a sad music mixed CD that Lisa made for me. The songs that make me cry with self-pity are David Gray's "This Year's

Love" and Jeff Buckley's "Hallelujah." I like tasting salt and soap run down my face and into my mouth.

I sit here and smoke weed. I don't like smoking because it hurts my throat, but I ran out of pot brownies (thanks, Dad, for digging into my stash), so I must settle for my trusty old glass pipe named Puff that I've had since college. My skin tingles. My headache persists, but it doesn't matter as much anymore.

I look at my small breasts with the nipples and areolas stretched from breastfeeding, the skin loose on my belly from the pregnancies, the stretch marks on my thighs—I call them my tiger stripes. I have been self-conscious about these signs of declining youth and motherhood. I rub my stubbly head, feel around my bloated face for the acne that has erupted all over my skin. I'm feeling less like a human, more like a mutant blob. I can't imagine myself as a sexual being, now or in the future. That I'd ever been sexual is a distant memory, another incarnation. I know that maybe there is desire somewhere—I think that's the part of me struggling to be put down. But that part is so weak, wounded, put down a long time ago, two weeks ago.

A sudden voice enters my mind. *Remember when you would pray to God for boobs in junior high school?* I startle myself by laughing out loud, which sounds foreign alongside the melancholy of the mixed CD. It's really funny because in fact, the last prayers I ever said to God were to get my first period, that magical time of the month when I would get to wear maxi pads and tampons like a real woman. "Please, God, let me get my period. And give me boobs, bigger than Sis's, though, please. She doesn't have big ones, but I just want boobs bigger than hers. That's all I'm asking for," my fourteen-year-old self prayed as I got out of the shower and rubbed my chest with the bath towel, as if praying and touching the spots that needed the prayer would double my chances for tits. I figured that if I didn't ask for big boobs, God would see my humility as a virtue and give me more than what I asked for.

The day after I got my period, Sis and I went shopping, and she bought her husband Rob a bottle of Drakkar Noir, his favourite cologne. I loved smelling the muskiness of it; it made me think of all the cute boys in school who wore the same scent. She went in the kitchen to give Rob the small black bag, but the only thing she found was a note saying that he was working out in the gym with his friends.

The night went by without much activity. I fell asleep with my niece and nephew, who were curled up in the fetal position on either side of me. I awoke the next morning when Rob tapped me on the shoulder.

"Hey, Brandy."

"Hm?"

"Listen—this might be a shock, but your sister and I talked, and we decided to get a divorce. She left this morning, upset. I don't know where she is. But I have to go to the shop. I'll see you when I get home. You can bring the kids by later."

"Uh, okay."

Then he was off to work in the hair salon he and Sis owned. Wait—did he say that he and Sis were getting a divorce? I hardly saw them fight, not like Mom and Dad.

My mind went insane with questions, and I never felt so confused in all my life.

I lay in bed until Nikki and Christian woke up, crawling all over me and pulling my arms to get out of bed.

"Okay," I said, "I'm up now. Let's get something to eat."

I took the kids into the kitchen, where I gave Nikki a bowl of Cheerios without milk and Christian a bowl of Cookie Crisp with milk. I watched them eat as I drank my cup of Maxwell House instant coffee with three large tablespoons of Coffeemate. The kids ate their cereal quietly, until Christian picked up a little chocolate chip cookie from his bowl and tried to shove it into Nikki's mouth.

"Hey, cut that out. Eat your own cereal, Christian. Nikki has her own."

He laughed at me, and suddenly I felt very sad for them. They were just little kids—they had no clue. But then again, neither did I.

For the next few hours, I treated them with extra care, letting them do whatever they felt like doing and being gentle when they did something bad. I also had a million imaginings about where Sis was and what she was doing. I wondered if Mom and Dad knew what was going on, if Rob had told them. I decided that this was unlikely and instead, tried to concentrate on the kids.

I bathed in a pool of nervous cold sweat, sitting on their floral plush couch blankly watching *Sesame Street*, when Sis phoned right after lunch.

"Brandy? Is anyone there with you now?"

"No, just me and the kids. Where are you?"

"You can't tell anyone—promise me now," Sis whispered into the phone.

"Okay, I won't. What's going on?"

"Okay, listen. This morning, when I got in the car to go to work, I saw that the seat was down the whole way."

"Yeah, so?"

"Brandy, Rob is gay. He's been sleeping with men."

"What are you talking about? How do you know?"

"Look, I know."

"I don't believe you. Just because the seat in the car was down. . ."

"I'm telling you the truth."

"Okay, but where are you now?"

"I'm in the basement of the salon. I'm trying to listen to what he says."

"What? You're spying on him?" I pictured Sis in the bowels of the hair salon. I didn't even know there was a basement. I couldn't imagine that it was very clean.

"I have to find out. It's disgusting down here—I saw some rats."

"Sis, please just come home. I'm so worried about you."

"I can't come home yet—and don't tell anyone where I am or what I told you. Please—you promised me."

"Yeah, I promise. When are you coming home?"

"I don't know. I'll call you later."

"Okay."

She hung up the phone. I stared at the earpiece in my

hand. Should I call someone? Is she crazy? What is she talking about, that Rob is gay? That's impossible. They have kids together.

I opened the medicine cabinet in the bathroom on the ground floor and took out the Drakkar Noir. I plucked the cap off the nozzle and spritzed it in the air. Before the cloud could dissipate, I thrust my head into it and spun around. The kids were watching me, got off the floor and ran over, laughing, as we whirled around together. I spun faster, trying to spin the chaos out of my head, laughing with them, trying to be a four-year-old, a one-year-old, protected by laughter and love.

PART FOUR

Betrayal

http://cancerfuckingsucks.blogspot.com
Monday, September 10, 2007
Betrayal (Part I)

I was pretty sure I've used the word "betrayal" in a post title previously, but looking back, I guess I haven't. Given that this probably won't be the last time I use this word, I'm parenthetically labelling it.

It's been almost a week since round deux from the attack of el diablo chemo, and it's been a tough week. On Thursday, Charles and I made a run across the U.S. border for some cheap American goods, and I was doing alright then, with the help of a handful or two of pills. On Friday, the big fundraiser dinner took place—almost 700 people in attendance! I donned my curly red wig and a cougar-like dress (even had a full-on boob slip when I took the camcorder bag off my shoulder! I felt soooo Paris Hilton, except that I probably blushed when it happened and not acted like it was just what I do every day). It was great seeing so many people and getting all the hugs, but truth be told, I was painfully pooped out after an hour. I was feeling kinda whoozy, and nothing tasted right. I was lucky that I got home and into my pjs by 10:30.

On Saturday, the fun continued with Charles's conference downtown. I was okay for most the day and spent the time working at the display table, content to hammer away at the food book that I should have finished editing and laying out by now. But by the time 3:00 PM rolled around, I hit a big wall of fatigue, which has continued up until now. Yesterday, Charles, the kids, Charles's sister and her family *and I went to a friend's brother's farm to ride horses, and the kids had a blast. Me, well again, the fatigue was nothing less than torture.*

It's hard to describe this feeling to anyone who hasn't experienced it. The closest I can come is probably something remotely similar to the fatigue a woman has when she's in the first trimester of her pregnancy. But it's not the type of tired that a nap can cure. Actually, I'm finding it very hard to sleep when I'm feeling like this. There's no comfort to be had in the body whatsoever.

This is where the betrayal comes in. If it's true that the mind and body are one, or can be one, how can the body betray the mind so heavily to the point of it being a full-scale attack? Loads of people have advised me on visualization, that if I talk to the cancer or imagine it going away, it will. But with my body betraying me in such a way, how am I to believe that? My body is doing things despite itself, and I know that's a product of the chemo. Even some of my moods are a product of the chemo. I have to say it again, even just to remind myself—I'm being poisoned. Right now, my body is not my own, that is, even if my mind is still my own.

Very recently, I've become obsessed with the name Moxie. I read it somewhere in a magazine called Craft, which was a handy distraction during my chemo session last week. I like the name, and the word, Moxie. I keep telling Charles that when we have another kid, whether boy or girl, I want to name him or her Moxie. I say "when," not "if." I know that against the better judgment and advice of some people, I probably shouldn't wish for or desire something that there's

a great chance I won't be able to have, which is a third child. But I just feel at this very moment that perhaps that kind of desire is exactly what I need.
Posted by Brandy Lotus Blossom at 10:17 PM

The doc told me that I'll likely experience early menopause because the chemo is going to kill off my reproductive system. This whole cancer thing just keeps getting better. Anyway, it's not like I'm in a baby-making mood lately.

The other day, I was walking with Charles and the kids to Main Street to get a newspaper to look at the interview he did about his conference. I hid under a bandanna, the kind I would have worn back in high school when grunge was all the rage. Not long into our walk, my scalp began to get unbearably itchy. I wanted to rip the bandanna off my head, but I also felt ashamed of my baldness.

"Just take it off. You look good bald," Charles gently said.

"That's easy for you to say. I look like a freak." I sounded annoyed, just so I could mask how I was on the verge of tears.

I scratched under my bandanna some more, until it slipped off entirely.

"Fuck," I said.

Charles stopped pushing the double stroller and waited

for me as I fiddled with the bandanna. "Oh, fuck it." I kept it off. The drizzle soothed my scalp.

When we got to Main, we had to wait for the light to turn before we could cross the intersection. People stared at us. I squirmed from my nakedness and the pity it was garnering. I wanted to run. Instead, I tied the bandanna around my head.

However, today I feel grand. I've been exercising, walking, and doing shit like crazy. I went to this hokey workshop at the Cancer Agency on how to put on makeup. Cosmetic companies donate free kits to women going through chemo, which sounds great and all, but I think about how toxic this makeup is and wonder how many of the ingredients could cause cancer. Fuck, what doesn't cause cancer? Not much.

So I'm at this thing, and everyone except me is over the age of sixty. Most of the information was therefore pretty useless to me since I don't have to worry about wrinkles and sagging skin. But what was helpful was how I began to think that I didn't look so bad being bald after all. Another woman commented on how nice, round and smooth my head looks. Another said that the absence of hair makes my eyes pop. They were probably just being nice, but it still felt ego-good. It was also cool how everyone was shouting out opinions about how good one shade of eye shadow looked, or how maybe the bright pink blush wasn't so great on our pale skin. For an hour, I basked in the sisterhood. It's not often that I don't feel completely alone and misunderstood.

Once I left the seminar, I heard Mom in my head, telling me that I don't look good at all, that I look sick, and that I need to get back into bed. Different voices, different appearances for different audiences. Brave face on the blog. Defiant face for the mother. Dejected face for myself. All those faces facing fear.

One cup of milk, one tablespoon of butter, ten saltines—that's what goes into what Mammy called Cracker Soup. When I was a kid, I craved very few things, but whatever I did want to eat was given to me quickly and abundantly. Nothing else filled my twig of a body like the hot buttery milk and soggy crackers, some still slightly crunchy if eaten quickly enough. The butter, or actually it was Country Crock margarine scooped from a brown plastic tub, melted into yellow circles floating on top of the boiled milk. The smell—I would now say that it is akin to salty brie—made my tummy grumble when Mammy put the bowl in front of me. I instantly felt warm inside when I slurped the first spoonful. When Mammy discovered my love for cracker soup, she was proud she could feed me like no one else.

Anything goopy, creamy, salty and fatty was the magic formula to get me to eat in those days when the medicine I took to quell my seizures simultaneously made me hyperactive and killed my appetite. To round out my diet, I got my protein from dippy eggs and Sunbeam bread lightly toasted and slathered with Country Crock. After Mammy fried up the dippy eggs and put them on the table with the toast, I would break into them with the corners of toast, halved into triangles, and stuff it in my mouth as the yolk dribbled down my chin.

Sitting at the table with his coffee and toast, Pappy would say, "You sure do like them dippy eggs. Look at that girl eat, Ida!"

"Of course, she likes my dippy eggs, Junior! Why wouldn't she?" Mammy teased Pappy in return.

Pappy leaned in close as I was taking my next bite. "Hey, you think your mammy is a good cook?"

"Mm-hm," I muttered with a mouthful of egg and toast.

"Well, lucky you, cause she sure don't cook like that for me, no sir!"

It was fun to see Mammy and Pappy do their little banter.

I caught the yolk before it dripped onto my shirt and licked my fingers, getting every last drop of the golden goop. I licked the plate clean of yolk and dug the hardened remainder out of the egg whites, savouring the last bit of yellow. When I finished eating, the emptied fried egg whites congealed on my plate. Mammy either threw the leftovers outside for the birds to eat (the cannibalism not escaping me even at that young age) or put them in the slop bucket for the pigs. Even though Mammy didn't believe that whatever I didn't eat would be waiting for me in hell and covered in maggots, like Mom told me it would, she agreed that life was best lived if nothing was ever wasted.

I think now to try cracker soup, but I can't even finish making it before I start dry heaving. I imagine a plate of dippy eggs and toast. It only takes me one second of that thought to know that's a totally bad idea. I just want to eat a piece of extra coarse sandpaper with Tabasco sauce.

I take a cracker from the package and nibble on it. I peek into the saucepan. The warm milk has formed a skin on top. I turn away from the stove, sit down with my cracker and glass of water, and dutifully eat.

I met my acupuncturist for the first time at Inspire Health today. Inspire is a place where cancer patients go to get support in the form of seminars, meditation, yoga, nutritionists, naturopaths, acupuncturists, and doctors. After you pay the initial lifetime membership fee, it's free to access most of the stuff there. It's nice to go sit in their living room, drink Rooibos tea, and browse the cancer resource library. Most patients are older, but I've come to accept that that's just how it is with cancer.

One of the first things my acupuncturist, Richard, told me is that according to Qigong, breast cancer is caused by too much worry. A number of people have echoed these sentiments, against which I've become defensive. That idea feels too much like blaming the victim. Still, as soon as Richard explained that idea, I was taken back to when I was pregnant with Chloe, and Charles had confessed that eight months into our relationship, he had cheated on me.

It was midnight on his thirty-sixth birthday when his cell phone rang. I looked up from the book I was reading. He answered the phone, glanced at me, and went into another room, out of earshot. I followed him, which clearly made him uncomfortable. He said, "Okay, I'll call you tomorrow, thanks," and hung up.

"Who's calling you at this hour?"

"Oh, I don't know—somebody wishing me a happy birthday."

"You don't know who it was?"

"Yeah, I think it might have been an ex-girlfriend or something."

"Did she tell you who she was?"

"She said happy birthday and asked me if I knew who it was, but she was coy. It's nothing."

"I don't think it's nothing. I think it's weird. Are you going to call her back tomorrow, like you said?"

"Probably not."

"Okay."

We went to bed, but the next morning I woke up with dread. Perhaps Charles knew that I wouldn't let it drop and that the more lies and vagueness he attempted to pull off would only fuel my suspicions further. So he did it—he told me how during the first summer we'd been together, he had had an affair with another woman. To get back at the wife to whom he'd still been married, he said. It had nothing to do with me. He did it to hurt his first wife, not me.

Yet upon that admission, I had felt very hurt. Something happened inside my breast, a very localized, focused crushing tightness. Why was this woman still calling if he'd broken it off a long time ago, as he said?

The pain of knowing that betrayal under normal circumstances—the relationship would have been over. Right? But I was carrying this guy's kid, and I loved him. That moment had been so traumatic that I had almost forgotten the agony, the anguish of five years ago. Now as I keep hearing in my head what Richard said about breast cancer being caused by worry, I believe that that was the moment I developed cancer. Of course, I'm not going to tell Charles that. But this is the upside of my logic for not repressing that belief—if I can get to a point where I forgive him and accept him for who he is at the core and his weaknesses, the cancer will go away. The cancer being a metaphor for wounds to the spirit—that will help me.

The more I go to Inspire, the more I believe in the mind-body-spirit connection. My dreams indicate I'm not totally at peace, but I'm starting to feel things calm down. The challenge is to see how it will be when I get my next chemo.

Right now, I'm sitting on the bathroom floor. I can hear my kids and parents one floor down, eating dinner. The incense has burned out, and suddenly I feel too warm. Richard told me I have too much yang—too much fire.

This is a dream. I am in this forest with Chloe, Mylo, and Dad. There was a downpour, and there are fallen tree limbs on the ground. After a brief respite from the rain, it starts up again. Suddenly, while Chloe and Mylo are playing, I notice that really heavy old tree branches are going to fall on us. I grab the kids and start running. But Dad continues to sit on a rock, not moving. I shout, "Dad, let's go!" Very slowly, like a turtle, he gets up and says, "Okay, I'm coming." The sense is of an urgency to get Dad, and us, out of danger.

I wake up to hear Mom screaming in her sleep, two floors below me. Usually I let her scream until she stops, but she isn't stopping, only getting louder. I trudge down the stairs, first checking on the kids. They are sound asleep.

Dad is snoring on the couch in the living room, and a Time Life music infomercial is on the television. I can't believe Mom's screaming isn't waking him up. How many meds did he take?

I go into her room. She's on her back, wrapped up in blankets like a cocoon, or like she's mummified, eyes half open and fluttering, mumbling in Vietnamese, groaning, then shouting. I shake her and say, "Mom, it's okay, wake up." I shake her again, but she keeps dreaming. She opens her eyes and looks at me, but she's not awake. Her breathing is raspy and gurgling. I have to snap her out of it. I don't want her to keep dreaming whatever nightmare is playing out in her head. Finally, she blinks and realizes that it's me. She deflates; her body loses the tension. She turns over and goes to sleep.

I stand there for a moment to make sure she's fine. Mom goes back to snoring softly, so I whisper "Sweet dreams, Mom," and go back upstairs. On the way to my bedroom, I hear Mylo whimpering in his sleep. I go in and sit with him. Here lie three generations of nightmares.

"Hey, I buy this chicken. Look good. You eat." Mom just got back from her shopping trip along Fraser Street. One thing I am grateful for when my parents come to stay with us is that Mom gets to go out on the bus on her own, do shopping and hang out with other Vietnamese women. She seems happy when she goes out and about, even if Dad worries that she will get lost or spend too much money.

"Thanks, Mom, but I can't. I really don't feel like eating. Nothing tastes good." My mouth feels like someone shoved a muddy boot in it.

"No, but you try. I try it. I tell you, it good," Mom insists. How can I get her to understand that I don't want to—that I can't—eat?

"Mom, please, I'm sorry, but. . ."

"You better eat, or you get more sick. If you get more sick, you die! Then what? You need get better. You need eat."

I look at the ground and release a long sigh. This is her way of taking care of me, of trying to take control of a situation that is vastly out of her hands. She wants to feed me. She wants to save me through food. I think many mothers who have survived tremendous hardship must want to do the same thing for their children. The gravity weighs on me, and I feel really old and really young all at once.

I take a small piece of chicken from the little Styrofoam tray. Normally, I love eating chicken skin, but all I want to do is retch out my guts. I peel off the chicken skin and place the meat in my mouth. I chew three times before running to the bathroom and spitting the chicken in the toilet. I gag and cough and long lines of saliva and mucous hit the toilet water. Mom stands by the door.

"Sorry, Mom, I just can't."

"Okay, but you need eat." We go back out to the kitchen, and she finishes putting away her groceries. She pulls out a bag of *xi muoi*, salted dried plums. I used to love those as a kid. They were my treat from the Vietnamese grocery store in Harrisburg we'd go to once a month. I'd take a little sandwich bag full of *xi muoi* to school, slipping one into my mouth to chew and suck on during class. I knew that there was a good chance I'd be ridiculed by my classmates for eating these exotic little snacks, but I took the chance.

"Mom, can I try one of the *xi muoi*?" I'm thinking the pungent saltiness might do some wonders on my dead tastebuds. She opens the package and hands me a shrivelled reddish plum. I pop it in my mouth and smile. It's good.

I return to bed and suck the shit out of the leathery plum. I try to make it last, but I can't help eating the skin off the plum and being left with the pit. I suck on the pit for a few more minutes, until all the salty sweet essence is gone. I spit out the pit. It's a bit smaller than the tumour I can still feel in my breast. I'd like to think that this plum is the antidote. I want more.

My parents are flying home to Pennsylvania soon. I'm trying to avoid my mother at all costs because she always loses her mind right before she goes home. She thinks that I'm going to fail without her and that she needs to tell me as much as possible about how to live the right way and not the way I'm currently living, or in this case, dying.

"Hey, you get something to eat?" I turn around. She's coming into the kitchen with Dad's dirty plate and cup. He eats his meals in the living room, in front of the television.

Shit. I didn't get my food and scramble back upstairs in time. "Yeah, I'm just getting some rice soup." I ladle the congee into my bowl and sit at the table.

"How come your husband always out? What he do, he never home?"

"He's busy, Mom. He's got lots of meetings and stuff. That's his job. You always have to be out when you're a professor."

"He have meeting late at night? Why? He need stay home with you, take care of you. You sick. What you do when Mommy Daddy go home next week, ha? Maybe we stay longer and help. You no can take care kids yourself."

No way, lady. You need to go home. "It's okay, Mom. I'm halfway through my chemo. I'm starting to feel better. Charles's parents help out too."

She winces at the mention of his parents. She wants me to need only her.

"Charles's parents, they get sick of taking care of kids sometimes. Your husband should be here. What do you think he doing at night?" She leaned in closer to my face. "You know, when I pregnant with your sister, her father cheat on me, sleep with another woman. I be in bed with baby, and he off sleep around. He left me three days when your sister born."

As much as I feel terrible that such a betrayal had happened to Mom and had clearly had a lasting effect on her, I don't want to hear her insinuations. "He's working, Mom! That's what he does. He needs to work so that he can take care of us."

"You need get better. You know, I can't take it if you die. If you die, how am I see kids? His parents no let me see them. I never see them again. I need see my grandkids. So what happens when you die, ha?"

"Mom, please don't do this again. I already told you I'm getting better, okay? I don't like it when you talk like that."

She's not hearing me. I can tell by the way she's looking past my shoulder to the wall, her eyes welling up with tears, her nose turning pink. "I need stay and take care of you. Nobody here for you. You no have family here, no friends. They all his friends, family. You only have your mother. That why I talk like this. I your mother."

"Mom, if you keep talking like this, I don't want you to come back."

I get up from my chair, leaving my mother sitting at the table. It hurts to sit there with her, and it hurts to walk away.

PART FIVE

Shrink

You know what don't go well together? CAMs and psychotherapy. What kind of idiot am I? Have I not learned in the almost thirty-two years of my life that my mother is beyond hope? The chemo must be fucking with my brain enough to make me think that it'd be a good idea to take my parents to see my shrink in order to get a message across about how not to stress me out.

Charles and I have been going to this therapist at the Cancer Agency for a couple months now. She's a young Jewish woman named Donna, who's doing her practicum at the Cancer Agency. After hearing me talk about my parents—how they've come to help but how my mother is stressing me out to the point that I don't want them to come back—she suggested that we bring them to our next appointment. Now that I think of it, I'm sure her textbooks didn't tell her what to do when face-to-face with an insane Vietnamese mother. Yeah, I'm betting that no amount of cultural sensitivity training could've prepared her for what was about to go down.

When Donna asked Mom about how I felt or how she felt or how anybody felt for that matter, Mom would repeat her line of defense: "I love Brandy, but she no love me. I no want her be sick, but she no like me take care of her. Fine. I go home." I sat there, secretly amused by how Donna was trying to deal with this stubborn lady. But as the session was coming to a close, I began to fear what I would face at home.

Dad sat back as Mom launched into an all-out attack in the living room.

"You mad at me, so you make me go see your doctor, ha? You want her tell me how talk to you? You want her correct me? She no correct me! She younger than me, why would listen to her, ha? I no can believe you make me sit there, that girl correct me like that!"

"Mom, please, I just want to talk normal with you."

"You no talk normal. You talk to me like I'm shit! You look down on me like I nothing!" She sobbed and pointed at me. "Fine, I go home and no come back!"

Holy fucking Jesus on a popsicle stick.

Dad pleaded with Mom to calm down. "Liên, she didn't mean nothing by it. Look, we're going home soon, can't you just. . ."

"Oh, yeah, she want be mean to me! That why she take me to doctor! She think I do all wrong, that I stupid!"

"Please, Honey. . ." Dad uses that term of endearment in desperate times. *cycle of emotional abuse*

I called Sis in the hopes of getting some sound advice.

"Sis, I need your help. I took Mom and Dad to see my shrink today. . ."

"You did what?" Sis interrupted. She cackled. "You took Mom to a shrink? Are you nuts?"

"No, she's nuts, that's why I took her to a shrink. She's driving me crazy."

"We already know she's nuts, so why do you need a shrink to tell her that? Well, how did that go?"

"How do you think it went? It was horrible. She's screaming and crying all over the place. I might have to hide the knives," I joked, kind of.

"Wow, I don't know what to tell you," Sis sighed. "Oh,

I'm sure she'll get over it soon. Maybe by the time she gets back to Pennsylvania, she'll forget about it."

"Yeah fucking right, she will. She's not going to forget. What did I do? I'll call you later, bye."

I picked up the shakuhachi that Roshi gave me three months ago. I brought it to my lips, but instead of playing, I hit myself on the head with it. It made a hollow clunk on my skull.

Ears under water, I can hear my breathing. It's the only way I can meditate. I picture nothing. Everything is black. The black is undulating with my breath.

My hands run over the acne on my face, head, and back. My skin has erupted because my body is excreting poison. I remember when my Vietnamese cousins first came to the U.S., their bodies were ravaged with scars, especially my cousin Lung. He's half-White like me (though he never knew who his father was) and has scars on his back from being tied to a tree and whipped, just because he was *bui doi*, a half-breed. Both he and his brother Nghia were also covered in chloracne. Dad told me their acne was a result of them being exposed to Agent Orange. My initial thoughts when I met my cousins for the first time were how I escaped the beatings and the toxins just because my mother was lucky to get out of Vietnam. Lung and I have very similar ethnic backgrounds, but the difference in how our lives ended up playing out was huge. Until now, I think. Perhaps the same chemicals that ran in his blood also run in mine. It's not hard to think that with the way my body's mutated from the cancer and the treatment.

I bring my arms to my sides and sink deeper into the water. The steam rises and goes through the skylight I cracked open.

Brrrring! The phone sounds an alarm on the bathtub deck. Shit. My heart just beat out of my chest.

I shake water off my hands and dry them on a cloth. I'm not a fan of ironic things happening, like me getting fatally electrocuted by the phone as I answer a call from my oncologist while sitting in the bathtub to ease the side effects of chemo.

"Hello?"

A cheery female voice asks, "Is this Brandy?"

"Yep."

"This might be an odd question, but would you by any chance have a ladybug tattoo around your arm?"

"Yep."

"Thank goodness," says the woman with an audible sigh of relief.

"Who are you?"

"Oh," the voice chuckles, "I'm calling from Dr. Lothlorien's office. She forgot to number and identify the pictures from your consult last week. We wanted to make sure we've correctly identified you for your chart."

"Well, that's a relief. I'm glad you were able to match my tattoo with my headless body."

The receptionist laughs. "Yes, good thing you have that tattoo! Bye."

What would have happened if I didn't have that tattoo? Would I have been asked to go into the office and identify my boobs in a line-up? Would my boobs have been assigned to some other patient, like in one of those baby-switching stories on soap operas? I'm glad that my lucky ladybug tattoo has come through for me.

Come to think of it, I am lucky. My trial nurse said so. I hit the breast cancer jackpot; I won the all-inclusive package to Cancerland. After finishing this exclusive chemo trial, I'll be subscribed to two months of tanning services at the radiation spa. Then I'll be whisked off to the operating room to get a cancer makeover, complete with new boobs and tummy. The nurse drove home the point about how lucky I am. There's a mega waiting list for reconstruction post-mastectomy. But I am part of the super-elite group of women who have hardcore yet operable breast cancer, and we are the only ones being accepted for reconstruction without waiting. Don't be jealous.

I have decided to get a TRAM-flap reconstruction. It's a breast reconstruction surgery in which one's abdominal muscles are cut and tunnelled up to the breast area to make new breasts. Then the belly fat is also removed to help make boobs. The surgeon then places a hardcore mesh in the area where the abdominal muscles used to be. I'm going to have a tight bod. Literally. It's going to feel tight, with all the switcherooing done, like a permanent corset.

I always thought my boobs were too small. Now my prayers are being answered, only not in the way I would have liked them to be.

Mom is a big fan of plastic surgery. She pretends it's natural, but she's not fooling anyone. Well, maybe she's fooling the White folk. They think that Asian women are ageless. She's had her nose and eyes done, three facelifts that I can remember, and even had the skin lifted off her neck and hands. She also has permanent, tattooed makeup. She looks good. Really, she got good results, even when she went to Vietnam for some procedures. She's offered to pay for plastic surgery for me, too, but heck, now she can save that money because I am getting it done for free.

I put my ears back under water. This time, all I can focus on is how my heart is beating out of my chest.

I had round five of chemo yesterday—a new cocktail. Docetaxel and Capecitabine. Docetaxel is administered through an IV, and Capecitabine is a pill I take twice a day. So far so good.

Mom and Dad have gone home. Now, I'm consumed with putting my life and house back together post-Mom. She rearranged my stuff to where she thought things should be. Apparently, she thought a lot of my stuff belonged in the garage in unlabeled black garbage bags. It's raining, it's cold, and I'm in the garage, digging through garbage bags as if I were dumpster diving, when in fact, I'm just trying to figure out where my hair dryer and Mylo's favourite Thomas train and Chloe's ballerina doll might have ended up. I've already gone through three garbage bags full of dishes, books, clothes, university notebooks, trinkets from my fireplace mantle, toys, utensils, and shoes—none of which were thrown together with any apparent logic. Mom's message is clear: my stuff is crap.

Life is much better without my parents living here. I walk around my house without fear of Mom coming after me, yelling at me to get back in bed and not die. I'm not holed up in my bathroom, and I can watch something other than *CSI* or *Law & Order* (all billion variations of it) on my living room television.

But Mom and Dad want to come back, like now. My art therapist makes sure I realize that their return would be for their benefit, not mine. My therapist said, "You do not need mommy to come take care of you and do all her crazy-making." I can do well on my own, thankyouverymuch.

Besides, if my mom saw me now—how I go out into the world—she'd definitely chain me to my bed. With my twice-weekly acupuncture sessions, my nightly pot brownie/sleeping pill/anti-depressant dose, and my morning greens/protein shakes, I'm feeling pretty freaking okay. My white blood cell count is up so much that I don't have to inject myself as often with Neupogen. I'm feeling so good that I've fooled myself into thinking that I look decent bald and sans makeup. I am the leader of my own cult. I'm beautiful in my own *ET*-looking way.

Frustrated with this search for my stuff, I get ready to throw this almost empty garbage bag back into the corner out of which I dug it. There is something heavy on the bottom. I use the length of my arm to reach in and grab it. It's my photo album, tattered and fat with family pictures, many of which I had taken secretly (meaning, I stole them) from my parents' house when I had visited over the years. I flip the album to the last page, where I keep an envelope of old pictures. Rediscovering this album reminds me of when I was a kid, and I'd search the living room hexagonal cabinet that contained all the photos from Vietnam in the 1960s, among others. Mom and Dad rarely talked about their time in Vietnam, but I would make up stories based on the photographs into which I stared.

A few years ago, I found these little black-and-white headshots of Mom and Dad in one of Mom's dresser drawers. I took some of them out and placed them with my kids' passport photos. I went into my bedroom at their house and sat down with the pictures. Even in her immigration photo, Mom is striking, especially in the way she looks at the camera with both innocence and knowing. She's wearing a simple white shirt with one of those rounded schoolgirl collars, like on a pinafore. Her hair is flowing and wavy, with a nice sheen coming off the top of her part. The hair and the collar perfectly frame her slender neck. There is only the tiniest glimpse of her right earlobe coming out from under her hair. Her eyes are wide and steady, holding the gaze of the camera with heavy intention. Her lips pursed together, even though she smiles ever so slightly, her cheekbones are raised with dignity. Her skin is smooth, coming off the image like rich heavy cream.

I looked at the picture for a long time.

I put Mom's immigration photo back in the album and carry it into the house. I trudge upstairs to my bedroom and stand before my ancestral altar, where I've kept the journal I made with Ba ngoai's picture on it.

I set it down on the journal, the first hardcover book I ever bound. I used the technique for exposed cord binding. On the front cover is a picture of Ba ngoai. It is the only picture of Ba ngoai that I have. The original is a black-and-white postage stamp-sized headshot, in which Ba ngoai's hair is pulled back into a severe bun. She's wearing a black shirt and pearl earrings. I blew up the image and transposed it onto the cover of my journal.

I compared Mom and Ba ngoai's pictures for resemblance—cheekbones, forehead, eyes—all the same. I pick up Mom's picture, and I feel calm, as if she has graced me with the heaven in which she is living in that picture. I turn my glance to Ba ngoai's picture. I realize that the difference between the two shots is the vastness between Ba ngoai's sadness for being left behind and Mom's hope for a better life in another country.

When Ba ngoai died when I was seven years old, the idea of having had another grandmother barely registered with me. As I got older, Ba ngoai was only mentioned when my mother would tell me how horrible of a daughter I was, and how she would never treat Ba ngoai like I treated her. In more recent years Mom would tell me how she left Ba ngoai behind in Vietnam, and how overcome with grief and depression at the end of the war, Ba ngoai committed suicide by eating rat poison. So it seems, as I stand here with this journal in my hands, that Ba ngoai and I have in common longing, isolation, and the poison that we take to get rid of it all.

um this is so weird

❦❦❦

Every day for the past three months, I wake up after a long night of not really sleeping, thinking about what I would like to do during the day but too tired to really do any of it. I go over in my head and in my journal and on my blog what cancer has done to my relationships with people and what I think of those relationships. It's really not that hard to come to the conclusion that people are better off without you—that being dead would relieve everybody of the expense and burden of dealing with this illness. *will the cycle continue?*

Self-pity is a sickness all its own. But I have two little people who are counting on me to get better. They bless me with their innocence and wisdom, and they are the only two people in my life who don't make me feel like a burden.

Charles wants Mom and Dad to come back. Then, I think, he can go off to his late-night meetings without as much guilt or sense of responsibility. Selfishly, I like it when he stays home and sits in bed with me, pretending to listen to my nonstop chatter about celebrity gossip, peppered with complaints about my agony. It's nice when he rubs my back, if only for a minute or two. His fingers draw light circles across the expanse of my skin, making me forget for a moment about the pains that wrack my body and about how inhuman I feel.

Right now, I'm in Richard's hands, in his care.

"Let's do the spleen, kidneys, liver, sexual organs, breasts. . ."

Richard taps a needle into the top of my right foot. I do not feel a thing. I'm not sure how many needles are sticking out of my legs and feet, but Richard knows what he's doing. I don't notice the effects of acupuncture until I skip an appointment, and then I feel like crap again.

"And for the spirit," Richard says, tapping one into the top of my head. I sit back and sigh. I let the healing properties of the needles course throughout my body.

"How are you doing with the chemo side effects?"

Richard's Maneki Neko Lucky Cat clock is waving at me. "Not so good. I always have a headache in my entire head, can't eat because of the mouth sores. Everything hurts. Look at my hands." I hold out my red, cracked hands for him to see.

"We need to build up your immune system. The chemo needs to do its job, so we won't try to interfere with that for now. Later, we will focus on getting rid of the toxins. Okay, so you relax now."

Before I know it, he disappears from the room. I'm the only one in here. Usually, there are one or two other cancer patients, mostly women, in here getting treatment from Richard. I look forward to hearing other people's cancer stories, but today I will settle for silence.

The problem with closing my eyes is that lately when I do, all I see and hear is Mom. She's telling me that I shouldn't be sick because when I'm sick, I'm no good. If I'm sick, what can I do? Nothing, is what. I never felt like she thought I was good in any way, sick or not. So what does it matter?

It's an Asian thing to not take pride in your kids, or at least, not to show them if you do. That's what Mom told me once when we were visiting her and Dad in Pennsylvania. She heard me praising Chloe's ability to stack blocks as high as she could before knocking them down. She followed me from my bedroom into the living room, where her ancestral altar glowed red and smoky from the lights and incense.

"If you Vietnamese, you no say good things about your kids. Bad luck."

I responded with my usual refrain. "Mom, I'm American." The wall clock chimed three as we sat down on the couch.

"Yeah, but you no teach her like that. Then she turn out no good."

"If my kids do good, I'm going to tell them so."

"No, you no do that. Then they get big head—like you."

"I'm not sure how I got my big head. You never said good things about me."

"Ha, but everyone say how good you are. I no hafta."

"Okay, well, I'm sure my kids won't have a big head."

Mom pshawed me. "Yeah, you see."

I'm not going to wait around for her prophecy to come

true, I thought, but if it does, then they deserve their big heads all the same.

Mom arched her back.

"Oh, my back so sore today! I pain so much."

"You want me to rub your back?"

"I go get medicine."

I waited for her on the old couch. Why did I offer to rub her back? It had been years since I'd done this—the last time probably when I was seventeen or so. Before I knew it, she returned to the living room, with the pungent green medicated oil and a penny in her hand.

She handed me the oil and the penny.

"Oh, Mom, do I have to?"

"You said you want to rub my back—if you no want to, I no make you." Her pout was as big as the couch.

"Okay, lie down, lie down."

She lay on her tummy, head turned toward the couch and away from the rest of the room. I lifted up the back of her shirt and stared at the thick flesh, the seemingly impenetrable rolls covering her shoulder blades. I unscrewed the cap of the bottle of oil and squirted some onto her back. I kneaded the oil into her rolls and mounds of skin and muscle. I thought, well, at least she's quiet. Until she talked.

"You should teach your kids, but no say about how good they are. That bad."

I kneaded more deeply into her muscle tissue, flexing my wrist and rubbing the inside of it along her vertebrae. My fingers grabbed one-inch pinches of skin and crimped them like doughy piecrust edges.

"I tell your daddy all the time, no tell you how good you are, but he no listen to me and still give you money for your grades. I say, why give money, she no get good grades for us! I say, she no go work like me when I was a kid. She go school, that all! But he no listen."

After I pounded on her with my fists for a few moments, I gathered the skin around her shoulders and neck and brought my forearms down on the length of her back. Her skin was warm and moist. I could feel the pores opening up into large receiving craters. I poured more oil onto her back and lightly rubbed it all over so that her skin glistened. My eyes burned from the smell.

"I never tell your sister she good, and now look. She listen to me—she good to me. She love me very much, she no talk back to me."

I looked at the penny in my hand. This is what she wants.

Starting from her left shoulder blade, I dragged the penny down, digging into her skin, drawing it down hard past her armpit, down her side, ending at her waistline. A bright angry welt flared up on the path I took. Mom let out a long moan.

"Did that hurt, Mom?" I asked, half-hoping.

"Feel good. Do more."

The welt sprouted beads of blood. Though that single act of coining only took but a few seconds, I exerted an incredible amount of energy over it, and already I felt spent. I continued on the opposite side, parallel to where the other welt was etched, and began the slow descent down her side.

"I think, oh, maybe someday Brandy be like her sister, she learn. You get older now, maybe soon you know why Mommy is right."

The welts became easier to make. I looked at the work of art on Mom's back—some concoction of sweat, oil, muscle, fat, blood, metal, and blood. Line after line, her flesh swelled with intensity. When I finished ten minutes later, I felt tremendously guilty yet strangely redeemed by the sight of raised flesh made shiny from copper, oil and blood. The heat from the penny in my fist was almost too hot to touch. Somewhere along the line, Mom had fallen asleep, still muttering in her dreams about my eventual transformation into a good daughter who will take care of her as she had done for her mother.

Her breathing slowed, and her words fell to silence. I leaned over to blow softly on her back, cooling the heat and drying the wetness. When the welts began to scab over, I pulled her shirt down. I got up from the couch and sat in the rocking chair, staring into the ancestral altar, wondering how I would be forgiven.

The red glow of the altar fades to black in my mind's eye. The door opens, and Richard re-enters. He's telling me that my *qi* feels stronger already, twenty minutes into the session. I tell him that my oncologist said that my tumours are responding well to the chemo and shrinking.

He twists some needles, squints at them, says that I need a few more minutes. My *qi* will be even stronger, with a little bit more time.

http://cancerfuckingsucks.blogspot.com
Thursday, November 22, 2007
On the Bus

    I was on the bus yesterday, going home after massage therapy. I take the bus a lot now, to go to and from all my appointments along Broadway. There are two buses that I could take: the 9 or the 99. The 9 is the everyday people bus—folks look a little more sullen and don't smell as good. The 99 is the express bus that goes to the university, so it's full of students. Most of the time, I take the 9 because I can't stand the chatter of students, even though the 9 takes longer than the 99. Yesterday, I caught the 99, as it was the first bus that pulled up.

    The bus was packed, but I was able to take a seat when a bunch of people got off at Granville. There were two women sitting across from me, bitching about their professors. I gathered that they were grad students from the way they were talking about theory and such. One of the girls was complaining about some criticism her professor made of her performance in class, and she began her sentence with "I appreciate what he's saying, but. . ." Which got me thinking about euphemisms in academia. Basically, when someone says they appreciate what you're saying, what they mean is that they think you're full of shit. When they say, "That's interesting," they really think what you're saying is completely idiotic. Now when someone says, "I find that fascinating," what that means is that they're not sure if you are full of shit or not, but they think what they're saying might be full of shit too, so they will investigate the comment to decide on the exact content of BS later.

What the fuck does this have to do with my cancer? I don't know.

But really, I wouldn't have been thinking about this if I didn't have cancer, because if I didn't have cancer, I wouldn't have been on that bus going home from massage therapy, which helps get rid of some of the pains of cancer.

The other meandering thought that I had while on the bus: there was a woman standing in front of me as I was sitting down. She was about twenty years older than I, or so she appeared. My first thought was, "I should let her sit down because that's the polite thing to do for older people." Then I thought, "Screw that. I have cancer, and she's only about fifty-five or whatever anyway." Just as I was about to whip off my hat to demonstrate the level of my sickness, I noticed that she was wearing a wig. I can spot fake hair a mile away now. Then I thought, "Shit, she probably has cancer too." I sat there anyway.

It got me thinking about the hierarchy of illness, especially when it comes to cancer. The day before, I was getting acupuncture, and there were two other women in the room with me. My acupuncturist said, "This is Blahblah. She's got a rare form of cancer. So rare that only three people in Canada have been diagnosed with it—and I'm treating two of them!" He beamed. The woman just sighed. The first word out of my mouth was "Wow." But then I thought, What a dumb thing to say. Wow, like impressive? Or wow, like unbelievable? Either way, my gut reaction was that I felt icky for saying "Wow." But yeah, I've noticed how people like to one-up everyone else with cancer stories. Makes me feel weird.

Like when people say to me, "My sister had cancer, and it was awful for her, but she didn't complain at all." Like, wow, good for her, she's such a fucking hero. What's with the heroics of not saying anything when you feel like you're going to die? It's like when women—or their husbands, which is worse for obvious reasons—brag that they didn't have an epidural or scream when they were pushing a melon-head out of their vaginas. Cause you know—it makes me feel better to bitch and moan and cry and wail when my body feels like it's being ripped open or aching with every little breath. Being silent is only an option for me when I'm really dead.

I guess that's the stigma of cancer. Not supposed to talk about pain and dying. Really, that's what's going on inside the head sometimes. I myself find that really interesting. Fascinating.

Posted by Brandy Lotus Blossom at 4:07 PM

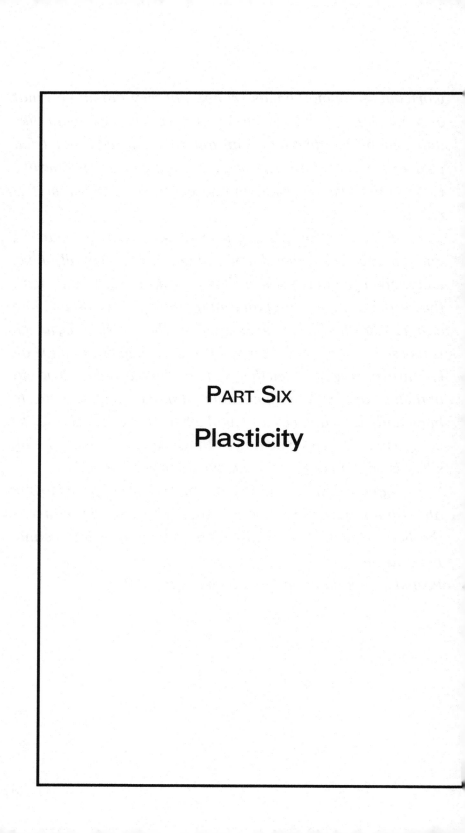

PART SIX
Plasticity

When I was eight years old, something very peculiar happened. When I woke up, both my parents were home, not just Mom. Usually, Dad would have left for work hours before I awoke. Not that morning. They were in the kitchen. Mom was frantically packing sandwiches and sodas into the red Igloo cooler, and Dad was organizing driving maps for Pennsylvania, Maryland, and Washington, D.C.

"Why are you home, Daddy?" I asked, rubbing confusion out of my eyes.

"We are going to Washington, D.C. today. You and I are going to all the monuments, and your mom has to go to the doctor."

"Is Mom sick?" It wasn't every day that we went to Washington, D.C. out of the blue on a school day. In fact, I'd never been there. And to take Mom to the doctor? It didn't make any sense. She didn't seem sick to me.

"Just a little. She's going to spend all day with the doctor."

"Why?"

"It's so she can sleep better. It's for her allergies."

Mom had really bad allergies—I knew that. She took loads of medicine and wore masks every time she did her gardening.

Before long, we were on the road. After a four-hour drive, we arrived at the doctor's office where Mom would spend the entire day being treated for her severe allergies. Dad and I promptly left to go tour the nation's capitol.

I felt very special. Our family didn't travel much or far from Mifflintown, and I loved hanging out with Dad. He was patient with me and took time to explain things.

Turns out that he and I were on a mission. Dad wanted to see the Vietnam Veterans Memorial that had just been built. He wanted to find his Uncle Raymond—Mammy's brother—who was killed in Binh Dinh province in 1966. Uncle Raymond had been the first casualty of the war from our town. After seeing the Lincoln Memorial, the Washington Monument, and the White House, we made our way to the big shiny black wall that had thousands of names etched on it. Dad located the directory and searched for his uncle's name. When he found it, we went to the panel. His finger travelled along the lines of the glossy stone until he found Uncle Raymond.

"Mammy wants to see his name," he said, taking a picture. I had always wondered about the young soldier in the portrait in my grandmother's living room. Unsmiling, Mammy's brother's youth was forever preserved in uniform, on canvas.

We meandered through the gardens and around the dancing Iskons to the National Mall. (Oddly enough, our mostly homogenous Protestant hometown had a substantial Hare Krishna farm community, so I knew about Iskons—or as we pronounced the word, "Ishcons.") Dad and I didn't really talk all that much during our walk back to the car. He didn't seem in the mood to talk, so I kept quiet.

When we got to the car, Dad said, "Now, don't be scared by how your mother looks. Her face is going to be all wrapped up in bandages from her operation, but she's okay."

I remembered going to the dentist and having a cavity filled, and I'd pictured it being something like that for my mother.

We went into the medical office building where we had dropped off Mom. The nurse told us that she was just waking up from the anaesthesia. I sat in the waiting room while Dad went to talk to the doctor and bring her out. My heart stopped when I saw her. Just like Dad said, her head was wrapped in bandages. She walked slowly, hunched over. She was still really groggy.

"Mom?" I held her hand, which wasn't something I'd done very often.

In a raspy voice she said, "Hey, you have fun with Daddy?"

"Yeah. Um. . .?" I looked at Dad, and he motioned for me to not ask questions.

After saying goodbye to the nurse, we began our drive back to Mifflintown. We got home so late that I had to go straight to bed. I had school the next day.

I lived in confusion for a few days. Mom and Dad whispered about her surgery, and she didn't go anywhere while her face was still swollen and different shades of purple, yellow, and green. All for allergies?

When my sister visited, she told me the truth.

"You know why Mom got that surgery, right?"

"Yeah, because her allergies are so bad."

Sis laughed. "Is that what she told you?"

"That's what she and Dad said."

"It's not for her allergies. Well, unless you count her allergy to aging," Sis laughed again. "Mom got a facelift. She is afraid to get wrinkles and look old, especially since she's ten years older than Dad."

"Huh? But she doesn't look old, and she's the same age as Dad."

"No, she's not. She just tells everybody that because she doesn't want Dad or anybody else to think she's too old for him."

"Dad doesn't know?"

"No."

I couldn't understand. First of all, I didn't really know what a face lift was, but I knew that rich people and celebrities got them to look younger. But after seeing Mom's bruised face, I didn't think it made her look younger, only beat up. Second, why would Mom lie about her age to everyone? Who cares if she's ten years older than Dad? Uncle Pen's fifteen years older than Aunt Linda.

"Hey, come do my eyebrows?" Mom shouted to Sis from her bedroom.

"Yeah, coming!" she shouted back at her, rolling her eyes and sighing. She grabbed the tweezers and left me there to think about why Mom was so worried about how she looked or how old she was when all any of us cared about was her.

My eyebrows just came off. I'm washing my face with a washcloth, and just like that, they're gone. I look really freaky now. There are a few scraggly hairs on my browline. Pathetic. I gotta pluck out those sonsofbitches.

"Hey, Mama, what you doing?"

I turn around. Chloe sits down on the bathtub deck. She looks at the lotions I have arranged there.

"Well, check this out. Mama's eyebrows just came out."

"What? Whoa," she said, running her finger over where my brow used to be. "Why, Mama?"

"You know that medicine Mama is taking to get better? I guess my eyebrows don't like it. They left until the medicine is gone. They went on vacation."

Chloe laughs. "I'm hungry, Mama." so sweet

"Okay, let's eat." I put on my slippers. I hold onto the wall and railing with one hand, and Chloe's got my other hand as we go down the stairs. I think of how I used to help my great-grandmother walk around her house when I was younger. Huh, I remind myself of a decrepit eighty-year-old woman. Fantastic.

"How about some *bao bao*?" I open the box of steamed Chinese chicken buns. Chloe nods and sits down at the table. I zap two buns in the microwave and sit down with her to eat.

My tastebuds are coming back a little bit, but my throat is still full of painful sores. I have to chew the bites until they are liquefied before I can swallow. I watch Chloe eat. She's a happy kid. She's a good big sister to Mylo, like Sis was to me. I hope she stays happy and good, always.

Mylo is lured from his bedroom by the smell of the buns. "*Bao bao*?" he asks.

Chloe hands him half of her bun. They finish eating and bound off to play. It always gets heavily quiet when I'm left alone at the table.

Charles is downstairs on his laptop. We still go to therapy at the Cancer Agency, but other than that, we don't talk much. I take it from him that he is done processing his brother's death and just wants to get through my treatment.

I worry about my husband. Edward and his wife used to say that cancer brought them closer together. A lot of people say that. I had hopes that the same would be true of us. If I have to go through this shit, something positive should come out of it, other than a great new pair of boobs. But I don't feel like we've become closer. I don't feel an urgency to live life to the max with him. It's more like, let's get through this and then get back to our life as usual. Cancer is annoying in the way it has interrupted our plans. That's all.

"Hey, I have to go soon. Are the kids ready?" Charles says as he comes up the stairs into the kitchen. His hair is greasy and dishevelled, and he's still in his t-shirt and boxers. He just asked me a simple question, but for some reason, I can't answer it.

Charles stands beside me. "Are you okay? Is something wrong?" he looks concerned. I can't explain to him this feeling of being stuck. I can't understand it.

I bend over and rest my head on the table. "I'm fine. I'm just—just really tired, and my joints ache like crazy." I regret having said any of that. I can't stand myself when I complain

116

to him about how I feel. "I'll be okay. I want to rest a while, and then I'll go out and do some errands. I almost forgot. I have acupuncture today."

I raise my head. Charles already went upstairs to change his clothes. "That's good," he calls down from our bedroom on the third floor.

What's good, Charles? That I feel like shit? Or that I said I won't feel like shit soon? I don't know what you mean anymore. Do you know what you mean anymore? Or are you just saying "That's good" so I'll shut up and you can get out of the house more quickly and not have to deal with my cancer bullshit?

I said that all in my head? I'm the only one who heard that rant? Okay, good.

Dressed and anxious as fuck to get away from me, Charles runs downstairs and grabs his keys.

"Hey, don't forget the kids!" I call down.

"Oh, yeah. I'm running late..."

"Well, just hold on, okay?" God! I can't believe him. He can't help me get the kids ready to go out the door?

"Come on, you two monkeys," I say, grabbing their hands and taking them downstairs. "Get your coats on. You're going to Yeh-Yeh and Nai-Nai's house."

"Why, Mama? I want to stay with you," Chloe says. At least someone wants to be around me.

"Sorry, baby, Mommy has some appointments. You won't be there for long."

"Okay," she says, pouting.

"You guys better go now before you get too hot in your

clothes." I look at Charles, who's halfway out the door. "What time do you think you'll be home?"

"I don't know. Probably around five o'clock," he says. He'll be home at 6:30.

"Okay. Have a good day." I close the door on my family. I watch them trudge out to the van and hop into their car seats. Charles will drive them to his parents' condo, wait outside for his mother or father to come get the kids, and then go to work. He will spend his day talking to students and colleagues, writing emails, making phone calls. Someone will likely ask him how I'm doing, and he will tell that person that it's a tough road, but I'm strong. The chemo is working, and there is nothing to worry about. I'll be back to normal before we know it. The inquirer will commend Charles on what a good supporter he is, and Charles will smile and shrug. Of course he takes care of me. He's my husband, isn't he?

Yes, we're all doing the best that we can.

http://cancerfuckingsucks.blogspot.com
Wednesday, December 5, 2007
Adventures

After acupuncture, I thought I was just going to go home on foot. I started walking on Broadway. There was a nightclub that had closed down, and a temporary thrift store had set up shop there. I walked by this place several times but never gave it a thought to go in. But yesterday, I was drawn upstairs to the store. I almost turned back upon entry—it was dark, sticky, smelled weird, and I couldn't see anyone in there. There were handwritten signs encouraging me to probe further: *"Come on in!" "Great deals!"* I reluctantly moved inside.

I walked around and saw a cute, clean-looking stuffed reindeer, and I decided that I would buy it since the sign outside said that proceeds go to the SPCA. I like animals. An older lady came to chat with me about it. She told me it was five bucks, but all I had was U.S. cash, which she gladly accepted. I walked around some more and found an awesome box for $1. I love boxes. This one had a mirror (that was falling off but could be glued back on) and a little drawer. Then I saw two pieces of cloth that would be great for reading tarot cards. I held onto my treasures and trudged to the front of the store.

I started talking with the lady, who told me I had a nice smile and a really good heart. She blessed me and hugged me and made me feel warm. We walked around the store together. When she couldn't figure out what some of the items were used for (some of it was really weird shit), we would try to figure it out. Then she said, *"What's this?"* I said, "A dirty diaper." She said, "Good heavens! Why would someone leave a diaper here like that?" She was disturbed and went to the back to bleach her hands after disposing the diaper. But she was happy that I told her what it was. She said, "I almost opened the thing to see."

I left and went to Toys R Us and dizzily walked around for an hour. I didn't buy much but just sort of observed the Christmas spirit. Everyone seemed in a daze.

With bags in hand, I decided to take the #9 home. I got on the bus, and a dude and his two daughters sat next to me. He was chewing them out for not getting good enough grades. I felt bad for the girls, who were about six and eight years old. Suddenly, the sun peeked through, and there was this gorgeous rainbow spreading across the city. I wiped the condensation off the window and told the guy, "Hey, there's a rainbow." He and his kids stopped fighting to admire the rainbow with the rest of us on the bus.

Instead of going all the way to the stop near my house, I decided to get off at Main Street. I hadn't seen my friend Burcu in ages. I felt compelled to show her the rainbow. When I reached Burcu's Angels, the vintage clothing store she owns, she was already standing out front. We both gazed at the rainbow. Then she realized who I was (after not being able to recognize me sans hair). She invited me to come in.

I sat on her couch in the living room in the back of her store and burst into tears. I just started crying, and she hugged me and introduced me to all the people who were in the store. In no time we were laughing, and they were giving me compliments on my baldness. One girl said I looked *cool and hardcore and that she had a male friend who was into beautiful bald chicks (she told me it's a good thing I'm beautiful, which made me blush). We joked about how there's no Buddhist monk fetish porn out there, and that I should pioneer the field.*

Burcu's Angels is a magical place where freaks feel at home—and I felt so at home. I wandered around the store and picked up a lovely blouse. Burcu insisted that I try it on, and when I came out with it on, she gave it to me! She also gave me a bag of dried lavender—and lavender is something that makes me feel calm and happy, like my spirit is at peace.
Posted by Brandy Lotus Blossom at 7:52 AM

I'm in my bed, staring at the wall. I'm thinking about this space I'm occupying and about what's occupying my space. Something is always going rogue inside me. Now it's cancer cells; back then it was neurons. From the age of three, I had upwards of 100 petit mal seizures everyday and took a cocktail of Valproic acid and Valium to quell the chaos in my brain. Now I'm trying to think of how to describe what it's like having a seizure. Maybe you can imagine.

You sit there, frozen by your brain and the lights shining bright colours inside your head and the hollow echoes of people near you talking far away. The *whoosh whoosh whorl* of the hazy, swirly tunnel is nowhere as apparent to anyone else as the Mona Lisa smile on your face, which always leaves them to wonder, What is that little girl thinking when she has these spells? You find it no different from the consciousness of infanthood or even of being in utero, and you'll always remember these gaps of time as such—some sweet metallic taste of pre-consciousness or pre-whatever people who don't remember what this is like think of as consciousness.

You'll be listening to what you're being told as a four-year-old, probably some such about getting something to eat or washing your hands or putting on socks so you don't catch cold, and then next thing you know these neurotransmitters (though you don't know that's what they're called) decide to have a little party in your head, shooting off in all sorts of directions, and you're in for the ride: one, two, three, four... And when you come out of it eon-seconds later, you hear them say, Lookit, she's staring like that again. Most people learn that it's no big deal really, except for your mother who will forever believe that number one, you're as fragile as the bright blue robin's egg you tragically crushed when you grabbed it out of the nest just to hold it in your hand, and number two, this is all her fault.

You have epilepsy, which means that everyday you take some nasty goopy pink medicine by the tablespoonful and that every month you get out of school to go see the doctor and that less frequently you get out of school for the whole day to drive faraway to Danville Hospital to have these sticky circle things hooked up to your head so they can read your brain. Everyone thinks that having epilepsy means that you'll be stupid, but as far as you know, you're the smartest kid you've ever met, which means you're even smarter because you're supposed to be stupid from the epilepsy.

You sit in your living room, trapped by your mother's paranoid fantasies of you being let out of her sight, just at the moment when the Big One hits, and you're thrown into a seizure that no one can save you from, keeping you enclosed in your mind for eternity. She thinks that if you stay home within earshot, she'll be able to tame the demons and keep them reined in, for she honestly believes that your condition is not just from you taking a tumble out of the highchair at the age of two, but rather it's a punishment from the gods for having left behind a brother that you won't learn about until many years later. It's just another karmic blow to add to the list of punishments doled out for her mistake: first there were the miscarriages, then the premature baby who died—then, she foolishly thought all sins were atoned for. You were born—a perfectly round, evenly breathing, squooshy pink ball of a baby. You cried loud, had bright wide eyes, and were loved by the whole family, even those who had questioned your mother's intentions for marrying your father. Why did she let herself believe to the point of arrogance that she had done right this time? She should have known that such bragging would be punished. And since you turned out to be damaged goods after all, you and your scrambled-egg brain possessed of unforgiving spirits, it was.

well that was a super brutal karmic mess

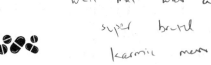

There was a red-orange line running across the sky and through the clouds. It was a Sunday morning, five o'clock, but at four years of age, I didn't mind getting up at that hour. Mom sat beside me, kneeling, eyes fixed on any number of Buddha figurines in the altar. She leaned over and put my hands together, fingers straight, and waved them up and down for me. Nearly certain that I was capable of doing this motion by myself, she let go and continued with her own hand-waving. I followed her lead and watched a line of smoke roll off the top of the incense, at times billowing and at others narrow and straight.

Da da da tick tock da da da. The cassette player on the coffee table contained some little bald monk in scratchy robes, chanting and instructing Mom on which way to turn and when to bow. She hunched forward, stretching her arms out above her head and toward the altar. I mimicked her, sticking my butt in the air just a little further. The stretch felt good.

I raised my head slightly to look at the two-foot brown vase covered in an elaborate black dragon print; I knew that it was filled to the top with quarters that I had no desire to pilfer (as opposed to taking change from my mother's purse). Each statuette, picture, and trinket was flanked by flowers—plastic, real, and dried.

Mom grabbed her bone-shaped gong stick, wrapped in red cloth, which was so worn at the joint end from Mom holding it tightly that the cloth was smooth like suede. She tapped the hollow yet heavy bronze rice bowl. *Bummmm. Bummmm. Bummmm.* Three times she gonged, and I wondered if she was summoning the spirits whose pictures adorned the altar among Buddha figurines and paintings. I had no idea who these people were, but they had achieved some status worthy of our worship, and I waved my hands at them as I did at all the Buddhas, though their eyes didn't follow me as much as Buddha's did. Buddha watched me from his lit painting with the gilded frame and orange background. He was being fanned by two women with blue eye shadow, blood red lips, gold tiaras on top of their black hair pulled up into two buns, and long dresses with high collars. Buddha and his attendants' eyes shone red and gold. I moved slightly to the left; so did his eyes. I moved slightly to the right, and he was still watching me. The women fanning him watched me as well—they wanted to protect him and do a good job of keeping him comfortable. I got sucked into the light—and his eyes.

Mom clicked off the cassette player and got up on her feet, while I sat still and had my staring contest with Buddha.

"Okay, all done. You do with Mommy every morning, okay?"

Mom left to make tea before I could give her my promise that I would.

I kept staring at Buddha and the fake candles glowing orange. I felt like I was starting to have a seizure but not quite. It was a different kind of trance—a kind that I knew you couldn't take medicine for.

Years later, I found myself seizing in the presence of bright lights eerily similar to those in Mom's Buddhist altar, orange and red and clear and white. I was out partying with my friends Jamie, Mae, and Hazel in Hollywood at some gay club where young, lithe, and bored Asian boys were dancing on tabletops to strobe lights timed to the house beat. I can't do strobe—the flashing causes those pesky neurons to engage in one hell of a mind-fuck as they dance more furiously than the light brown bodies on the tables that night. I held onto my girlfriend's clammy hand and got dragged along in my trance through the crowd of onlookers. I squeezed her hand, and she looked back at me with concern. Without a word, I sat down at the first cherry vinyl seat I came to, holding my head with both hands, large clutches of hair knotting between my fingers. The *boom boom thump* moved further and further away until it was so distant that I swore there was a valley between the source and my body. The lights came in the psychedelic whirl. I came out of it, but I closed my eyes and told my friend that I couldn't stay—the lights were making me sick. She led me out the door into the cool Los Angeles air. I took several breaths and focused on the sign above the club's entrance: Buddha Lounge. Before I knew it, we were headed to the butch dyke club down the Strip, where they had two-dollar beers and no strobe lights. I breathed a huge sigh of relief.

When Mom and Dad were here at my house, I'd sit on the couch and watch Mom chant under her breath, eyes closed, right hand clutching a string of dark brown beads. I rubbed my bald head and stared at her mouth. She had been listening to her chants through her portable CD player and headphones. The volume was turned up high since she's hard of hearing from years of working in a sweatshop, all those sewing machines buzzing in her ears. I could hear *nam mo di da phat* coming from her headphones and her whispers. I closed my eyes to the lights that started appearing before me.

PART SEVEN

Homespun

How long have I been rotting in this way? It feels like since before I was born, before the epilepsy, before the hypothyroidism, before the cancer—Agent Orange that seeped into Mom and Dad's skin, eyes, noses, mouths, into their blood, mutating despite optimism or blind faith that it all was completely harmless, to the point of creating me—a successful mutant, when the ones before me have failed and died. I've been made to have bones that creek and hurt, and being able to only half-breathe way before I hit my golden years, if I even make it to that. Aging before your time is a surreal process made more surreal by the drugs you take to try to stop the time warp.

Since I'm living what must be a parallel universe, I might as well go to my hometown. Yes, this is a parallel universe because, I'll tell you why, I WANT to go home, looking forward to it, that's how nuts I've become. The chemo is also turning my brain to mush because I've almost forgotten how psycho my mother is and how there's nothing to do in Mifflintown and how everyone always stares at me when I go home because I'm Asian-looking and mostly everyone else is not. This time I feel so calm and peaceful about it. I imagine some sort of divine hand guiding me there. I want to go to a place where people remember me as a weird little girl who danced and flailed to her own beat and didn't give a goshdarn and was happy about it all.

Today, January 10, 2008, marks the last day of chemotherapy. I still feel like shit, but I never wanted a day to come more in my life than I do today. Because it's my last chemo, I've planned a trip home to Pennsylvania, before I begin radiation.

There's the cool rush of the drugs flooding into my veins when the nurse starts the pump. Beside the big bag of toxins is a smaller bag of Benedryl, to prevent the nasty allergic reaction of not being able to breathe and getting super flushed. I'm an expert in this shit now. So is Charles.

I look at him. He's pounding away on his laptop—some grant or other that's due. Eyes closed, I listen to the pump *click, pause, click, pause, click. . .*

"Excuse me, this is my last day here," I say to the nurse.

"Yes, I see that! I bet you're pretty happy about that," she smiles at me.

"Someone said that sometimes people get certificates when they're done with chemo. Do you do that here?" I want a certificate, damn it.

She laughs. "We should! You're not the first person to ask. But no, we don't."

That's fucking lame, especially if I'm not the first person to ask about it.

"That's too bad," I say, closing my eyes again and putting my head back against the headrest.

I laugh to myself, and I don't care if the other people in the room think I'm crazy. I'm just like Dad. This chemical, metallic smell of the drip—it takes me back to that time two years ago when Charles, the kids, and I were staying with my folks for a couple months. I smelled burnt rubber as I lay in bed with Mylo, snuggling my baby boy to sleep. Charles had left his flip-flops on the gas stove, forgetting that it was in use since the weather had turned cold. I heard Charles swear as he shoved the smoking shoes off the stove.

My parents were in Camp Hill for my dad's weekly veterans PTSD support group. My mom's sister lived a few blocks from the VA hospital, so she hung out with her while my dad went to his meeting. I've always had my doubts about how useful these meetings were, especially when my dad came home from them completely high off his ass. This one particular night when he brought home a special certificate was no exception.

I had just gotten Mylo to sleep when I heard the glass door slide open. When Dad walked in, his voice boomed across rooms. I couldn't tell what he was saying, but I knew that it was some substance-filled babble. I tiptoed out of the bedroom to see what the commotion was.

Dad shouted, "Hey, Charles, you need help there?"

Charles looked up from his laptop and muttered, "Uh, no thanks."

"Looks like—" Dad grabbed the wall to keep from falling over—"you're working hard there."

I searched his eyes for consciousness. He swayed before me in a cool high, I imagined, hearing everything with a surrounding echo. I knew what that was like—I've been high enough times to know the tunnel in which one travels when others around you are solidly stuck to the ground.

Dad reached into the cupboard to see what kind of prescription drug cocktail he was going to concoct to enhance this true-blue good feeling rolling through his body. Grinning at me, Dad said, "Hey, you wanna see what they gave me tonight?"

Annoyed, I sat down at my laptop and waited for him to do his show-and-tell. He left the room and came back with a piece of paper. I took it from him and read:

For you it was the News; For me it was Reality.
You called for Pizzas; I called for Medics.
You watched Construction; I performed Destruction.
You watched children Play; I watched them Die.
You learned of Life; I learned of Death.
Your passion was to Succeed; Mine was to Survive.
You served Dinner; I served my Country.
You Forgot.......I Can't.......

I didn't know what to say. The words were framed by a border of little yellow stars in a band of blue. There was a medal of whatever in the top centre.

Dad looked at me, or at least, I thought he was looking at me.

"Wow, that's pretty fucked up," I said, feeling the bite of accusation from the certificate.

He shook his head slowly. I was afraid he was going to topple over. He stared at me, his bloodshot eyes getting wide long enough to blink, then folded again. I wasn't sure if he was shaking his head because he was agreeing with me that it was fucked up, or if he couldn't believe that I thought it was fucked up.

"I want it back." Sway. Sway. "I'm gonna..." Sway. "...hang it on the wall."

"Here you go." I returned the certificate to him.

Overhearing our conversation and Dad's sudden desire to redecorate the family room, Mom piped up, "What you do? What you have?"

"I got this at the VA."

"What is it?"

"It's a certi. . ." Sway. "ficate that says I was in Vietnam."

"Oh, it say you in Vietnam?"

"Yeah."

"Okay."

Dad somehow managed to find a pushpin, which he used to display the certificate, right below our latest Worrall family picture, taken at Thanksgiving three years ago. While hanging up the certificate, he knocked the family picture off-centre.

"Dad, what's wrong with watching kids play? I watch kids play all the time."

"Cause when you was watching kids play, I was fighting a war."

Never mind that I wasn't even born yet—this time warp was freaking me out.

The certificate, given on what special occasion I did not know, disturbed me with its bitterness. I was angry with Dad for wanting to put this out there, where I and anyone else would have to see it everyday. I was angry with him for being proud of it, smug even—his smugness embarrassed me. I was angry because Mom didn't know what it really said, and I was sure if she did, she wouldn't want it hanging there. But if I told her and she made him take it down, I would be an agent of what he can't forget.   complicul

The next day, I looked at the certificate some more. It was hung below and kitty-cornered to another certificate he received for the twenty-five years he spent "in service working for the Government of the United States of America." Then I went to "my" wall in the hallway, with my academic honours certificates from high school, college, societies and organizations. I thought of my 4-H blue ribbons from the county fair, my Mifflinette trophies from walking in parades in a bright green polyester cowgirl dress with white fringe, my trophies from my track and field days when I would come in third place (out of three girls) in the 1600 meter run, trophies from playing flute in band and from being a candidate (coming in last place) of the Veteran's Queen Ball.

I returned to Dad's wall in the family room, now boasting of two certificates, both proclaiming his loyalty to the U.S. of A.

I read the last lines, "You Forgot.......I Can't......."—the words capitalized as if to announce the official and concrete status of memory and action. I kept staring at those last words, the line reverberating in my mind, driving me into a trance reminiscent of my seizure years, falling into my father's high, in a vacuum of unrelenting memory and the sickening comfort of amnesia, voices fingers hands glances freezing bodies and blood, one breath in, one breath forever gone.

sooo well written

Now, I release another breath, the one I held throughout this memory. I listen to the IV drip. Click. Pause. I suck in another breath, this sudden connection with my dad, of the violence done on the body, mind, and soul, and how now, after all these years, I understand, sort of, maybe. Dad, I won't forget. I can't.

Dante forgot to list Chicago O'Hare International Airport as one of the circles of hell. Hell becomes more hellish in the height of winter. Unfortunately for me, I have to go through hell to get from Vancouver to Mifflintown.

Long, yet sadly familiar, story short—my flight from Chicago to Harrisburg was delayed, changed, erased, and reinstated an annoying amount of times because of shitty weather. Finally, running back and forth between terminals in confusion and frustration—including running through that one corridor with the flashing neon lights along the moving walkway that always almost cause me to have a seizure—I realized that I could take a detour to Pittsburgh instead of trying to get on a flight to Harrisburg. My best friend Lisa lives in Pitt, and she'd been planning on driving to Mifflintown to see me the next day anyway. It was a rare flash of genius on my part.

Lisa and her friend Larry picked me up at the airport, and even though we were all tired, we were hopped up on excitement to see each other.

"Hey, can I rub your head?" Lisa said in her characteristically awkward way that I love so much. In junior high and high school, she was the shy nerd, and I was the obnoxious geek.

"Go for it," I said. "It's like when people want to rub my belly when I'm pregnant, except this is kinda morbid," I said, smiling.

"I think you look pretty hardcore and awesome," Lisa said.

"Hey, Larry, wanna give 'er a rub? It's for good luck." I bent my bald head in his direction. Oh yeah, this was the first time I've met Larry.

"Sure." He rubbed the top of my noggin. "Stubbly."

"Yeah, my hair's growing back now. Fuck, I'm starving."

"Let's go to Eat 'n Park. It's the only thing I can think of open right now."

"Fuck yeah." The three of us were off into the bitter cold.

Fifteen minutes later, we arrived at the restaurant. Mmm, oh god, mmm. Did I mention the Mmm? With my tastebuds coming back to life and the sores in my mouth and throat going away, enjoying food is back on the agenda, big time. I scarfed down two poached eggs, corned beef hash, and potato pancakes. It was one of the biggest foodgasms EVER. Actually, it was a mutiple foodgasm. Seriously though, it was the first time I felt sexy in six months. Too bad the sexiness was with a mega breakfast plate and not with my husband.

Larry drove Lisa and me to her apartment, and she popped in an ancient VHS tape, which documented our summer of 1995. We drove around Mifflintown and reported on road kill and our numerous shitty temp jobs, including working in a warehouse packing books for a monthly book club service.

"Oh no, was that when we stole the phone book from the loading dock of the warehouse?" I shouted. My cheeks hurt from laughing so much.

Lisa snorted. "Yeah, why the hell did we do that?"

"God, we were so dumb. And bored. And pathetic!"

We both snorted.

"Hey, do you remember the time your grandma called me a whore who was going to die of AIDS?" I said. "Man, your grandma is whack. I don't get why she didn't like me."

Lisa rolled her eyes. "She's a sad woman. She's just a little racist and prejudiced sometimes."

"The joke's on her. I don't have AIDS, but I got cancer!"

"Yeah, and you're not going to die either."

"Nope! I'm going to live just to spite your grandma! But, Lise, why is it that both my mom and your grandma think that when I'm hanging out with you, I'm whoring around—but you're not? What the hell is that all about?"

More laughter. It had been so long since I had a release like that. I could feel the laughter helping the chemo kill off the cancer. I wanted to laugh it all away.

Mom's invited the family over to visit with me, as she always does when I make a trip home. Mammy, Pappy, Aunt Linda, Uncle Pen, Sis and her kids, who are now adults, are here. As soon as they walk through the door, before they even have a chance to take off their coats, Mom takes her cue to stuff everyone as full as possible, making the rounds, asking, "Eggroll? Baghetti meatbah? Pizza? Pepsi? Cookie? Coffee? Chips?" She's like a relentless kitchen robot when my dad's family are sitting in our TV room. She needs to feed them, and dammit, they had better fucking eat or else. I escape the insistence of food before she gets to me and decide to go to my old bedroom to lie down for a moment. The excitement is too much.

In order to get to my bedroom, you have to pass through the office/laundry room and my parents' bedroom. Sounds like a weird floor plan, and it is. But that's what happens when your mother tells your father that the porch is a waste of space, and that he needs to close it off and make a new TV room and office, essentially adding onto the original house structure. More repurposing, in other words.

I pause when I get to my parents' bedroom. Hanging on the wall beside the door is a black-and-white portrait on an eighteen-by-twenty-four canvas of Mom when she was probably in her thirties. The artist did not miss a beat or stroke in sketching her beauty. A Vietnamese Mona Lisa. But her Mona Lisa Smile was in her eyes, not on her mouth. At the time of the creation of that portrait, what had those eyes already seen?

"What you do in here?" Mom shouts from behind me. "Your Mammy and Pappy sit out there wait for you. You better go give them kiss, hug."

"Oh, okay." I turn around and go back to the TV room.

I sandwich myself between Mammy and Sis. I squeeze Mammy's delicate hand and smile. She says, "How you doing, my sweetie pie?"

"I'm good, Mammy. Getting some energy back. I'm happy to be home."

"We missed you. I wish Chloe and Mylo was here with you."

"Me too," I sadly say. I pinch my sister on her thigh. "Hey, what do you think of this crowd?"

"It's nice they all come to see you," Sis says quietly.

I sense there's something up with her. "What's wrong?"

"Nothing. It's just I get lonely this time of year, you know, after the holidays, when everyone goes back to their lives. I don't see my kids much anymore. They're too busy. I'm glad you're back. Gives people a reason to get together."

"I have something for you. Come with me so I can give it to you."

We tell Mammy that we'll be right back, so she doesn't feel like that we're ditching her. Aunt Linda and Uncle Pen take over our spots anyway.

We go into my bedroom, and I pull a folder out of my

backpack. I hand Sis a copy of a picture that I had found in Mom's drawer. When my parents were busy in the garage kitchen, I copied it on their printer.

She gasps. "Where did you find this?"

"It was just in Mom's drawer, with a bunch of old letters and other photographs."

Sis stares at the photo. "Mom told me she lost this picture. I even asked her if she had it, and she said she didn't. She lied to me."

"This is a copy. You can have this one."

We stand in silence behind the closed door as Sis gazes at the image of herself and her brother Hieu, when they were babies. Hieu is older than Sis by a couple years; he's about three years old in the picture, she is one. He holds her hand. He protects her, even at that young age.

I learned about Hieu when I was twenty years old, and Sis came back from one of her trips with Mom to Vietnam. She placed a framed black-and-white photograph of a teenage Vietnamese boy on her kitchen table beside my high school graduation picture. "This is your brother, Hieu."

Sis was speaking English, but I didn't know what she was saying.

Much like she's staring at the photo I gave her just now, back then I stared for a long time at the picture on her table. His skin was smooth, his hair jet-black and parted on the left side. He looked a lot like I did in my graduation picture. This boy looked like me.

Sis said, "He's dead."

I repeated in my head what I heard. *I have a brother, but he's dead.*

"Don't tell Mom that I told you. Dad doesn't know that she had a son."

The questions I had were too crowded to come out of my mouth.

"The real reason I went back to that awful place was to see Hieu's grave." She started crying. "But no one let me go there. I begged them. I told Mom I needed to go. But they said if I went there, someone would kidnap and kill me! They told me I'd be tortured and stabbed." Sis broke down into a wave of sobs.

Shortly after she told me this, Mom showed up at her apartment to pick me up. She saw Hieu's picture beside mine and started yelling at my sister in Vietnamese. My sister took her tongue-lashing, and even though I didn't know what she was saying, I knew what she was yelling about. Sis grabbed Hieu's picture off the table, took it back to her bedroom, and shut the door. Mom and I went home.

All that I had ever known about Vietnam before then was through thick worn photographs piled and rubberbanded in shoeboxes from department stores that don't exist in our town anymore. Before that moment, Vietnam was where my parents met, under bombs and mosquito nets and Agent Orange, married at the U.S. Embassy in Saigon, a rescue mission for both of them. Now, this visit for Mom and Sis— and the idea that I'd had while they were gone of a happy, tearful family reunion—it actually wasn't like that at all.

Every time I come back to Mifflintown, I want to find out more. I either ask Mom, Dad, or Sis questions about gaps in the stories, or I search drawers and cabinets for remnants of narrative buried among jewellery, papers, old Vietnamese currency, and tiny Buddhas. How did Hieu die? Sis said he killed himself after being homeless for years after she and Mom left Vietnam. Mom's family was supposed to take care of him—he was just nine years old at the time. But they threw him out into the street where he lived for around five years. Mom said he stepped on a punji stick. She opened her eyes as wide as she could and rolled them into the back of her head to show me what his face looked like when he died. Mom ended her story with quiet tears rolling down her cheeks. She said, "I make mistake." That was the moment that all the anger I had about her leaving him behind washed away.

I want to unearth pieces of us that fell to tragedy. I don't want forgotten deaths to be my family's legacy.

Now, years later, I was standing with my sister, reuniting her with someone she had lost. "Thank you," Sis said, softly crying and hugging me. "He was just a little boy. She left him alone. She left him behind." Sis started moaning from somewhere deep within. I could feel the pain.

"I have the picture on my computer. If you ever need another copy, just tell me, okay?" She nodded. "Hey, don't worry. Someday, I promise you and I will go to see Hieu's grave. This picture is just the start. I'm going to make it happen."

"Where you two go? Mammy, Pappy, Linda, Pen, they want go home now!" Mom shrilled from the other side of the door.

"We're coming, Mom!" We dried our faces and left the bedroom to say goodbye to our family.

The *Juniata Sentinel*—our local newspaper since 1846. When I was growing up, being in the newspaper was a big deal, especially since the town is so small. When I think of all my family's moments of glory that were immortalized in the *Juniata Sentinel*, I recall the photograph of Mom with her gigantic squash that won her a blue ribbon at the county fair in the 1980s; the letters that my father had sent from Vietnam in the late 1960s, asking the good people of Mifflintown for donations to the orphanages in Saigon; and all the letters to the editor that I'd written in high school, denouncing the school board for its violation of the separation of church and state, and chastising the locals for their racism and intolerance toward other religions and cultures (namely, Mom and her Buddhism). Now, the greatest glory of all—me and my baldness and my family and friends, on the front page of the *Juniata Sentinel* with the headline "Accomplished Communicator Spreading Vital New Message." Wow. Huh? (I must note the unfortunate placement of an article entitled "Man Facing Over 1,000 Sex Offense Counts Enters Guilty Plea in Juniata County Court" right above my awesomely dysfunctional family picture for my article, making it appear as if it were perhaps I who was this sex offender.)

My sister's high school friend, Carol, was the reporter who came to my parents' house to interview me and take pictures. It was like one of those oral history assignments I had done during graduate school at UCLA, except instead of being the interviewer, this time I was the subject. Carol asked me everything from my life growing up in Mifflintown (I happily described to her the kind of racist fuckheads I had to deal with from age four) to my current life in the big city in a different country. Then she took my family's pictures— Lisa was in the pictures too—and even my gay ex-brother-in-law, who happened to drop by, popped into the frame. (My sister was pissed.) Aw, wonderful dysfunctional family photo! Screw quilts. This picture is the best souvenir yet from Amish country.

Right now, back in Vancouver, I'm sitting with one of my besties, Irene. She came up from Los Angeles yesterday. I think it's awesome how my best friends have been coming for visits. It has been difficult feeling connected with people ever since I moved to Vancouver. Before I got married, every time I'd moved to a new city, I quickly made friends because the reason for my move was school. But when I moved to Vancouver, it was all about Charles and his friends and family. Then I had kids and even less of a social life. But look at this, my besties are coming to see me!

Because I might die, and they want to make sure they see me before I do.

Shit, Brandy, why do you think like that? Fucking head. Appreciate sitting here. Be girly. It's about living.

"When are your parents coming back?" Irene asks.

"I don't know. I don't want them to come back til March, but Charles wants them to come back now. Of course, they also want to come back now. But I can't take how controlling my mom is."

"Crazy immigrant mothers—gotta love them! They make us who we are," Irene chuckles.

"That's why I have all this!" I point to shelves upon shelves of self-help books. "Here, look at this one." I hand her *Mama Drama: Making Peace with the One Woman Who Can Push Your Buttons, Make You Cry, and Drive You Crazy.*

"Really? You know this is for White people, right?" She grins.

"Yeah, I'm pretty sure this chick never ran into our Crazy Asian Mother brand of crazy. But there's no harm in trying." Irene's Filipina, so she knows all about the CAM because she has one too.

"Let me know how that goes. Hey, you have some really cool books here," she says, looking at my other creative therapy books. She pulls one off the shelf. "Wanna do some of these exercises?"

"Okay, pick one."

Irene and I used to do creative therapy books during our lunch hour when we worked together at UCLA, stuff like Julia Cameron and Eckhart Tolle.

She reads for a few moments. "Here's an interesting one."

I take out my journal. Irene continues, "We're supposed to write 'if-then' statements of things we want to improve in life. The 'if' statement is a positive action you can take. The 'then' statement is the positive outcome that you want to happen."

We settle down with our journals and pens and begin scribbling. The words come easily, as if they are writing themselves.

If I think more about Mom, Dad, Sis and me, then I can broaden my perspective about them and myself beyond my subjectivity.

If I assess what my needs are by periods of time, then I can keep in touch with my parents in a way that allows them to see why I need space now and also so they can still have some contact with the kids.

If I make an effort to connect more with Charles, then he will express what he needs and be healthier.

If I start a creative ritual with Charles (like leaving each other love notes at night, to be read the next morning), then we can end our nights and begin our mornings with love for each other.

If I teach the kids to write letters, then I teach them how to express themselves and show them the value of offering creativity to loved ones—and I get to spend more time with them.

I stop writing and look at my list. It strikes me how much human connection for which I yearn.

But if I try to make these connections, then I might be let down and abandoned.

"Did you finish your list, girl?" Irene asks.

"Yeah, I'm done for now."

"Want to share it?"

"Maybe later."

We decide on another exercise. Like the last exercise we just finished, this one flows easily. It feels like a cleanse, or a baptism. We are supposed to keep completing the phrase "I come from. . ." and see where we go.

I come from a war that went on too long and a little trailer that someone else lives in today. I come from the beginnings of a state on one side, and the end of a republic on the other. I come from timber and creeks and hills and the speedway on the other side of those hills and the drive-in movie theatre down the road and the river that sometimes floods. I come from the smell of leather Bibles (King James version and The Living Bible) and the fine powder of burnt incense. I come from land mowed and ploughed by John Deeres and Cub Cadets. I come from nightly nightmares that shattered God-given country silence and prayers that the whole valley didn't hear. I come from hollows. I come from overflows. I come from being secure under my sissy's armpit at age five, to being left with a cold robin egg blue wall to face at age six when she moved out, the sound of her car tires on gravel taking her away. I come from Arch Rock village, Mifflintown, Pennsylvania, USA and Long An province, Vietnam, though I now live in Canada. I come from a country where White

people have been, and I have not yet stepped foot on. I come
from places to which I am afraid to go.

When Mom was a couple months pregnant with me in 1975, she was getting ready to make the trip to Vietnam by herself to get Hieu. But the U.S. government abruptly voided her visa and paperwork, and refunded her airfare. The government knew it was going to pull its troops from Vietnam, thus ending the war, and it couldn't allow its citizens to travel there, knowing the danger and chaos that would ensue. So Mom never got to bring Hieu to the U.S. He ended up dying there alone.

When I pieced together that story from what little I knew of Hieu and from what Dad had told me about Mom's first attempt to return to Vietnam, it struck me how paths are laid down by sudden circumstances. If Mom had been allowed to return to Vietnam, she and I would probably have been trapped there when Saigon fell, with Sis and Dad still in Mifflintown. I would have been born in Vietnam, and Hieu might still be alive. How different my life would have been. Instead, I was born in Pennsylvania, safe and sound, and Hieu died. Does Mom think about these things too? Is she thinking that my cancer is her second chance to rescue one of her children?

I look at my altar, which occupies the shelf above the books I've been meaning to read. There are Charles's grandparents and my Vietnamese grandmother. There's a picture of Hieu when he was a boy, cropped from the photo of him and Sis. Behind Hieu's picture, I've hidden a picture of Edward. I don't think Charles is ready to see a picture of his brother in the altar, but it comforts me to have Edward there. I scan their images. Three of them—old. Two of them—so young. Variations of life and experience and loss; in the end, only death. Roshi is right, about how it all ends, but damn, doesn't it just seem like an empty, meaningless life without attachments?

Fuzzy, electric buzz—solitary noise of air around me. I'm being either electrocuted or electrified. Why do all the radiation and imaging rooms sound metallic? It's the same quality that air has when I'm having a seizure.

I'm getting a new tattoo. It's a constellation of three dots—an isosceles triangle. Or wait, maybe it's obtuse. I can't remember simple geometry.

The technician draws the second dot, right between my boobs, and checks with his assistant to make sure the coordinates are correct. I'm lying as still as possible. Wouldn't want them to fuck this up.

I look at the first dot he drew, two inches below my collarbone on the right side. He's finishing with the third dot, just below my armpit.

"Now this might hurt," the technician warns me, wielding a tattooing needle.

I laugh. This kid is younger than I am. He looks to be the same age as my nephew Christian. "Do you know how many tattoos I have?" I say.

"Yeah, then this shouldn't hurt. Ready?"

"Yup." He tattoos the dots one by one. "Do you take requests for something cooler than dots?"

He grins. "No, but one lady once said she was going to tattoo flowers where her dots were when she was finished with treatment."

"See—you've brought out the creative side of people," I say.

"Hm, I never thought of it that way. That's cool." He finishes tattooing the last dot. "Are you okay?"

"Why, did you do something?"

"Tough, I see. Okay, when you come in here for your treatment, we will have you lie down on this same table. These dots tell us where to aim the radiation. The treatments will be ten to fifteen minutes long each time you come in. Any questions?"

Buzz. Buzz. I'm plugged into this room.

"No, the doc already explained to me the side effects." I hop off the table.

"After chemo, this'll be a walk in the park," Mr. Young Radiation Dude says.

"Good." I open the door. I can't wait to get out of this giant circuit board.

"Enjoy the afternoon," he says.

"You too."

I walk to the elevator. Old people are waiting to get on. They look at my head. That's right, old people, I got the same disease as you.

Fuck, every time I come to the Cancer Agency, I feel like I'm a resident in an old folks' home, except I don't do the fun things they do, like play shuffleboard and Bingo or clap to sing-a-longs.

I'm stopping at Blenz café before heading home. My legs hurt already, and it's gonna be a long walk. I feel like a billion years old. I somehow managed to get a hernia and arthritis in my pelvis. Because I didn't have enough things wrong with me.

I'm overwhelmed, depressed, and fed up. Apparently, Charles is too. He's taken on a more combative tone with me, questioning everything I do and say.

At least it's snowing. I like snow.

Last night, I got super pissed at Charles. First, I was irritated that he went out to drink with grad students before coming home. I realize this is irrational and unfair, but whenever he hangs out with grad students, I become jealous and suspicious. I suppose if one were to psychoanalyze this, it would be easy enough to relate it to our beginning, when I was his student—and many times, I probably subconsciously get triggered into seeing myself as or feeling like I'm his student. So when I called him and he said he was having drinks with grad students, I got pissed. When he came home, we had a talk.

"Charles, do you want my parents to come now? It'll be another couple of months til they do if you don't want them to come now," I said, looking at him for signs other than what was coming out of his mouth. "They help a lot, right?"

He gave me a long stare, then abruptly turned his back toward me. "It's up to you. They're your parents."

"This concerns us both—and our whole family, really. It's a big deal when they come, so I want to have your take on it. Please."

He started walking away from me, to the bathroom. "I don't know what to say to you. It's up to you. It's your decision to make, not mine."

WHAT THE FUCK IS WRONG WITH YOU, CHARLES! HELLO, I NEED HELP HERE!

I started sobbing and hyperventilating. I lay there in our bed, crumpled and tired, while he was in the bathroom brushing his teeth. When he emerged and saw what a mess I had made of myself, he came over and hugged me.

He finally spoke, "Okay, I think it's best if they come now. We need help." *this is really sad...*

"I'll ask them," I said. "I just needed your input, that's all. I need support from you too. Please stop saying this is all about me. It's about us, okay?" I said, managing a small smile between sobs.

"Okay. I'm glad we had this talk." He kissed me on the top of my head and sat down at his desk to do email.

This was the best conversation that we've had in a long time. And you know what? That's really fucking sad.

When I get home, I'm going to make myself a bowl of cracker soup. So creamy and fattilicious. I totally need to eat cracker soup and watch the snowfall.

I have tremendous fears and hesitation about having Mom and Dad come here so early and for so long. But I can't go back and change that now. I wouldn't want to disappoint any of them: my parents, Charles and his parents, and the kids. Like all the times before, I try to mentally prepare myself for the interaction with Mom. She's become one of my wellness goals. How do I accept her as she is, even when she's constantly talking at me? I was thinking about this on the bus—made me think of my relationship with Charles and my path toward acceptance of who he is in terms of how he does or doesn't connect with me. In therapy I am able to articulate an understanding of her. How do I transfer that understanding to real interactions?

Mom is coming to help out—I have to make sure to remember that. She's not here to cause me misery and pain. Her instinct to control everyone and everything is her way—the only way she knows. I need not scoff at or belittle her efforts.

One exercise I might try—one that no shrink has ever suggested—is to pretend she's not my mother. I'm more apt to feel empathy and understanding with someone who is not as close to me—because I don't allow them to affect me as much psychologically. When my mother is pushing my buttons, can I say, "She is just a woman who believes such and such"? Or consider deeper reasons as to why she'd say such things? Really—is she out to hurt me? Or even if she is, why? Fear? Anger at the situation? I can drag my ego away from what I perceive to be her negativity. I can do this. Oh boy, is this self-help crap working or what?

I'm also reading self-help books to not be bitter, resentful, and suspicious of Charles. Often, if he's not in his office when I call (like yesterday), or if he's meeting with a grad student (like yesterday), I start thinking he's cheating on me, and I take on an angry tone with him. In my calmer times—basically, when my ego doesn't feel as threatened—I tell myself that I need to trust him—and that I can't control anyone but myself, that he's only human.

All that goes out the window when I get the slightest inkling that he's intimately involved with someone else—or even that he would like to be. Then I look at myself and think that if I were Charles, I'd probably want to be with someone else too. I've got bad skin, no hair, am damaged goods, will have my boobs cut off soon, might die. That's an awful way to think of myself. I also know that those thoughts stem from what Mom has told me—I need to be a better, prettier wife. I have to work hard to change my thinking, and I'm more than happy to do that. That's the kicker—I can change my body to get rid of something terrible like cancer, but it's much harder to get rid of terrible thoughts and mindsets. $s \circ \circ \infty$ open

Okay, but honestly, Charles hasn't been the biggest help, even though he might think he's been. Once in a while, he does something with the kids, like yesterday when he took them to the park. It's been a while since he's done anything like that on a regular basis. And when he's watching them at home, the house becomes a mess. Cleaning? Hardly. But he thinks he tries. I just have to not expect too much, even so far as him paying attention goes. He does what he feels he can, and I need to appreciate his efforts.

Last night, I dreamt that I was really sick, so sick that I couldn't talk. And then I had a baby—a newborn, even though I couldn't remember giving birth to this child. Even though I couldn't remember how or why, I was a mother again, and I was in love again.

PART EIGHT

Limpky

This self-help stuff? Total and utter bullshit. My parents have been here for over a week now, and I'm thinking they need to leave. Oh, wait. Do you hear that—that shrilling, grating sound? That's my mother, annoying the shit out of me.

"You no better give your kids old juice. They get sick, and then you have big trouble." Mom just found Mylo's sippy cup, which had been missing for the past two days. She gave him diluted juice, and he dropped it under his bed. I knew it had been missing, but I didn't know that she had given him the cup. I found it when I was looking for his stuffed ladybug. When I unscrewed the lid, the bite of rancid juice made me cough.

"Mom, I would never give them old juice. You don't need to yell."

"I just telling you—you no give kids old juice or food. Make them sick! I no want them be sick like you sick!"

"I don't want them to be sick either, Mom."

So maybe this whole sippy cup thing isn't a big deal. I know that. But why can't she trust that I am a good mother? Why does she think that I would automatically do stupid shit like give my kid food poisoning? It's insulting.

"You know, you better no give your kids bad stuff, then they have limpky like you," Mom says.

Limpky: the sickness inside. I've come to understand "limpky" as a word my mom made up from the words "limp," "slimy," and possibly "slinky." Limpky. It's bad. You don't want it. If you have it, you must get rid of it. You can get rid of the limpky by various methods, including but not limited to drinking tarry Chinese concoctions, soaking your feet in a hot bath of fresh herbs, or screaming at your daughter until the limpky gets scared out of her.

Right now, I'm going to slowly and deeply exhale the limpky.

Self-help Brandy says, "It's her way of caring, of taking care of us." She just cares. Remove the ego. It's not important.

Chloe interrupts my inner chant. "Mama, I love you," she says. It's so simple. Just like that, she says she loves me. I can't remember if I ever said that to my mom when I was little. I must've, right? It's so instinctual for children to love and be loved.

I always thought I learned from my mom how not to be a mother—the way she's overprotective, smothering, nagging. But I haven't learned how to be a good daughter. Honestly, I don't want my children to take after me in terms of how I've treated my parents. I haven't been entirely cruel, but I have a difficult time talking nicely to my mom. I would like to soften my tone, my gaze. There's too much hardness in my life. Too much limpky.

We are getting down to the wire. It's almost time to amputate my tits. It's the event of the year.

Okay, this is so not funny. I'm trying, really, to see the humour in this. I mean, they're just two blobs of fat, right? Just boobs. That's all. And a boob is also someone who is dumb. This whole cancer thing is dumb. If I had anal cancer (please don't ever let me get anal cancer), I would say that cancer is an asshole. I could keep going with this, but inevitably, I would just end up feeling like crap. . .which is what comes out of an anus.

The Brandy Bake is done this week. No more radiation. My skin is so itchy that when I walk by a cool edge of wall, I stop and rub up and down on it. And my nails are peeling away. I think that's the last side effect of the chemo. I'm moulting.

One final side effect for now: time is pressing on and paralyzing me. Everyday I compare myself to Edward and think of how he made the most of his last three years. He had all these ambitions and didn't stop going for them. Me, I get tired, depressed, and crawl under the blankets. I live alone with the pain. Sometimes I'll push harder on the places where it hurts so that when I release the pressure, it feels better. I hurt myself more in order to be fine with the constant pain.

Massage therapy, aromatherapy, reflexology, reiki, yoga, and acupuncture help. I get all these wonderful services at Friends for Life, an organization where professionals volunteer services for people with life-threatening illnesses, mainly cancer, HIV/AIDS, and Hepatitis C. Charles and I are going to therapy there, with a lovely therapist named Natalie.

And—I still can't believe it—Charles cried. During our first therapy session with Natalie, he broke down and just bawled. He looked scared and vulnerable.

Natalie asked, "Are you afraid of Brandy dying?"

He nodded and let loose a muffled "Mm hm."

"State your fears out loud. I want you to say, 'I am afraid of Brandy dying.'"

He gave her a deer-in-headlights look. I could see his matter-of-fact, rational brain working furiously to meet her request.

"I am. . .afraid of. . .Brandy dying," Charles said. He released a desperate sob. I didn't know what to do. Do I rub his back and comfort him? I felt awkward in even just thinking about doing that. Is this what we've become—strangers to each other, drawn apart by fear?

I started crying, but not because I was sorry for Charles. In fact, I was happy that he felt this way. I was thrilled that he was sitting beside me sobbing. He was scared of me dying, at least in that moment. Finally. But when I cried, it was for the fact that I had become so cold and detached from our marriage. It was like I was preparing both of us for my departure.

I looked at him. Natalie gave us silence. She let us sit with our emotions. But sitting together, we were not. I wondered if he was crying because he felt sorry for himself that he might end up alone, his wife in the grave, a single dad. I couldn't grasp the meaning behind his tears. If he was so scared of me dying, then why didn't he spend more time with me? I suppose he didn't want to be reminded of my illness and misery—he didn't want to have to interact with it. He was running away from his fears, with which he was forced to cohabitate.

Natalie interrupted my inward analysis. "Brandy, do you want to comfort Charles?"

I was startled by her question because it was if she were reading my mind. "Yeah, I suppose."

I reached over and took Charles's hand in mine. He gave me a crooked smile.

"How does it make you feel to see Charles crying like this?"

"I feel relieved. He doesn't allow himself to show his emotions about my cancer. I don't think it's healthy for him to not talk about it."

"Would you like him to share his emotions with you more?"

"Yes. He has difficulty doing so. He says that this cancer is all about me, whatever I want to do to make myself feel better. It makes me feel so alone."

Charles remained quiet. He held a soggy tissue in his fist. The look on his face reminded me of Mylo's when he gets hurt.

"Charles, do you think you can talk with Brandy about where you're at?"

He nodded vigorously, as if to convince me and Natalie that he was ready to do what he was being told to do, like a good student.

"Can we start now?"

"Oh. Well, I just think that I will do what Brandy wants."

FUCKING SAY WHAT, CHARLES?

Natalie didn't take her eyes off him. "First of all, when you want to tell Brandy something, tell it to her, not to me. Second, I don't think you heard what she said. I want you to say what she said to you back to her. Say, 'What I'm hearing you say is. . .' Then respond to what she said."

Charles turned and looked me in the eyes. His gaze felt strange, so forced and devoid of emotion. "What I'm hearing you say is that you want me to talk to you about my feelings."

Natalie interrupted once again. "Is Charles's understanding correct, Brandy?"

"Yes," I said.

Charles turned away from me. "I just don't want to bother her with my feelings. I think my feelings are irrelevant anyway."

"Charles, look at Brandy when you are saying this," Natalie instructed.

"I—," he started.

"I heard what he said. He doesn't have to repeat it," I broke in. This was a waste of time. Charles was missing the point.

"I know you heard him, Brandy, but I want him to say it to you. You both need to learn the importance of being physically present—even if it's as simple as eye contact—when you talk to each other. You need to realize how important it is to physically and mentally pay attention to what the other person is saying."

Natalie was starting to annoy the shit out of me, just like Roshi had.

Charles looked at me. "I don't think my feelings should matter. You're more important right now."

"No, Charles, your feelings matter! How do I make you understand? I feel alone, like you don't want to deal with me. I feel like when you tell me that it's all up to me, it's because you're revoking all responsibility in anything in our lives. We are married—in sickness and in health, right?" I stopped because I was crying so hard I couldn't talk. It was always a letdown with him.

Holy fucking A, the two of us were a mess. If I didn't have cancer, what would our relationship look like? Would we just keep back-pedalling through the inertia? And now that I could be dying, we are erupting and melting into the quagmire that our marriage has become.

"Well, I'm sorry to say that time is almost up. I want you to try connecting to each other this week, in the way that I described here, if only for one moment. Next time, would you like me to book you for two hours? I'm thinking you could benefit from a longer session," Natalie said. Okay, she's not so bad. I believe that she actually cares when she looks at us and forces us to do these exercises.

"Yes, that sounds good, if Charles's okay with it," I said. I knew he'd go along with whatever I wanted since that's his default, even if he does detest couples therapy.

He nodded in agreement.

We booked our next appointment with Natalie and headed out the door. The walk down the winding staircase of the heritage house felt like a march to solitary confinement.

I've begun thinking that I'm better off by myself.

If I resolve to be okay with myself and not rely on support from others, then I will be fine, right? Because attachment and dependence breed expectation. All these sappy Lifetime Network movies about love becoming realized through cancer journeys (by the way, every time I hear the term "cancer journey," I seriously want to pull out someone's hair—cause I'm bald, right, so I have to pull out someone else's hair since I don't have any of my own. I fucking HATE that term! Journey is like going on a vacation, or a cheesy 1980s rock band, not something shitty like cancer)? They're not real life.

Still, the little girl who played with Barbie and Ken and their house made out of shoeboxes duct-taped together wants someone to rescue her. No one told her that when you grow up, sometimes the only person to rescue you is yourself.

In my experience people are honoured by an organization at the end of their long years of service or when they're dead. So it came as both a surprise and a point of concern to me when the historical society decided to honour me at the Annual General Meeting and Dinner. The honourees in the years before me were old dudes. And then me. I taught writing workshops for the society and published books resulting from the workshops, which gave them a hefty pool of funds to create some scholarships, so the honour was not unwarranted. Of course, my first thought was, "Are they honouring me in case I die?"

All my family went to the event: Mom and Dad, Charles' parents, and Charles' sister Liz and her family. Mom had no idea why we were there or why people were saying stuff about me at the microphone. She just knew I did something, even though she didn't know what that thing was. When I got up to the mic to accept the award and bouquet of roses, I pointed out my parents in the audience. Dad sat there and gave a shy nod, but Mom stood up with a big smile on her face and pageant-waved to the crowd. For once, she was proud of me!

At the dinner I met author Wayson Choy, whose work I respect and admire greatly. He talked about his memoir-in-progress, in which he recounts his near-death experiences and the lessons he learned from them. He spoke with me quite pointedly, telling me that now is not my time to go or give up. Perhaps it was my chemo brain or the pot I ate to combat the chemo brain, but I felt that Wayson was an angel. A white-haired Chinese Canadian gay angel. I mean, how often do you meet a famous writer who's working on a topic that is affecting you in the very present moment, and who delivers a personal message and support in this most crucial time? Talking with Wayson fuelled me. And it possibly fuelled Charles too, as I think he was proud and impressed that his wife was being encouraged by Wayson Choy.

At the next therapy session with Natalie, Charles immediately told her about how I was honoured. I smiled sheepishly. I didn't really want to talk about it. I was caught between feeling honoured and feeling scared and ashamed.

Sensing my hesitation, Natalie asked, "What would you like to do during this last month before your big surgery, Brandy?"

Oddly, I found myself practically mute. Where I've always had so much to say about all that had been going on or all that I had wished would happen, I had no words for what I wanted to do next.

Here's my problem with all this. It's a countdown. Or more like, The Countdown. I am scared shitless of April 15th. The way everyone is talking about it scares me even more. What would I like to do in this last month before surgery? Sounds so final. I get that it's a major surgery and the recovery time is long. And oh yeah—the fact that they're chopping off my breasts and that my body is going to be changed forever. There's this dance with death. But it shouldn't be bad. Most people survive. What if I'm not most people? Already I'm not in the category of "most people," being that I was diagnosed with cancer at the age of thirty-one. Most people at the age of thirty-one do not get cancer. Fact.

Everyone wants to think that I think I'm okay. I am okay, I say to everyone, especially on my blog. People read the blog and think, Wow, she's so brave, and she's got a great sense of humour. All this cancer business—no big deal. What a fucking lie. And I am not a liar. Or at least, I don't like to be.

So you have someone tell you that you have cancer and you're going to have to have your tits chopped off and the doctors are gonna move your shit around like a jigsaw puzzle with missing pieces and then add pieces from another puzzle, and you don't know what you'll end up looking like, feeling like, or even if you'll end up alive at all—how about someone tells you that, and then you tell me how it's not a big deal, how you're going to spend your last month before surgery as if it might be your last because it really might be your last, but how you're okay anyway because everyone wants you to be okay. Because it's not okay, and I'm not sure if it will be ever again.

It is Edward's birthday, and Charles, his sister Liz, and I are on a full flight, headed to Los Angeles for Edward's burial. It took a long time for Edward's wife Cindy to have his grave marker made. Being the artsy architect, Edward had a specific design in mind, which wasn't to be compromised. We get into LA late tonight. Tomorrow, we'll be at the burial ceremony. Edward is being buried at the cemetery to the stars in Westwood. I'll get to say hey to the likes of Marilyn Monroe, Merv Griffin, and Don Knotts.

When I die, I don't want to take up any real estate. Charles and I bought a cemetery plot with his family, but I just want my ashes to scatter throughout time. The thought of having my body trapped underground freaks me out. Plus, not to disrespect the dead, but I think actual land is better used for the living, and there are too many living people without homes. Being buried seems so excessive.

Come to think of it, I'm not sure I've written down my wishes. Charles and I have a will, but I never really told him what I wanted him to do in the somewhat likely event of an early death. Thinking about this makes me feel like it was when I was making a birth plan with Chloe. In that case, I thought about how I wanted labour to go, if I wanted to hold her all bloody and slimy right after birth or if I wanted her cleaned up before I held her for the first time—stuff like that. Now I'm thinking about stuff like what's going to happen to my journals, what a memorial service would look like, and what kind of booze people should drink in my honour. Maybe even what kind of writer's scholarship would be established in my name. The Brandy Liên Worrall Scholarship for Creative Writing. Or maybe even a writer's retreat—Charles should build a goddamn writer's retreat.

We've begun our descent into Hell-A. I prefer flying into LAX at night rather than in the daytime. The lights cast a fanciful hazy aura over the city. So many lights twinkling. You could definitely get lost, but you'd never be in the dark.

LA is lunch and pedis in Beverly Hills with my friend Victoria, who walks red carpet events, asking celebrities whom they're wearing. LA is karaoke and kimchi pancake in Koreatown with Mae and George, eyeing the hoards of lanky Asian kids trying to hook up with each other past midnight. LA is dinner parties with UCLA professors, who talk about the latest HBO original series being their guilty pleasure because real scholars don't watch television and instead read *The New Yorker* and listen to NPR. LA is where Charles and Edward used to play roller hockey religiously at Santa Monica beach every Sunday morning, dumping balls into nets and garbage cans turned onto their sides.

Charles gave up his position at UCLA, finally. He had had tenure in both LA and Vancouver for the past five years. I've lost track of how many times we moved back and forth between the two cities, between blinding sunshine and relentless rain. He couldn't make up his mind where he wanted to settle. UCLA has more prestige, but Vancouver is a nicer city in which to raise children. My cancer made the decision for him. We would have to settle in Vancouver because otherwise we would be driven to poverty with all the medical expenses for my treatment and post-treatment in the U.S. We keenly remembered how hard a time his brother had financially from the beginning of his diagnosis, even though he had top-notch medical insurance. One brutal fight that Cindy had with the insurance companies was over getting them to help cover the expensive drainage kits used to clear the fluid from Edward's collapsed lung on a daily basis. The companies didn't want to lose money on a patient who was going to die soon.

After Edward's burial, after the pedis, the karaoke and kimchi pancake, and the beach hockey, we are here cleaning out Charles's UCLA office for good. I wonder how many trees were slaughtered for the advancement of a single professor's career. I start indiscriminately throwing away shit. I could ask Charles if he wants to keep this and that, but if I did that, we'd never get out of here, and we would also end up preserving a mountain of bullshit that he probably has forgotten about. Still, I know how many minutes-hours-days-weeks-months-years went into this pile of words. I say a little prayer for all of them and send them off to be reincarnated.

Maybe I should take more care and ask him about all this stuff. I certainly don't want bad word karma. . .like, when I'm gone, will he just go through my journals, papers, and books and throw them in a pit and light them on fire, their importance becoming nothing but ash? That would be such a violation of my spirit. But these things—notes from faculty meetings, graded papers he never handed back, ungraded papers he never bothered to read—who gives a shit? What if he throws out all my papers when I'm dead, all those thousands of words written over all those years? Does his word count mean as much to him as mine does? I'll never know.

We are home. Back in Vancouver. Back to the rain. Back to the madness that is my mother.

Mom's fighting with me. I don't even know what we are fighting over. I don't even care anymore. Something to do with me not listening to her or understanding her or blah blah fucking blah. I took her to acupuncture with me because she was complaining about her arthritis. She wanted me to tell Richard something, but apparently I got it wrong or some shit like that, and now we're on the bus, and she's going on about me not listening to her. And she's right—I'm not listening to her. She could be talking to her imaginary friend beside her for all I care.

So, Natalie, what I will tell you during our next session is that I am spending my last month before surgery being annoyed to high hell. Oh, the few days in LA were short and sweet. Lord knows I needed that vitamin D. But now I'm back here, trying to fight the urge to throw myself off the bus at the next stop.

Maybe, Natalie, you could tell me how I could get out of feeling stuck between wanting to be brave and wanting to cower. Would you advise that it would involve a hotel room that I can check into and hide out for a while and not tell anyone where I am or when I will be back? I'd like to have an affair with my journal and a few bottles of Yellow Tail Shiraz. I'd like to lie in a bed in which so many others have lain before, maybe even on the bed spread that never gets washed, and watch shitty reality television, stare deep into the Panasonic's soul. I'd like to be drunk off filth and sin; I'd be glad to be mad.

That's how I'd like to spend my last couple weeks.

I was on the phone with Mammy yesterday. She's now eighty years old with Parkinson's and other pains. Mammy was telling me about what ails her, and I said, "Mam, you know what you need? You need to smoke some weed."

Long pause.

Then she said slowly in her lilting voice, "Why, Brandy, don't you go puttin' the devilment in my mind!" She chuckled.

I thought, jeez, how much would that rock if I got Mammy stoned?

But yeah, it's highly unlikely I will ever smoke a bowl with my grandmother. I can't imagine what other awesome words like "devilment" she would teach me if she were high. Something to put on the bucket list.

I actually don't have an official bucket list—which is odd, considering how much I love lists. I have lists about lists I should make. Bucket list item #1: Get Mammy high.

There was a time when having big boobs was number one on my bucket list. This is my chance to fulfil that wish. What's it going to be like to have my rack stared at when I walk around in the city, as opposed to people staring over my head at some other chick, who's sporting a great pair of tits? Why is it that when we're not objectified, we would like to be?

Touching myself now. I can feel the big tumour. Reminds me of those 3-D implants that those body modification freaks get. I used to be one of those freaks.

How can something so small be so deadly? Looking at my boobs in the mirror. They look sad, unwanted. I draw a happy face and a sad face on a scrap of paper and cut out the faces. The cut-outs are slightly bigger than my areolas, about the size of a toonie (a Canadian two-dollar coin, in case I lose my mind and forget what that is). I tape them over my nipples, and now I can perform my own boobie tragicomedy. There will come a time when the stories of my boobs will rise to the likes of Medea, Antigone, and Penelope. I intone: *carpe diem, deus ex machina, in media res, nota bene, memento mori*, and some other gobbledeegook. *Wingardium leviosa.* Indeed.

I am inspired. I will give my boobs a proper send-off. They shall be groped. They shall be immortalized. They shall not be forgotten.

I will run this idea by Charles to see what he thinks.

He is sitting in bed, tap-tap-tapping away on his laptop, periodically raising his head to watch *Rome* on the History Channel.

I slide under the blankets and nuzzle his arm. "Don't you think it would be cool if I asked people to grab my tits? You know, cuz they're going to be gone soon anyway." I look up at him and smile.

He stops tapping long enough to deliver a quizzical glance.

"Seriously, like, what does it matter?" I shrug.

"You're disembodying yourself from your boobs already?" He really does talk like that.

"I guess so."

"If that's what you want," he says, returning to his tap-tap-tapping. Are you disembodying my boobs from me, Charles? Cuz it sure sounds like it. I move away from him and turn on my side toward the stairwell and wall.

I'll make a bunch of boob casts. I have two belly casts from when I was pregnant with Chloe and Mylo. I've been keeping them so that someday, when they are older and more interested, the kids can paint their casts and commemorate the belly that they inhabited for nine months. Yes—I'm going to make a shitload of boob casts. People can come to this bye-bye-boobies thing, give donations, and paint my boob casts. I give my boobs a squeeze. They are going to end up doing something for a good community cause after all.

I turn on my back and watch the ceiling fan go round and round. I become anxious watching the blades rotate on the lowest speed. I've felt anxiety ever since the diagnosis. The C word is so much bigger than I am. When my friends my age heard about me having cancer, the whirlwind became even more furious. They thought of the madness, the random chaos, and it scared the shit out of them. How it could have been them. How it could be them someday. The thought and all the what-if's behind it move so quickly, and even watching from a distance takes your breath away.

When I focus on one blade, my eyes following its circular path, I feel calmer. Even something that moves too quickly with a push-and-pull of everything else around it can slow down, slow enough to glimpse the pace and see the exact positioning at a fraction of a second. I watch the blade. The blade is me. I'm moving round and round with the rush of uncertainty, but I am still moving, of that I am sure.

I stand in front of the mirror, only the top half of my naked body visible in the reflection. I have dried plaster specks all over me. The old *Vancouver Couriers* covering the bathroom floor crunch and slide under my feet. I put a tub of warm water on top of the toilet and place plasters strips that I cut three-inches wide on my rolling cart that serves as a vanity table. Vaseline, iPod, candles, towels. This all sounds like a setup for some kinky fetish. But no. It's not sexy like that.

I called Lisa and Vinetta, my friends who own Rhizome Café, and asked them if I could have my last-minute boobie fundraiser there. They thought it was an amazing idea. Ever since speaking with them, I've been busy making these boob casts. I have almost thirty of them so far.

I didn't anticipate how ritualistic, symbolic, and therapeutic this would be. As I was doing the first cast, I was struck by how I felt like I was surgically treating my cancer before the doctors got their turn in a few days. Looking at myself in the mirror—with my fuzzy head and skin discoloured from radiation—I was shocked by how the wet plaster strips on my breasts looked like dressings on wounds. I felt both profoundly sad and liberated.

Even now, as I move from the twenty-eighth cast to the twenty-ninth, I feel like I'm performing some kind of sacrament. I carefully remove the damp, limp cast from my chest and look at it. I like how my nipples make little indents inside the cast and protrusions on the outside. My nipples ache from the thought of how time is running out for them. I place the cast on the newspaper and move into the bathtub, scraping dried plaster scabs off my midriff with my fingernails. I prep my skin for the next cast with Vaseline.

I hear the pitter-patter of kid feet.

"Hi, Mama. You still making boobies? Whoa, Mama, you have a lot of boobies! So many!" Chloe stands at the door, wide-eyed.

"You like them?" I ask, smiling.

"Oh, yes, can I have one?" Chloe's eyes scan the army of boobs on the floor.

"You can paint one at the party."

Chloe kneels down and inspects one. "Can I have two?"

"Um, sure, if there are extras after everyone who comes gets one to decorate."

She spies another one. "Can I have three?"

I laugh. My daughter, the hoarder. "We will see, Chloe Bean. You can help me dry them soon, okay?"

"Okay!"

"Go see what Mammy's doing. I'm going to clean up and bring the boobies down to the kitchen."

"Okay, Mama." My little girl takes off, excited by the boobies party.

After finishing the last cast, I carry them down to the kitchen table and line them up. Mom is getting ready to eat, so I reserve the last quarter of the round table for her.

"Oh my, what you do all that for?" Mom says, sitting down with her chopsticks and bowl of noodles. She faces rows and columns of my boobs. It's quite a sight—all these boobs on one side, and my mother and her noodles on the other.

"I told you, Mom. I'm having a party before I get my boobs cut off to raise money for places that have helped me get better. People are going to come paint these and donate money."

She laughs. "You weird! Why people come see-do like that?"

"I'm not as weird as you think I am," I say, smiling. Who's the weird one here, lady? "Don't worry, it'll be fun. Maybe you'll even have fun."

"Ha, I no have fun! I like sit here, boring." (To the average listener, it sounds like she says "bowling," but no, she means she likes to be bored.)

"Suit yourself."

Chloe and I put the finishing touches on the boob casts, making sure they're dry, and packing them in a box layered with bubble wrap. They are imperfect and fragile; some of them are deformed. That's okay. They'll be unique and unforgettable.

I look at my army of boobs. It's their last battle against cancer.

Even though I had to wake up at the buttcrack of dawn to go to the CBC Radio studio for an interview about the boobies bash, I'm feeling so jazzed. The event got some press, and now a TV crew from CBC is here at Rhizome filming it. The most awesome thing so far? Shortly after my family and I got to the restaurant and started setting up, two young women whom I didn't know were the first to arrive. They showed up because they'd just started chemo and wanted to meet other people who understand what they're going through. That's when it hit me again—the enormity of cancer, the isolation, and the intimacy with people whom I don't know but who understand so well the incredible darkness that can only be experienced once there is a diagnosis. That, contrasted with and complimented by this room now full of people—including lots of little kids—decorating boob casts with paint, glitter, markers, and pastels, has made me feel so complete.

With Mylo by my side, I hold on to his hand and approach the mic to welcome the crowd to this event. "Thank you all for coming out tonight. Looking around the room at all the beautifully decorated casts, I can say that my boobs have never looked any better." The crowd laughs. Charles is walking over to me. He gives me a great big hug, and I try not to cry. Now's not the time to get down about how unaccustomed I've become to his displays of affection. I accept his hug with gratitude and love.

Dad is planted in a seat by the door, manning the donations can. He stares in front of him. I wonder if he's feeling loss, like when he was in Vietnam. He comes out of his reverie and thanks people, who approach him and introduce themselves. His demeanour changes. He looks proud to be my dad.

Mom is sitting beside Chloe, helping her decorate her sixth cast. (I suspect that Chloe has roped various people into helping her decorate as many as possible.) Mom is smiling.

I breathe deeply. Charles, Dad, and Mom—three people who've suffered so much because of me. Who knows the depths of their pain, or how much they've kept to themselves? I'm so distant from them. This isn't how it's supposed to be.

Sitting beside Dad on the bench, I pick up the donations can and peer inside it. "You think we raised a lot of money, Dad?"

He nods. "Oh, yeah, some people gave $20 or more." He looks at me and smiles. His eyes are sleepy, but his demeanour is gentle and a little bit sad.

"There are a lot of people here, huh?"

Dad chuckles. "Of course there are. You have a lot of friends, people who care about you." His tone makes me feel guilty for not practicing gratitude more often.

"I just hope that people had a good time tonight," I say.

"Did you have a good time?" Dad asks.

"Yeah, I did, Dad. Look at Mom. She's painting a cast too."

"I know your mom drives you crazy, she always has. But she loves you very much. Sometimes she just worries too much, you know. We are all worried about you. You and the kids, you're our lives. We just want you to get better."

Dad stops and stares in front of him. I can't hear the crowd around us anymore.

I choke out, "I know, Dad." I squeeze his arm. "I better go check on things," I say and get up to leave.

I keep wondering why I can't stay with these feelings I have with Mom, Dad, and Charles. As much as I talk in therapy about how much I want for there to be a connection between us, when an opportunity for connection arises, I flee. It hurts, these moments.

In the hour of one of the scariest times of my life, I have no problem widening my circle into a community. But when those people in the community go home to their beds and their own lives, I find myself in the centre of the circle, alone. I stay quiet, eyes shut tight.

I woke up this morning slightly hung over but still pumped from last night's event. We raised $1200 for the Canadian Cancer Society and Friends for Life. Then I read the headline on the CBC website, "Cancer patient readies for surgery with boobies bash." It's a pretty nice article about the event, detailing the communal spirit of the fundraiser.

Unfortunately, some of the comments about the article are not so nice. Why would someone call me "pathetic and gross," or say that I have "the wrong attitude" and "no shame and no brains"? I felt completely demeaned at a time when I'm trying to not get down on myself and be depressed.

Then it hit me—this is why women are silent about having cancer, whether it be breast, ovarian, or cervical cancer. They think that no one understands—cancer is a lonely place. And what cancer patients DON'T need is more loneliness or judgment.

I am not ashamed, and I believe I have the right attitude. Excuse me for a moment. I must do this.

FUCK YOU! Fuck you, you ignorant fucking assholes, who insult me and judge me and call me pathetic. You know what? You're fucking pathetic, you sad little shits! You think you'd have much more grace and dignity if you were diagnosed? Because you have zero grace and dignity from where I'm sitting. You can suck my balls, bitches!

That felt good.

Still, it has been quite strange to get negative comments about my boob party, all this judgment about my character for trying to bring empowerment to a shitty situation and to raise money. This one particular person would not cut me any slack. After a few of her scathing comments on the CBC article, Charles wrote a touching, passionate comment:

"Do any of you who have made dismissive or insulting comments about this brave woman have any idea what it is like to go through six months of debilitating chemotherapy, where you spend most of your days poisoned to the extent that you can barely move and your veins and arteries and much of your body will never be the same, another five weeks of radiation where you are literally being burned from the inside and you wonder what the side effects of being irradiated will be if you survive the initial cancer being treated, and then ponder the prospects of major surgery that will require months of recovery and the possibility that you may not survive?

"Are you so pathetic and lonely or, worse yet, so lacking in human empathy that you cannot imagine what it might be to be this woman or someone who cares for her, who has seen her courage and sense of humour in the face of

such pain and fear, and who might cherish her generosity in throwing a party so that those who care about her can laugh along with her and support her in her hour of need?

"If you use words such as 'pathetic' or 'self-indulgent' to describe her, I am afraid they mirror your own flaws and not hers, and that you truly lack a fundamental humanity that allows you to see the grace and courage another shows in spite of their suffering. This has nothing to do with the sexuality of breasts, or your views about your own breasts or your sexuality. This is about the loss of a part of her body that has held great meaning, and how the fears about how that might change her life reflect the fears about how cancer may alter or end her life in the most profound way. To face one's mortality with a sense of humour, and among friends, is such a contrast to the superficial attempts at humour and insult displayed by some of the commentators that I truly marvel at the emotional poverty of their lives.

"I pity you and hope that you will not have to discover what it means to go through cancer yourself, or to see a loved one suffer through it and feel powerless to take their pain away. May you remain blissfully mean-spirited, so that you will not have to learn in the most difficult way what it means to be fully human and humane."

I read and re-read Charles's comment. It said so much more than what he had said to me in the past nine months. The first time I read it, I was sitting in the bed, and he was at the desk, looking at his laptop.

"Wow, thanks for that comment. That was sweet of you," I said.

"That woman's an idiot. Don't read any more comments, though. You don't need to worry about that bullshit."

"Do you feel powerless?" I asked suddenly.

"What? Oh, well, yes, of course, in a way," Charles said, running his fingers through his hair, one hand after the other—one of his nervous ticks.

"I love you," I said, my voice cracking.

He smiled. "I love you too," he said. He turned back to his laptop.

I used telepathy to tell him how much I wanted to take away his pain. I stared at the back of his head and told him that I'm sorry for bringing this sorrow into his life, and that if I get a second chance, I'm going to be the best wife I can be. I told him that things will be better the next time around, when I wake up from surgery and start over. We will both start over and find our way back to each other. I told him that I've forgotten how we grew apart in the first place, but that it doesn't matter. It will be different this time. I heard him tell me that he's sorry too, and that he will try harder too, and that we will be in love forever because that's how it was always meant to be. UGH

It's time. Charles's parents come over to watch the kids, who are still sleeping, and Charles, Dad, Mom, and I walk to the hospital. Who knew when we bought our house a few

years ago that I'd end up at this hospital, three blocks from the house, getting a bilateral mastectomy?

Even though it's only 6:00 in the morning, Dad is enjoying the kind of high that's more appropriate in the evening. I certainly don't think it's appropriate now. His eyes are glassy, and he stumbles over his own feet. I'm fuming and trying to ignore him. Now, Dad? You have to get high now, when my anxiety is through the roof and I need all the stability I can get?

The sepia quality of the dewy morning light softens the rage I feel toward him. He's walking his daughter to the hospital to get her boobs amputated. Maybe this is some sort of trigger for his PTSD. He needs to get high to make it through this.

When we make it to the surgical daycare door, I'm the first patient to register. Before I go to the registration desk, I tell Mom, Dad, and Charles that I'm ready.

"Okay, honey, I pray for you," Mom says. For once, I don't have the urge to snap at her that I don't believe in prayer.

Dad nods his head and stares past me.

Charles and I hug. "It won't be long. I'll be fine," I tell him.

"I know. I'll see you when you get out of surgery."

"I love you."

"Me too," he says, letting me go and sitting down beside Mom and Dad.

After I register, the nurse takes me over to a bed to ask me questions and prep me. I strip my clothes and get into hospital gowns.

The nurse looks at her chart. "Did you have anything to eat or drink after midnight?"

"I had a coughing fit at 4:00 AM, so I had two sips of water."

She looks up from her clipboard. "What? You were told not to drink anything after midnight."

"No, what I was told at the pre-admission clinic was that I could take sips of water before surgery."

She's adamant. "You shouldn't have drunk anything. I'll let it go, but your surgery could have been cancelled."

Bitch, please.

I'm on the verge of a meltdown. Breathe.

She finishes asking me questions and takes me to the operating room triage, where my body is going to be marked up for surgery.

I feel like I'm going to vomit. Of course, there's nothing to vomit, except for two goddamn sips of water.

I start singing the chorus to "Living on a Prayer" by Bon Jovi. Singing my karaoke favourites always calms me down, and right now I don't give a rat's ass who hears me.

"I've smoked forty-five cigarettes a day for forty years. Can I smoke after surgery?" An old dude on the other side of the curtain is fiending for his next ciggie.

"You can't smoke, but we have instructions for your nicotine patches after surgery," the nurse is telling him.

I'm definitely the youngest person in here. I can hear other patients give their ages to nurses, and all of them are over the age of eighty.

Finally, my oncology surgeon and my plastic surgeon come in to mark up my torso with a Sharpie, drawing circles and dotted lines. Dr. Lothlorien tells me that she'll try to not destroy the black widow tattoo that's near my bellybutton.

I pretend I'm in some Shakespearean tragicomedy. Enter the anaesthesiologist.

"I heard about you," he says.

"Oh, you read my blog?" I ask, surprised.

He gives me a funny look.

"No, I read your chart," he says.

"Oh." Normally, I would be mortified by my erroneous presumption, but I've pretty much adopted a fuck-it attitude since I got into triage. After all, I'm naked, and I look like an animal carcass about to be butchered in an ice locker.

The paparazzi clear the way, and now I'm being wheeled into the operating room. There are huge lights, so many machines that go "ping!" (just like in Monty Python's *The Meaning of Life*), and people hovering around me, trying to calm me down. Unfortunately, I must tell you, ladies and gents, that all your hovering is freaking me the fuck out.

The anaesthesiologist appears to the right of me and puts a plastic mask over my nose and mouth.

"I want you to tell me the months of the year," he says.

Huh? "Okay, January, Febru. . .ar. . ."

I wake up and look at the clock. 11:30. Didn't they just put me to sleep?

Panic. "Can you put me back to sleep? I'm still awake."

A nurse rushes over. "No, dear. We're done. It's over."

"Really? No way."

Did that just happen? Was that real? I'm done? My breasts are gone?

I can't stop sobbing. I can't catch my breath.

Oh my god, that hurts!

"It hurts! Ah, I'm sorry!"

The nurse rubs my arm, and she's telling me something about taking me to the recovery room. I just want to stop the pain. It's burning and aching all across my chest, like someone simultaneously pounding on me with hammers and rolling me in fire. Where's Charles?

"I'll go see if we can find your husband, dear. Go ahead and cry. The medicine should start working soon. Everything is fine," the nurse is saying. She leaves me alone in the excruciatingly bright room.

I'm terrified of being left alone with this pain. What if no one comes back? What if they forget me here? I'm pretty forgettable, especially at sushi restaurants, it seems. The server always takes my order, then forgets to put it in. I hope I don't have the same luck in hospitals. Where is Charles? I always expect him to be late, but for once, I'd like him to be on time.

"In there? I can go in?" I hear him say from the other side of the curtain.

He's here! This is the best moment ever. I'm so happy to see him.

He comes over and squeezes my arm.

"How are you feeling?" he asks.

"Like shit," I say, even though the words sound like marbles rolling around in my mouth. "How are Mom and Dad?"

"They went home to eat. I told them that you were out of surgery."

I want him to bend over and kiss me, like in *Sleeping Beauty*. He looks tired.

"You should go home and eat. I don't know how long I'll be here," I say.

"Okay, I'll check on the kids. I'll be back soon."

"I might be in a room by then." *Charles ---*

"I'll find you when I come back," he says. He bends over and kisses my forehead. Or did I imagine that? I'm feeling out-of-body.

Charles leaves. I begin to think that this is one of those transitory places between death and afterlife. Everything is so bright and white; the energy is confused. There's panic, there's calm. But even the panic feels calm, like a terrified child being consoled by her dad.

I can barely lift my head. Instead, I roll my head from one side to the other. I see other people—super old people—

coming out of their surgical sleeps. Nurses go to their sides and reassure them that they haven't passed yet. I wonder if nurses are trained in responding to this type of am-I-alive-or-dead confusion. I wonder how many times these nurses have had to tell people that no, they are not angels and that this is not heaven. I wonder how many times the nurses have seen looks of disappointment on people's faces.

One of the nurse angels says, "Ms. Worrall, your room is ready." So polite. It's like I'm at a resort. Except that the porters could use less aggression as they're pushing me through the halls, smashing through doors and into musty elevators.

My room is big and stuffy. The light coming through the window is dull and gray—typical Vancouver aura.

Dr. Lothlorien breezes in and says, "You have a nice flat tummy."

"Just in time for swimsuit season," I say.

"How are you feeling?" she smiles and puts a hand on my knee.

"Terrible."

"You have a morphine drip here. It should help you be more comfortable."

"I'm pretty itchy inside the compression wrap," I tell her.

"I'll tell the nurse to set up a Benedryl IV. I'll check in with you later."

"Thanks, Dr. Lothlorien." She smiles and breezes out of the room.

I can hear Charles in the hallway, asking someone about which room I'm in. He appears at the door, looking rushed and exhausted. He brought me a pillow from home and a picture of the kids and us in a horse carriage in Victoria last summer, a month before my diagnosis.

Charles sits beside me, and we watch television. I'm not really watching it. I'm wondering what kind of horror movie lies beneath my dressing. If the pain is any indication of what I look like. . .I can't complete that thought. I just hope that my imagination is worse than reality.

It's so hot and stuffy. I'm in a reverse pressure room, intended for patients who require isolation. There's a vent that sucks out air, and the window is sealed shut. I am sweating like crazy, which adds to the itchiness under the dressing. This is a little bit of hell right now. I want to tear off my skin, rip open my muscles, claw out my bones. I want to be left with nothing.

How? How can Charles still love me after all of this? I'm a thing, a non-human, or less than human. The morphine is puppeteering me. Charles is so alive. Go home, I tell him in my head. But I don't really want him to go.

I want to sleep and forget this ever happened. Shouldn't I be sleeping? Why am I so awake and wired? Fuck me. I'm one of those people who have the opposite reaction to morphine.

The day is long, the night longer. Charles is snoring on the pullout bed/chair thing. A nurse named Kelly comes in to check my IV's. She's younger than I am. I'm starting to realize that I'm not that young anymore. To her, I'm not some young woman with breast cancer. I'm just another woman with breast cancer. I want to tell her that I'm not as old as she thinks I am, that there are maybe five years between the two of us. She leaves before I can break the news to her.

It's 9:00 a.m., and Charles went home to get some sleep. Dad has come to take his place by my bedside. Dad is completely doped up on something again, whether it's prescription meds or weed or both, I don't know. He's wobbly and slurring. Dad, why can't you be sober for once? Fuck it. He probably figures that since I'm on morphine, he can be stoned. Fair is fair.

We're saying words to each other, but I don't know what they are. We're saying stuff despite ourselves—stuff we'll never remember beyond the moment it's been said.

"Dad, remember when you'd play P-I-G with me?" He laughs. "What's so funny?"

"That game is really called 'H-O-R-S-E,' but I told ya it was P-I-G so it was shorter. I couldn't play that long."

"What? Come on, Dad, two letters? You couldn't shoot the basketball for two extra letters?" I laugh too. I cherish the moments I spent with Dad when I was little, but now that I'm a parent, I know how exhausting it can be sometimes to try to entertain children. "Well, I liked it. It made me feel that I was somewhat good at basketball."

Dad laughs again. "No, Brandy, you was never good at basketball. You was too short and skinny."

"Remember when I ran track?"

Dad guffaws and slaps his knee. "You dropped outta half of them races because of your asthma. I tell ya, I was glad cuz them was long races. What were you thinking, running the two-mile race?"

Oh, Daddy. I love you. And do you remember when you'd take me fishing and I'd get my line and hook caught in a tree? Or when we used to rent horror movies from DC Video on Saturday nights and watch them in the basement living room, and how every time you went upstairs to get Diet Pepsi, I'd follow you because I was too scared to stay downstairs by myself? Do you remember any of that, Dad?

"Well, I'm gonna have a smoke," he says. "I'll be back. You gonna be okay?" Dad gingerly gets out of his chair.

"Yeah, Dad, I'm not going anywhere," I say, closing my eyes.

I hear him moseying on out the door.

A few minutes later, the shrill of Mom's voice makes me open my eyes.

"Charles' parents come watch Chloe Mylo, so I come here see how you doing. You in lot of pain?" Mom stands by my side, gently touching my arm.

"I'm okay, Mom."

"You better take it easy. You no want rip nothing," she admonishes me and looks at me from head to toe.

Nurse Tina pops in and tells me that I should get out of bed and take small walks down the hall. She looks at Mom when she talks, as if Mom knows what she's saying. I tell Tina that we will try it in a few minutes, and satisfied with my promise, she leaves.

"Mom, that nurse said that I need to get out of bed and walk down the hall."

Mom is horrified. "What? I no can help you outta bed! I might let you fall!"

"You're not going to let me fall. Just hold onto my one arm, and I will use my other arm to hold onto the IV cart." She looks unconvinced. "I have to, Mom. That's what the doctor wants me to do. It's what the nurse said."

"Okay, but you be careful! Oh my! I no want you fall!"

I hold onto my mother's leathery hand and swing my legs over the side of the bed. She puts my slippers beneath my dangling feet. My legs feel like jelly, and I have to admit that even I'm a bit scared to get out of bed. I hold onto the ring of the IV cart and wiggle my left foot into the slipper. I bear my weight on the left and put my right foot in the other slipper. All that effort, just to get out of bed? Fucking epic.

Mom and I make it into the hall without casualty, and now we are doing the shuffle down the hall. The nurses cheer me on and clap as I take my baby steps. Reminds me of when Mylo took his first steps on his first birthday. Are they going to give me a cookie when I drop my first load too?

"You know, I understand how hard, how much pain you have. When I have you, they cut me open and take you out, and oh my, I feel so much pain. Nobody come help me, take care of me. Not your mammy or Aunt Linda. I have pain, but I wash clothes and cook. No one come see me," Mom says.

I stay quiet.

"When you Chloe's age now, I want to leave your daddy. I no can stand no more. But I stay because I love you, and I say, 'Oh, Brandy need mommy and daddy. I no can leave.'"

One time, when Mom and Dad went to get pig gall bladders for one of Mom's medicinal recipes, I went through their stuff. I remember finding a letter addressed to Mom from her friend Nga in Vietnam. Surprisingly, it was written in English. From it I learned that Mom wanted to go back to Vietnam after having lived there a couple years, that she couldn't stand living in Pennsylvania any longer. But Nga was telling her how horrible it was in Vietnam, with people dying all over the place. She told Mom that being in Pennsylvania was for the best, and that she needed to think of her daughter too. It was best for her and her daughter. But what about Hieu? I don't recall Nga mentioning him in the letter, even though she signed the letter with "All my warmest sympathy."

"I think I need to be back in bed, Mom. I'm getting dizzy." *so much sorrow and loss*

"Okay, you better lay down. Too much standing," she says, helping me turn around.

Back in the room. Dad's returned from his smoke. Mom helps me into bed, and Dad settles into the chair in the corner.

"You know, I tell Brandy how I almost leave you when she was little. I tell her I stay with you because of her."

What? No! She's not doing this here, is she?

"I no want to leave you because she little girl. . ."

"Oh, shut the hell up, Liên." Dad closes his eyes and shakes his head in frustration. I frantically push the morphine

193

button, hoping that I can trip it up and OD.

I close my eyes to the dysfunction being played out with me lying in the middle. This is where it would be useful to be Christian. I could pray to God for respite. The Zen thing isn't kicking in. The noise, inside and out, is too loud.

"Please, can you not fight right now? I'm tired. I want to take a nap. Please."

The bickering ceases, and I close my eyes, pretending to go to sleep. I can hear them "hmph!" and hiss at each other, and after a few more seconds, they are completely quiet. I gather from the movement and angry whispers that Dad has decided to go home. I can hear Mom situating herself in the chair in the corner where Dad had been sitting.

Eyes closed, I remember seeing the letter from Nga. It was rubberbanded in a bundle of correspondence in the bottom of their dresser drawer. In that bundle was a letter from Dad to some governmental authority figure, explaining his PTSD and his substance abuse in order to clarify a psychiatric evaluation done on him. Most surprisingly, Dad detailed the emotional distance between him and Mom, how his PTSD had affected his marriage, which he'd hoped to rescue and repair. He said that they have been unable to communicate very well, and though she's been trying hard, he withdraws from her, and she is forced to coexist with him as long as she chooses to remain in the relationship. Reading that letter knocked the wind out of me, and I hurriedly bundled all the documents back together, secured the rubberband, and threw the bundle back in the dresser, pushing shut the drawer.

I don't know how much time is passing. I fall in and out of consciousness. I know at some point, Mom has gone back to my house. The skin on my chest feels like it's burning. I try to focus on the time I got my wisdom teeth cut out, and Lisa came over to hang out. It was prom night, but of course, neither of us had dates. She couldn't help laughing at the sight of my swollen face. I'm glad there were no camera phones and Facebook back then.

"Mama! Mama!" I open my eyes to see Chloe and Mylo inching into the room. They are excited to see me, but they seem a bit afraid too. It must be scary to see your mommy looking like a mummy. Actually, I can relate.

"Mama, how do you feel good?" Chloe asks with endearingly awkward syntax.

"I'm so much better now that you're here, baby girl!" Chloe hugs my arm.

"Mama, I bring kitty kat," says Mylo. He offers me his little black-and-white stuffed cat doll. I take it and hug it, and Mylo smiles and sucks on his bottom lip. He looks like he's trying hard not to come over and pinch my elbow.

Charles's family is here—his parents, his sister Liz, her husband Bennett and their kid, Sarah. Everyone has come to see how I'm doing. I remember what it'd been like to visit my great-aunts in the hospital, and Uncle Pen when he had surgery for cancer. It's uncomfortable, not knowing what to say or how to act. But they've tried to make this into a party and brought a bunch of food. The amount of people in here exceeds the legal capacity, but no one's come in to say anything. So we eat, and

I pretend that this is just another family gathering and that I'm not naked and disfigured under these sheets.

Yes, this fried rice is the best I've ever eaten. Thanks.

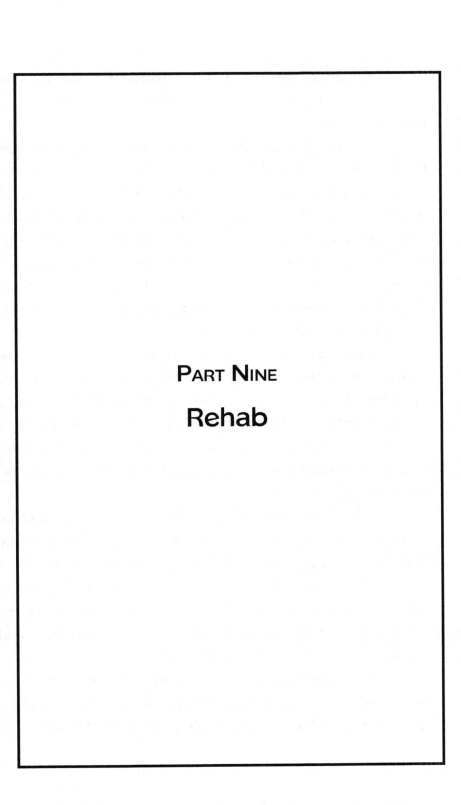

PART NINE

Rehab

Instead of staying in the hospital for five days as expected, they let me out on the third day, just like Jesus rising from the dead.

As I was leaving the hospital, I was so hunched over that the super ancient old people were staring at me. I thought, "Fuck you, old people" as I hobbled out the automatic sliding door that wouldn't slide open at first because I was too hunched over to be detected. Charles parked at the curb and had to get out of the car and stand in front of the door so it would open. When we pulled up to our house and I walked to our front door, I wanted to point my finger and shout, "You rascally young people, get outta my yard!"

Not long after I made the journey from the first floor up to my third-floor bedroom, one of my best friends showed up. Jamie drove from Seattle with his friend Sharon. I was so happy to see him. Jamie makes me laugh all the time, and it was then that I realized that laughing hurts like a motherfucker. Laughing and coughing—two things I don't want to do now. I'm ripping apart at the seams.

As if I don't already feel like I'm inhabiting an alternate universe, it started snowing today. Snow in Vancouver in the middle of April is unusual. At first, it had been raining. Then the rain turned into big balls of hail. Now the hail has turned into snow. It's coming down hard. I can see it piling up on the skylight across from my bed. I feel like I'm living in a cave, and I'm safe from an impending avalanche.

Jamie and Sharon have gone to the hostel downtown where they're staying. I've shuffled to the bathroom to empty the two drains that are still coming out of me. I take off my robe and look in the mirror. The dressing is crusted with dried blood. Small bits of tissue float in the red-brown liquid in my surgical drains. Was it really just last week that I was looking in the mirror, applying plaster to my chest to make boob casts?

I can't just peel off this dressing like I did the plaster. I don't know what I look like. Is the flesh black and rotting? There's a possibility that the tissue and muscles that were transplanted from my abdominal area to my breasts won't take, that the blood supply could get cut off and that the flesh will die. What kind of Frankensteinian monster have I become?

A couple hours ago, I had a major coughing fit. Since I knew that coughing would cause me a lot of pain, I tried stifling the cough, which made it much worse. I began crying, choking, sputtering, and moaning. Chloe and Mylo rushed upstairs.

Mylo, who derives his greatest comfort from touching elbows, rolled up his sleeve and said, "Mama, you can touch my elbow."

Still trying to quiet my cough, I just stared. He asked, "Mama, can I hug you?"

Chloe pushed Mylo forward and instructed me, "Mama, hug Mylo!" As painful as it was to lean over and accept his hug, it was more comforting to hold my son in that moment, to receive the care he offered me.

I may feel like a thing now, but I know that I'm still Mama to two kids who know that the surest way to heal is by hugging their mother and holding her tight.

Dr. Lothlorien and her nurse Rachel removed the drains and the dressing today. My skin is irritated from the adhesive on the dressings. It was excruciating when the drain to my abdominal wound was yanked out, with the remaining hole stinging when I move. But I don't look as horrific as I'd thought I would.

The stitches at my nipple area (though I have no nipples to speak of) and at my abdominal area from hip to hip are still oozing, so there are gauze strips covering them. My "boobs" are tinged greenish yellow. They are tight mounds of flesh. The new bellybutton that Dr. Lothlorien cut into my belly is crusting. These scars and scabs are my cocoon.

I've all but disappeared from the blogosphere. I'm trying to forget or not think about the people out there who are waiting for an update, a success story, a happy ending. I don't think I can give them a happy ending yet without lying. Trying to be present is exhausting. I just want to wallow. I want my old body and my old life back. I don't want to repurpose this one. It was fine the way it was before.

http://cancerfuckingsucks.blogspot.com
Friday, April 25, 2008
This is why America rules: motorized carts

These past few days have been different kinds of weirdness. A couple days ago, I noticed that my whole torso was numb. It was a very odd sensation to touch my stomach with my hands, but there was no sensation whatsoever that registered on my stomach. In other words, under normal circumstances, your hand feels what it is touching, and whatever is being touched can sense being touched by the hand. Now when I touch my stomach, my hand senses my stomach while my stomach senses nothing at all. It's as if I'm touching someone other than myself—a one-way touch. In fact, if I closed my eyes and lay there naked, and someone came over and touched me on my stomach, I would never be able to tell.

Additionally, I seemed to have developed lymphedema, a common condition that develops after a woman's lymph nodes are removed along with the breasts. I'm doing the best I can with the exercises I'm supposed to do, and I'm also going to a physiotherapy group on Monday for mastectomy patients.

Good news—I'm slightly more mobile. Despite the trauma my body's experienced in the past nine months, I'm feeling pretty good.

Charles and I always go to Walmart in Bellingham to pick up stuff. I know, I know! Walmart's this evil gigantor monster that's out to suck the souls of humanity, but I wanted to go to Walmart. More importantly, I wanted something that

I've dreamed of ever since Walmart existed in my world: to ride their motorized carts, the ones for customers who "need a lift," as the little sign on the cart's basket says. Yes, I am finally one of those people! I rode a Walmart cart—and IT WAS FUCKING AWESOME.

As soon as I hobbled into the store, I walked over to a group of ladies standing around chatting. This was the moment that Charles and I were talking about for the past hour—of whether or not I should get one of those motorized carts.

I said, "Yeah, I mean, I really don't need a cart."

Charles insisted, "Yes you do! If they give you any shit, just raise your shirt."

I conceded, "Yeah, I suppose you're right. I'll give it a try."

I got all worked up on the way to Walmart—getting pumped up to the moment when I could show my bodily disfigurement as proof to the incredulous attendant that I needed a cart. Instead, when I asked for the cart, one of greeters immediately spoke up, "No problem. See you gals, I gotta get a cart for this young lady." The way she said it, it sounded like she was doing the most important job that she's qualified to do. She said as I did my hobbly-hunch, "Don't mind if I walk faster, do you? Get a head start?" "Go ahead," I said, and she sped-walk to the carts. Even though I caught up to her in about two seconds, she still hopped on the cart, drove six inches, stopped it at my feet and said, "There you are! Ooh, the seat's still warm. I assume you know how to work this thing?" I said, "Uh, I never had one of these before."

She said, "It's easy—just put your thumb on that button and steer and go!" I was off!

I have to say, this weird life goal of mine—to someday ride in Walmart's motorized carts—falls in the category of "exceeds expectations." I totally want to pretend for the rest of my life that I'm somehow physically challenged and never have my shoes touch the ground at Walmart ever again.
Posted by Brandy Lotus Blossom at 11:13 PM

Mom's taken it upon herself to secure my life thoroughly here so that I can survive without her. She doesn't think I can survive without her. Not only that, she thinks my kids won't be able to survive without her either.

I'm trying really hard not to be annoyed. When she says, "You hafta cut apple like this so Chloe Mylo no choke. You no let them choke," I try to remember she's being helpful, not critical. But really, I know she's being critical, and come on, like I don't know how to cut fruit so my kids won't choke? What kind of mother does she think I am? Does she think I have cheese for brains because of cancer?

See—it doesn't work. Sometimes, the conversation ends pretty badly. This morning, she came up to my bedroom, armed with one of those lint remover tape rollers that are normally used on clothes. Mom likes to use them on carpets and rugs after she's vacuumed. The thing is, I don't have any carpets or rugs in my bedroom. The floor is laminate. There is nothing that you can use the lint roller on in my room.

Or so you think. While I was resting in bed (when I heard her coming up the stairs, I quickly turned on my side and pretended to be asleep), Mom appeared, lint roller poised. I heard *squeak squeak squeak*. She was de-linting my floor. Back and forth, round and round, the roll of tape moved along the laminate, all the while making a super annoying squeaking noise. I couldn't take it anymore.

"Mom, what are you doing?"

"I clean floor. You no can get dust with sweeper. I no want you sick again."

I started to say something, but what was the point?

"Your mother-, father-in-law take Chloe Mylo all the time? They no get sick of watching them?" she asked in an accusatory tone.

Charles's parents picked up the kids today to take them shopping. I was trying to cherish my quiet time, which was not so quiet anymore.

"No, they like watching them."

"You better not be sick no more. You hafta watch your kids. You no want Charles's parents get mad at you." *Squeak, squeak, squeak.* "You shoulda let Mommy Daddy take kids home with us to Pennsylvania." *Squeak, squeak, squeak.* "You can rest, and they like be with me. I take care of them good." *Squeak, squeak, squeak.*

"Mom, I'm really tired."

The squeaking stopped. Mom stiffened. "You no want

hear Mommy talk, I no talk." She skulked off to the bathroom, where the squeaking recommenced, as did the lecturing.

"You no want hear what I say all time. You like your daddy. That fine. I no talk. I no allowed talk. You and Daddy always tell me stop talking."

I could hear her sobbing between sentences, during which she'd hold her breath to be able to finish the thought.

"I just try help you, and you push me away." She said "push" forcefully, with a high-pitched breath. "You no want me here, your husband no want me here. Fine. I go home, I no come back."

I stuck my head under the pillow and groaned. Yes, I did feel bad that she was freaking out. But what was I supposed to do? Right, I was supposed to endure. Why couldn't I just keep my mouth shut and let her download in the first place? It's not like she's staying here much longer anyway. I just couldn't, okay?

The talking stopped. All I could hear was *squeak squeak squeak* with some quiet sniffles. Even though it hurt to move, it hurt more at that moment to stay in bed with her so close by. I got out of bed, went downstairs, put on my runners, and went for a walk. I wanted to get lost and disappear.

Charles's dad was asked to give a Chinese translation workshop to some university students. Ba-Ba had done the Chinese translation of an anthology of family stories that I edited. His involvement in the project happened because of the fact that he's Charles's dad, and Charles needed a translator. Ba-Ba also dabbles in translating classical Tang dynasty poems into English for fun. He then sends his translations to his buddies in China, and they discuss meaning, poetics, evolution of words—word nerd stuff like that. So he's always been happy to do translations when Charles asks.

Ba-Ba had been freaking out all week about his presentation. He'd ask Charles questions about what kind of material to present and how to present it, but Charles had been too busy with other meetings to pay much attention to Ba-Ba. I'd help out as much as I could. On the day of the workshop, Ba-Ba called and asked me if Charles could pick him up to take him to the workshop, since Charles was already in his neighbourhood for a meeting. I told him that it shouldn't be a problem, and that I'd relay the message to Charles.

I called Charles and got his voicemail. It was two hours before the workshop. I called him again, half an hour later. Nothing. I kept calling. Finally, when it was half an hour before the presentation, I called the office where he was having his meeting. The secretary told me that he had left a while ago. I called Ba-Ba and told him that I couldn't get a hold of Charles and that he should just drive himself to the university. I then set out to catch a bus to go watch Ba-Ba's presentation.

As I waited at the bus stop, Charles called me, telling me he was on his way home. "Ba-Ba's presentation is in ten minutes," I told him. "Where have you been?"

"What? I thought it was at 7:00 PM," he said.

"I don't know where you got that idea. It's on the calendar, 5:00-7:00," I said.

He told me that he was on the way to pick me up. My face burned; I was sure that the one inch of fuzz on my head was singed with anger. In fact, my scalp became unbearably itchy.

This is what has plagued me since my diagnosis—his irresponsibility and self-centredness. How in the world is he going to do right by the kids if something happens to me? Why does he always have his head up his ass? Why can't he tear himself away from his desire to talk, inform, educate, entertain and enlighten and teach? Why can't he think of his wife, his kids, his parents, who need his attention now and then? He supported me through my cancer journey? Bullshit. He only did so to save face because he knew that was what was expected of him. But he resented the fact that he had to give up conferences and other social and career engagements to take care of his needy, sick wife.

My mind raged, and raged some more. I kicked the bus stop bench as I saw the van approaching and coming to a quick halt by the sidewalk where I'd been standing.

I said nothing to him on the way to the university. I said nothing to him as we parked the car. When we got home after the workshop, I said nothing.

I waited until our therapy session a few days later to say something. Guess what? I had lots to say. I told him I was sick of him being irresponsible and self-centred. He looked mortified that I would say such a thing in front of somebody else. It hurt his ego and his reputation, I could tell, and I wanted to lay it on more thickly.

My failure is expecting him to change. My failure was listening to all those stories of how people are transformed after a cancer diagnosis—they become grateful and more attentive to their loved ones. In some way I had convinced myself that my cancer happened because it was finally the chance for Charles to change, for us to change as a couple. Our fissures would close; we would become one again because we would know how fragile life is. He would realize that all that time spent talking to people who were so enraptured by what he'd been saying was petty compared to the valuable time spent with family. He'd realize that at his deathbed, the people who love you—your wife, your kids, your best friends—they'd be by your side, not a conference full of peers or a seminar of grad students. Those other people—the people who went to hear him give a lecture—they were there to help his career. We were here to spend his life with him. He would see that, I was sure of it.

He didn't see it in the least. That was why his fuck-up over Ba-Ba's workshop enraged me. Maybe I couldn't outright tell Charles I'd been disappointed by how much he had not been there for me when I was going through the deepest, darkest shit of my life—because I didn't want to hurt him, make him feel so much of a failure, that he couldn't even be

208

there for his wife while she was going through fucking cancer. Yet it was true.

But he didn't think so. He thought he'd been there, that he'd made an effort. Didn't he cancel his trip to that one conference where he was supposed to be the keynote speaker? If that's not a sacrifice, I don't know what is. Yes, I'm being sarcastic.

To him, that was a sacrifice. To him, he had made quite a number of them. I was a bitch for not seeing it. Worse yet, I didn't understand him because I didn't understand how much of a sacrifice those types of things had been.

BUT I HAD FUCKING CANCER! I'd shout back in my head. I would give up everything to take care of him if he had cancer—didn't he know that?

So this is what happened.

After therapy, I took a bath when the kids went to bed. It was the first bath I'd taken since the surgery. I sat in the tub for an hour and cried. I cried because I look and feel like a freak. I cried because Charles would never understand. Because I've had images in my head of me cutting my veins out and letting them dangle and cutting them in half so I could die. I cried because I realized that I have no memory of the time before I had thoughts about killing myself or running away every day. I remember being four and wanting to take a bunch of pills. That's Chloe's age. I cried because so much has happened, so much is gone. I love my children more than anything—they saved me, but I'm never going to tell them that. I'm not going to guilt them like my mother did to me. They're happy children who only know the words "kill" and "die" in an abstract sense. They'd never apply those words to themselves or to anyone they love, and I'd like to keep it that way for as long as possible.

When I got out of the bathtub, I sat down on the floor and cried some more. I closed my eyes and tilted my head. The bathroom lights were bright against my closed eyes. I felt like I was back on the operating table, right before I lost consciousness, and the air was so electric, it hummed. Everyone became angels, and when I first woke up, I wondered if I were dead. All these quick memories of right before and right after the operation flooded back as I sat on the bathroom floor. After a few moments, I got up and crawled into bed.

Eventually, Charles came upstairs. I told him about these operating room memories. He didn't say anything. He was busy thinking about the day and our therapy session. He asked me why I was so angry with him. I said I wasn't angry all the time, that I'm trying to change old patterns and habits. I realized during therapy that my issues with trust stem from growing up with parents who didn't trust each other, with a mother who didn't trust anyone, not even her own daughters. I told him about my history of anger: how I was angry at him for taking years to divorce his first wife; how I was angry and hurt when I found out he cheated on me during the first year of our relationship; how I sometimes become angry when I feel like he's not around as much as I'd like him to be.

We left it at that. I still felt so alone, like the little girl who ate dinner by herself in front of the television, waiting for her daddy to come home to pre-packaged TV dinners of

Salisbury steak and fake mashed potatoes with carrot cubes and peas.

This week, we've had more intense conversations. There was a point at which he sounded like he was giving up on the relationship because, as he said, our dynamic isn't what he thinks it should be after eight years. It hurt to hear him say that because I felt I had been trying to not be bitter and angry—but I guess I'm not as happy as he would like me to be. When I tried to resume our conversation when he returned from hockey the other night, he didn't want to talk about it anymore. He said that he was just saying stuff—that that's the problem with talking: that you just say things and maybe you don't know what you're saying anymore. I know that's really an excuse to get out of talking because there's got to be some truth in what one is saying, or else why bother putting words out there to be heard, to be thought about?

So we stopped the talking. And all of a sudden, we were happy. We purged and were left with a desire to make each other happy. It's a new era, a new way of being. The old, the past are gone.

One day you're doing yoga. The next day you're getting a MUGA scan on your heart. I'm not saying that metaphorically or wistfully. That's really what my days consist of. I'm in limbo, this nippleless place between cancerous boob and numb mounds of flesh that used to be my abdominal muscles on my chest wall. It's a place where on the outside, I look like I could kick almost anyone's ass, but on the inside, I want to curl up anywhere at all and take a nice three-hour nap, wake up, pee, and take another nice three-hour nap. On the other side of this limbo is a place called What I Used to be Except Way Better. I cannot wait to get there. It sounds really dope.

I keep thinking of when Dad was in rehab. Which time in rehab? I don't know. Pick a time; they're all the same. Okay, let's say the most recent stint, for kicks. Before, I used to speak as his daughter who got whittled down after each visit, patience whittled away by expectations, promises, hope, disappointment, defeat, anger, bitterness. Resignation. Now when I think of Dad being in rehab, I'm not doing so as his daughter. I'm relating to him as someone who's been through the shit.

PTSD—those four letters don't do the illness justice. Post-traumatic stress disorder sounds so clinical and pat. Dad has hardcorefuckedup trauma that has not gone away. It leaves him alone sometimes, but it's always there. All the drugs he gets from the government for bipolar disorder, depression, anxiety, insomnia, and pain only do so much to numb the trauma. I know Mom has trauma too; she screams like crazy in her sleep every night. Since she screams in Vietnamese, I don't know what she's saying, but I'm pretty sure it has something to do with being killed, tortured, or abandoned. Because she's not a veteran, and because she doesn't understand all the psychobabble, she doesn't get treated for her trauma. She prays to Buddha but not about her trauma. She just prays and chants, and she teaches us to pray and chant too.

When Dad goes into rehab, it's gotten to the point where his trauma is unmanageable. Everyone around him has had enough. They are tired of holding him up, rushing to the house to help out Mom, watching him come to family gatherings drunk and belligerent. They tell him, "Why don't you pray to God and get over it? The war is over. You need to stop moaning about it." Of course, none of them has been to the war. They've barely left Pennsylvania. They don't know what it's like to live in his head, see that shit when he closes his eyes or when he wakes up and watches the news. Mom is the only one who knows, but she thinks he should do what she does, not understanding that each brain processes trauma differently.

Dad is tired of it too. He wants an off-switch to his brain—hence, the alcohol. He goes into rehab to numb that part of his brain. He leaves rehab, hoping that he's cured for good this time. He leaves tired but hopeful. Everyone watches him, and they say, "He looks good. He looks a lot better. I think he'll be okay this time." They turn their backs on him and return to their lives, newly unburdened by the demons in his head manifesting into substance abuse.

He's tired. Everybody else is happy that he's back to normal, but it's a daily struggle to be normal. It's exhausting to not think about how the hardcorefuckedup trauma could just come back full force at any moment. You can't control it—no one gets that. They think you just get treated, and you're good for the rest of your life, and you don't have to burden anyone with your illness anymore. You can't control the memories of that intense darkness, that isolation and loneliness, agony, helplessness that make you pray to God even if you don't believe in one, because what kind of God would make all this suffering possible?

You try to do things to get better: go for walks, read self-help books, take vitamins, exercise, go to therapy. Sometimes it works. A lot of times you feel stuck, like you're spinning your wheels and at any second, the mud is going to smooth out and give, and you're suddenly careening out of control off a bank. That stuck feeling, that muck and inertia, is indescribably painful. That's why you get the shakes. You have this twitch. You take pills. Ativan. Xanax. You drink Scotch. You smoke weed.

Back and forth, back and forth. The movement makes you nauseous, and you just want a constant feeling of moving forward, for at least twenty-four hours. But your mind doesn't work like that. No one around you understands. At all.

I'm trying to put it out of my mind. Today, I met this woman who was getting acupuncture the same time I was. She said she has faith in her abilities to heal herself. Instead of getting the recommended chemo, she's seeing a naturopath for intravenous supplements and Richard for acupuncture. She's doing visualization, and she's sure that the lump in her breast is just a fibroid and not cancer. My first thought: how can you be so sure? If I found a lump in my breast, you can be certain I'd get the first available appointment to see my oncologist and proceed to freak out in all sorts of dysfunctional ways. But this woman was so calm. I admired her in a way. She reminded me of Mom, while I felt like Dad. There we were, the two of us, together, still fighting.

This woman left acupuncture to get her intravenous vitamin C dose; I went to do my physiotherapy session and to talk to my oncologist. She explained my pathology report. She said that even though I had a good response to chemo and radiation, it wasn't a perfect outcome since one lymph node tested positive. But since the lymph node was taken out during surgery, it wasn't anything to worry about. She talked to me about fear of recurrence, about being vigilant about my health. She also mentioned that maybe I should try to find a support group for breast cancer patients and survivors. I wrote down some book titles she recommended and thanked her, but I know I don't need that stuff. Normal is all I need.

Now that Mom and Dad have gone home, I've been trying to work my way back to life by going on trips with Charles and the kids. Earlier in the month, we went to Whistler, a major ski destination in the winter. In the summer there are hiking and other outdoorsy activities like ziplining and horseback riding. We went with Charles's best friend, his wife, and his kid. I had a good time, but it was exhausting having to keep up appearances. I just wanted to sleep.

Not long after that, we went to Osoyoos, which is in Canada's wine country, the Okanagan. Charles's entire family went with us—his parents, his sister Liz and her family. That was less exhausting for me because I felt I could just be me around his family, and they'd understand. It was a retreat for all of us—it's been nearly a year since Edward died and I was diagnosed. Four years total of dealing with cancer. We've had enough.

There was a carpe diem aura about our family. We looked at each other in sad appreciation and gratitude of what remained. Charles's parents watched the three kids, and the rest of us grown-ups got shitfaced, played golf, and went to the spa. I tried to relax, but for some reason, I felt like an impostor. I had intruded on all of them. Only my kids looked at me without judgment or pity, without thinking that I'm fragile and temporary. I hugged them tight when I put them to bed each night.

Two more big trips, and I can get on with life. Next up, Pennsylvania. We skipped going last year because of my diagnosis, so my family (other than Mom and Dad) hasn't seen the kids in two years. Then Charles and I are going on a gourmet kayaking excursion with eight friends. I'm not sure how I'm going to cope with a weekend full of physical activity and heavy drinking, but I'll do my best.

Family vacations when I was growing up were driving to Ocean City, Maryland with the Ungs, one of the three Asian families in our town. We'd load up Mom's cherry red Chevy Nova with two coolers filled with cold cuts, sodas, and condiments, and the Ungs packed their station wagon to the gills with five kids, two parents, and the uncle. We'd take the morning to drive there, and we'd reach our destination by mid-afternoon. Before we got to our cheap motel, we'd stop by the highway to do some illegal harvesting of mussels. The Ungs were Cambodian, and Southeast Asians don't give a fuck. If there are living things lying by the side of the road that are free and edible, they will get plucked up and hoarded in huge garbage bags to be steamed later on in the evening— never mind the huge sign right beside where we parked that said, "Do not pick the mussels. $250 fine." If we got caught, our plan was that Mom and Mrs. Ung would do their best "we no speak English" routine while Dad, being the only White person, would pretend not to know any of us.

These trips to Whistler, wine country, and gourmet kayaking expeditions are a far cry from Ocean City, Maryland and illegal harvesting of mussels. Back then, I had all the time in the world, and it didn't take much money to make us happy. Now I know how time is precious, and all the money in the world wasn't going to make me feel normal ever again.

http://cancerfuckingsucks.blogspot.com
Monday, September 22, 2008
Funny Cancer Thought of the Day
        Nothing will take you out of wallowing in self-pity faster than your kid vomiting deep-fried bananas and chocolate ice cream at 11:30 at night.
Posted by Brandy Lotus Blossom at 10:53 AM

PART TEN

Dr. Big

Chloe and I were sitting in the Costco food court after we'd done some shopping. She was munching on roasted seaweed when she asked me out of the blue, "Mama, did you die when you went to the big doctor?"

"You mean when I went to the hospital? I didn't die. See, I'm alive, talking to you," I told her.

"Yeah, you're right," she said, nodding her head. "Cuz when you die, you go under the ground. Then aliens come and take you away, and you never come back."

"Yeah, something like that," I agreed. "Some people think there's God, and they either go to heaven or hell. Some people think you come back as an animal or another person. Some think that nothing happens. No one knows for sure. So aliens are a good idea too."

She said, "Yep," and took another bite of her seaweed.

I wanted to tell her that I didn't really think it mattered what happened in the afterlife because this life now is all we really know about, but I kept that to myself. Now wasn't the time to rule out Santa Claus, Easter Bunny, Tooth Fairy, God, Buddha, or even aliens. She'd learn someday, soon enough.

Charles and I are in the office of the Hereditary Cancer Program. I've been called in to discuss the possibility of doing genetic testing for the BRCA-1 and BRCA-2 gene mutations, which indicate hereditary breast and ovarian cancers.

The geneticist has a bunch of papers waiting for me to review and sign. She begins, "As you know, you've had Triple Negative breast cancer, and because of that and because you were only thirty-one years old at the time of diagnosis, you qualify for genetic testing. If you test positive for either the BRCA-1 or -2 mutations, you will likely be advised to have a hysterectomy because such mutations would place you at high risk for ovarian cancer."

She pauses, waits for my reaction. I'm not sure what she's expecting, but all she's gonna get out of me is, "Okay." Charles is oddly quiet, his mind elsewhere.

She continues, "Great, so now I need to ask you some questions about your family's medical history." With pen in hand, the geneticist asks me about Dad's side of the family, basically what his family's history with cancer was. I tell her to the best of my knowledge that a few of my great-aunts and great-uncles had cancer, but no one I know of in my immediate family has a history of it.

"Okay," she says, "so let's review your mother's side."

Before she can go down her list of relations, I stop her. "I don't know anything about my mom's side of the family. She's from Vietnam, and I don't know any of my family from there, other than my sister, my mom's sister, and two of my cousins. The rest I don't know, and I don't think they've ever kept any medical records or kept track of who died from what. Some of them were also killed in the Vietnam War, so you could probably rule out that they died from cancer."

The geneticist looks stunned by my admission. "Okay, well, maybe you could try to find out some more information somehow?" she asks, handing me a paper with a family tree on it.

"I'll try, but I don't think I'll find out much more than what I know today. But I do want to ask you something." I take a deep breath. My hands are clammy. I don't know why I'm nervous. "My mother and father were both exposed to Agent Orange in Vietnam. They saw the planes fly right above their heads and drop the chemical. Do you think my cancer has anything to do with that? I've been wondering that, since it's strange that I was diagnosed young, with such an aggressive and advanced cancer, and I don't think I have any family history of it." I search her eyes for answers.

"I'm sorry, but I have to say that while it is an intriguing notion, there's not much research that's been done on the link between cancer in the children of veterans and exposure to Agent Orange." She writes down "exposure to Agent Orange" on her notes anyway. This gives me a glimmer of hope that maybe somebody does care.

She hands me a consent form. She explains how sometimes patients will back out of genetic testing when they come to realize the psychological impact it might have on themselves or their children. The consent form makes both patient and researcher aware of these possible psychological implications.

"I, Brandy Liên Worrall, hereby consent to have DNA analyzed from a sample of my blood to attempt whether or not I carry an abnormal gene, or gene mutation, that is known to predispose to breast and/or ovarian cancer.

I understand that despite a personal or family history of breast and/or ovarian cancer, an inherited gene mutation may not be identifiable based on the current testing methodologies.

Choosing to know my genetic test results may reduce or increase my anxiety or worry about developing cancer. I understand that the emotional impact of receiving cancer risk information is not predictable, and the decision-making process regarding genetic testing may affect interpersonal relationships within my family.

If a specific gene mutation is identified by my DNA, genetic carrier testing will then be possible for my family members to determine whether or not they have inherited the same gene mutation. This means that if I choose not to know my DNA test result, with my consent my result could still be available for use by other family members. Further testing in my family may imply that a gene mutation was identified in my DNA. I understand that other family members knowing information about me that I have chosen not to know may affect interpersonal relationships within my family."

After I finish reading the form, I hand it to Charles. He skims it and returns it to me. "Looks good," I say and smile. I scribble my signature on the line and hand the geneticist the form, which has become dimpled from my sweaty hands. What will I pass on to the kids? What have Mom and Dad passed on to me?

It's hard for me to remember the time before now. Let's see. Before I came here, I was there. Before that, I was trying to put my life in order, one Rubbermaid tub at a time. Before that, Mae and her husband George came here from Los Angeles for a holiday visit. Before that, Lisa flew here from Pittsburgh for my thirty-third birthday and to go fulfil a teenage fantasy of ours, which was to see New Kids on the Block in concert. Before that my uncle back home killed himself because he couldn't take the pain anymore. When I was growing up, he was like a second dad to me, and he often reminded me of my own father. Before that, Charles was in Albuquerque for a conference. Before that, I was here, probably.

I'm at Starbucks on 14th and Main. I have no idea where Charles is. He and I are at a bad place. It's a place that's so bad that it might be good for us. Or not. But first, I want to talk about the weather.

It started snowing on December 20th, and it has hardly stopped since. You can't buy a shovel anywhere in this city. They're sold out. The snow stopped for eight hours last night before it started up again a few hours ago. It's coming down hard.

Charles and I argued after dropping the kids off at his parents'. About what, I can't remember. Quite possibly the argument had to do with. . . Oh, yes, I remember now. He was on the phone with a woman who is helping him get a bilingual

A Unwin

Mandarin program established in the public schools. Except that this lengthy conversation happened on Christmas, during our family time, and I wasn't too happy about it. So I emailed this woman and told her that she needs to not take up my husband's time so much during the holidays. Of course, he became angry with me for doing so. Perhaps he was right to be angry. I knew I was overstepping some line. But, I told myself, wasn't he overstepping boundaries, too—using up sacred family time by politicking with some woman, of whom I was quickly becoming jealous? We just talked around the true issue at heart and confined the conversation to how he uses his time, not bothering to touch upon my obvious insecurities. At least, they're obvious to me.

Finally, he gave up talking and said he was going somewhere to think. I cried myself to sleep. Then I woke up to the sound of someone shovelling. I looked out the window and saw Charles's best friend shovelling our walk. He and his wife came to drop off presents, but I pretended that no one was home, so they left them by the door. I waited around for Charles to come home. I texted and called him, but nothing. Then I walked here to Starbucks in this blizzard.

I'm waiting. I suppose this has been a long time coming. I'm sitting here watching cars slide by, tires not equipped for this kind of weather. Every time I see a beige Honda minivan, I'm hoping it's my knight in shining armour coming to rescue me and tell me that all is forgiven, and love is still there, still possible. Unfortunately, there are a lot of beige Honda minivans in this city. And it seems none of them are coming for me.

White Horse

http://cancerfuckingsucks.blogspot.com
Friday, January 30, 2009
12 Days and Counting

It's only twelve days until I get boobs. . .again. This isn't like the first time I got boobs, when I was about fourteen years old, praying to God every night (still a believer back then) to give me boobs—any boobs—so the junior high ridicule would stop (it didn't). I stared at my flat chest in the full-length mirror in the bathroom, rubbed the small nubs, and did some ritualistic chant after my Christian prayer. Eventually, I got boobs, but dammit, for all that anxiety and work and concentration, all I ended up with were barely-B's? Beggars can't be choosers, but this time, I get some choice.

I met with my plastic surgeon a week and a bit ago. She took a good hard look at my chest, and she said that full B/small C cup would probably be the way to go. For some reason, I felt bashful and didn't pipe up that perhaps I wanted to go up a size or so. She's the expert, after all. She showed me a saline implant that would be about my size, and I said, "Looks good to me."

I agonized over this for a good part of the morning after my appointment. I kept thinking, "What's wrong with you? It's now or never. Get the big boobies you want!" So I sheepishly sent her an email.

Hello Dr. Lothlorien:

I was just in to see you this morning concerning my surgery scheduled for February 11th. You had talked about giving me saline implants to make me a full B/small C cup. I was giving this some more thought, and I was wondering if I could get more volume to make me a full/bigger C/small D? I just keep hearing my girlfriends say in my head, "Go for the gusto!" so I thought maybe now's not the time to be bashful, especially since I know very well that you only live once.

Cheers, Brandy

A few days later, I got this reply:

Brandy,

No problem. Dr. Lothlorien has ordered you bigger implants.

Sincerely, Melissa

So I'm like, great! Big boobs! But a part of me was weirded out that the size of my boobs was decided over email, just like that.

I thought of how Chloe and Mylo have gotten used to seeing my nippleless chest, with the big scars and mottled tissue. I'm grateful in a way that I exposed my children to my body image issues rather than hid them, and that we were able to communicate about them. Chloe still asks me now and then if my boobs feel better or if they still hurt (her words), and we talk about it. I find it so easy to talk to the kids about

226

my body because they are the only ones who don't see me as deformed.
Posted by Brandy Lotus Blossom at 2:32 PM

PART ELEVEN

Fool

I'm so fucking sick of this rollercoaster. Is it me that's the problem? My insecurities, my paranoia, the lessons Mom has taught me about not ever trusting anybody, especially men? Why am I always wondering what Charles's doing or where he is or how he feels about me? Why do I discover these things that only support what I keep trying to deny?

This morning I was getting ready to write notes to put in the kids' lunchboxes like I do every morning. Using notepads that Charles gets from the university, I draw cartoons of the kids having various fantastical adventures. They look forward to reading them to their friends. I ran out of paper, so I looked in Charles's briefcase for a new notepad. When I searched the side pocket, I found a receipt from a bar downtown. The date and time was when he was supposed to have been playing hockey. He came into the room just as I found it.

"You didn't tell me you went to this bar. I thought you were at the community centre playing hockey," I said, narrowing my eyes.

"The teams were full by the time I got there," he said.

"Whom did you go with?"

"Some guys."

"How many guys?" I asked, my face getting hotter.

"I don't know. Like four or five." He left the room. I kept standing there, holding the receipt in my hand.

When he and the kids were leaving, I followed them out to the minivan.

"It says here that there was a party of two," I said.

"You don't trust me?" he asked with a biting tone.

"No."

"There were other guys, sitting at another table," he replied, getting in the van.

"I still don't trust that," I retorted, mostly to myself since he was already in the van with the door shut.

This is where I am. What am I supposed to do? Trust him? Smile and say, Oh, yes, it's perfectly normal and logical that my husband goes to have some glasses of expensive wine and fancy hors d'oeuvres with dudes who couldn't get into a hockey game at the community centre at 10:00 at night. Yes, I can just picture him sitting at a small candlelit table with one other dude dressed in hockey sweats, enjoying libations as they have a tête-à-tête. Makes sense.

I recalled how I told him last week how much I love him and how I've felt hurt by his actions. But he talked all that away. He thinks that as my husband, he has made a certain commitment, and that should be good enough. He kept going back to me being dissatisfied with how he sees me, like it's my problem and he can't or won't do anything about it. He almost had me convinced.

It was hard for me to get out of the house after he and the kids left this morning. I went back to sleep and didn't roll out of bed until noon. My doctor put me on new meds for sleep, which are actually anti-depressants in higher doses. My head is in a thick, grey fog. This is not a bad thing. Otherwise, I'd be seething with torment.

The time between not-knowing and knowing is the worst. It's the limbo of not knowing what to do with yourself. Just like when I've had biopsies. "Biopsy"—the word comes from Greek words meaning "life" and "sight." That's the problem. I have no vision about where this life is going.

Before Chloe's ballet class this morning, I apologized to Charles for being suspicious of him yesterday.

"I'm sorry that I didn't trust you about the bar receipt," I said, looking straight at him. He was sitting at the kitchen table, tapping away on his computer.

He stopped typing and looked up at me. I stood by the stove, palms getting sweaty around my mug of cold coffee.

"I'm sorry I didn't talk to you about it. I felt like you were ambushing me, and I reacted," he said apologetically.

"I should tell you that I checked our credit card statement. I didn't see the charge for the bar on it. I realized that you must have paid with cash. Why would you pay with cash? You always use your credit card for everything, Charles. I'm not sure what I'm supposed to think," I said, my voice cracking. I felt bad for snooping around and doing detective work, but at the same time, I wasn't sure what to do with what seemed like irrefutable evidence.

The silence between us grew heavier by the second. After what seemed like hours but was probably only a minute, he asked, "Do you think I'm cheating on you?"

The bluntness of his question took me by surprise. The bluntness of my answer was more of a shock. "Yes."

ooooh snap

Closing his laptop, Charles said, "You're right. I've been cheating on you."

One second passed. I was still standing here. He was still sitting there.

I looked at the clock. Chloe had to go to ballet.

I went into Chloe's bedroom and helped her put on her leotard and tutu. I put her hair up in a ponytail and wiped her face with a washcloth. Charles was waiting for her downstairs. She took his hand, and they got into the van and drove off.

I went into Mylo's bedroom and sat down on his Thomas the Tank Engine rug. He was playing with his trains. He didn't know what just happened. I felt so alone, control slipping quickly through my fingers like the finest grains of sand.

Flashes of signs, hints, and memories came quickly. First, foremost, and always is the ever-present voice of my mother, admonishing me with her I-told-you-so's. The loudest story of all was when she warned me against having my friend Irene be at my side when Chloe was born. I wanted a girlfriend, not my crazy mother, there to coach me through the birthing process, but I knew that my mother would also be jealous of me choosing a friend over her to be there. I didn't expect Mom telling me what a big mistake it would be because Charles would just end up having sex with Irene while I was giving birth.

"Are you insane? That would never happen, Mom!" I laughed wryly, the two of us standing on Santa Monica beach. "That's just nuts."

"Yeah, you think so much your friends, your husband. When I pregnant with your sister, her dad no around. He go off, be with other woman. I no know where he go. I by myself when your sister born," Mom said stiffly, staring into the ocean.

Even now, with the knowledge that Charles had been cheating on me, the idea of him and Irene hooking up is ridiculous. But I was so affronted by Mom's suspicion and accusation that I ignored the negative side to Charles's charm, or I tried to ignore it. I also neglected to hear how Mom was speaking from experience and not pure delusion. And while she was completely wrong about Irene (Mom's default is to suspect every woman as a trollop, her perception having nothing to do with Irene's character at all), she was right on the money about Charles.

As I sat on Mylo's bedroom floor, mindlessly putting together a curvy train track, I felt fated to be sitting there, battling with an unknown enemy, the other woman. It happened to Mom; it happened to my sister (in her case, it was another man). Why wouldn't it happen to me? Why would I think I'd be different from either of them, that I'd somehow escape being cheated on and abandoned, that I somehow was better at enduring, surviving, carrying on, that I'd be rewarded with loyalty and fidelity? From where I sat, I was the delusional one waking up to the same old reality.

This is what it must be like to have survived something catastrophic, only to end up wishing you hadn't survived after all. That you had died. And that all this would then go away. To be killed so as to not have to live in agony, in despair.

I easily figured out who Charles's lover is and realized that I'd had a gut feeling about her for some time. I remember back in August, when I was using his laptop to check my Facebook account, and he'd had his email account open. This woman tried chatting with him, asking "Are you feeling alright?" Some time later, she asked, "Are you feeling better?" I wondered, who is this person, and why is she talking to Charles like that?

Now this stranger has taken over my life, and what do I know of her? Very little. None of any of her biographical details matter, given the fact that she's stripped me of all that I am. Would she care to ask me now, "Are you feeling better? Are you feeling alright?"

I suppose it might be easier if I were just pissed off, told you to go fuck yourself, and wanted to not be with you because of your deception, period, end of story. But I'm not like that. While the angry ego side of me raises questions like—"Did he see her last week? What did they do? Was he happy then? How did he come home to me after being with her? Where's he going to be today?"—a larger part of me is just sad for everyone. I don't want anyone to be hurt—not

myself, not our children if they ever find out what you've done, not you, not her. Still, I find myself grovelling and actually literally praying to God (something I have not done in a while) that we can start our lives anew and happy. For a moment last night, it seemed quite absurd and ridiculous to me that you were the one who caused this grief, yet I was the one apologizing for making your life miserable to the point that you've gone astray. I was angry with myself for this, but the anger quickly melted into sadness, despair, depression, and a whole lot of "what if?" thoughts of me not being around anymore. You probably don't want to hear about my desire to be dead whether by my own hand or illness or wishful thinking, but it's true. I don't think you have to worry about it though—those are just thoughts that come up in spurts of depression, but I could never do that to you or the kids. I promised you that I wouldn't abandon you.

Yesterday morning when they took me back to the evaluation area before the surgery, my mind was racing with thoughts about us. When they put the mask over my face and told me to go to sleep and think happy thoughts, I thought of us growing old together and seeing our children grow up and be happy. I've always had this picture in my mind; it's what has been sustaining me over the last couple of years.

I don't want this; I don't want us to be miserable. I don't want to live in misery at the thought of you not loving me anymore or the possibility of us not working out. I don't want you to live in misery and longing for someone else because I've taken you for granted and you've lost faith in us. How do we honestly, sincerely, with our hearts achieve *happiness together? Is that possible? I want you to be honest and not give me any bullshit because you think that I need to be positive in order to recover and all that. I don't want you to *try* to love me out of guilt or because our children need a mother or because I'm good with your family, or any reason outside the fact that you honestly love me for me.*

When I woke up on Sunday, I thought, this is another day, another opportunity to live. And when I thought that, the world didn't seem so bad. I can't have my happiness depend on another person.

I keep replaying that thought, and each time I beat it down to a bloody pulp.

We keep talking. It keeps hurting. Yesterday, Charles said, "I just realized that you didn't have the luxury of having a respite from all this, like I had when I would go to see her." He stood there, earnestly telling me about his epiphany. It dawned on him like some fucking neon billboard in the middle of a pitch-black desert.

I looked at him and said, "Why would you think that I would have had that luxury, given the fact that my breasts were amputated and I had no nipples, and my self-esteem was buried in some forgotten place? Not only that, but what kind of relationship is it when one person needs to escape?"

He kicked me when I was down; he kicked me for being down. I don't know how I'm supposed to get back up this time.

It's been over two weeks of hell. Sixteen days of wondering what the future holds for me, if the man I've loved will ever love me in the way I've loved him, wondering how this came to be, wondering if Chloe and Mylo will get hurt by this. I've never felt so lost, damned, cursed. I've never felt so sorry as I do now.

Life is full of reminders and clues. Even our piano, which we've only had for about a month. Charles used to play the piano and compose music when he was younger, and recently, he's become really into doing so again. When we bought the piano, Charles wrote a song called "Waiting," and he played it for us. I thought it was lovely and touching when I first heard him play. Now all I can think of is that he wrote that song with her in mind. Had he been waiting to go to her and be with her the whole time he'd been here? Had he been waiting for the right time to leave me? Is he still waiting for that moment? What kills me is that the kids like that song. Mylo has even dubbed it "Good Night, Moon" because it reminds him of the children's book with the same name. I've come to see the song as born out of deception and betrayal against the kids and me, but the kids don't know that. I want to long for someone who longs for me. That's what Charles was looking for and getting with his lover.

I talk myself into circles. First, I feel consumed by pain. Then I begin to understand why he did what he did. Then I become angry that he abandoned me.

I had my reconstructive surgery on the 11th, four days after Charles told me about his affair. I got my dressing off a few days ago. Right after, I wanted to go to Charles's lover's office, sit outside, smoke cigarettes, and wait for her, since my surgeon's office is just a couple blocks from where she works.

Instead of stalking her, I went shopping for bras. I was actually having a lot of fun picking out bras and trying them on, discovering with glee that I can comfortably fill out a D cup. I was really excited about my new body, and I couldn't wait to show it off to Charles. I thought maybe seeing the new me would arouse new feelings in both of us. I wanted to work it out. I wanted a new start.

We went out to dinner and had a pleasant time. When we came home, we were lying around. But instead of being affectionate, he started grilling me on how I think I've supported him. We talked until he was too tired to talk anymore. What the hell had just happened?

I was pissed. I've gone through hell and have finally come to a point where I'm starting to feel good about myself again. Instead of being able to relish that, I was feeling like a piece of shit again. I couldn't sleep, and all I wanted to do was cry and smoke cigarettes. I wanted to ruin this body that has betrayed me and disgusted the man whom I loved. I took extra sleep medication and eventually passed out.

The next morning, I felt odd. I felt light, like nothing bad was really happening, and the most serious thing I needed to do was to clean my house. Nothing bad was happening to me. People's husbands have affairs all the time, and it was like, no big deal. Just another weather pattern passing through.

Later in the afternoon, I walked to Charles's sister's house. I sat down, accepted the glass of wine that his sister Liz offered me, and told her and her husband Bennett what had been going on in the last two weeks. When I told them, I just expected them to say, "Oh, that's interesting." But they were in complete shock. They couldn't understand why he would cheat. It was at that moment when I realized I wasn't a freak for thinking that this was catastrophic. I'd convinced myself that this was just another bump in the road, not a total break in the track of the rollercoaster. Seeing the looks on Liz and Bennett's faces, I broke down, overcome with grief. I drank wine and smoked about ten cigarettes before I walked home, drunk and useless.

When I told Charles that Liz and Bennett knew, he chalked it up to another instance in which I was being controlling. When I tried to be affectionate with him, he sarcastically asked me if I was doing this so I could tell everyone that we'd had sex. His cruelty cut through me, and I shook uncontrollably.

He keeps bringing up how hurt he was when he thought I didn't appreciate his support while I was sick. He told me how he hated me sometimes. I don't know why, but I felt relieved when he said that. I felt sorry that he had been feeling the way he did for a year and a half. I felt like I had been a bad person, like there was no end to this misery. When I told Charles what I was experiencing, he became nicer and gentler toward me.

This morning, he hugged me a few times and told me that he loved me and that I am a good person. Why is it that he wants me to be a wounded bird?

Now, it is 5:17 PM, and life continues to beat with uncertainty.

I find that lately, I've been spilling stuff just to make a mess that I can clean up. I'll pour coffee into my mug, missing it by a quarter of an inch, letting coffee spill on the counter and running on the floor. Instead of my characteristic "Shit!" or "Puta!" when I have accidents, I silently and calmly put down whatever I'm holding, pick up a dishcloth, wipe up the mess, every single drop. This morning, I was spilling some expensive Scotch onto the kitchen table when into my head came the words, "He did this to me."

"He did this to me." I kept trying to fight that phrase. I went to the sink to get the dishcloth, and all I could hear, one foot after the other, was "He did this to me." I wanted to wipe out that voice, stuff this dirty rag into its mouth, choke it. It kept going on and on. "He did this to me." I wiped up the Scotch, put the rag to my nose, and inhaled deeply. "He did this to me. This is worse than having cancer." I was calm and on the brink of something. I was livid.

Then the current became swift. I took the pitcher of water and spilled it all over the table. I watched the water run off. *Drip drip drip.* I watched the dripping slow down. I felt so foolish and unloved. My whole life, running away from me. I couldn't catch all the drips, there were too many. I lay down on the floor with my head in a small puddle, making the puddle bigger with my tears.

Sometimes I just want to swallow all my pills and go to sleep forever. I'd rather have cancer ten times over than to have this pain he put inside me. There is no chemo, radiation, or surgery for this pain. I can't shake it. I can't clean up this mess.

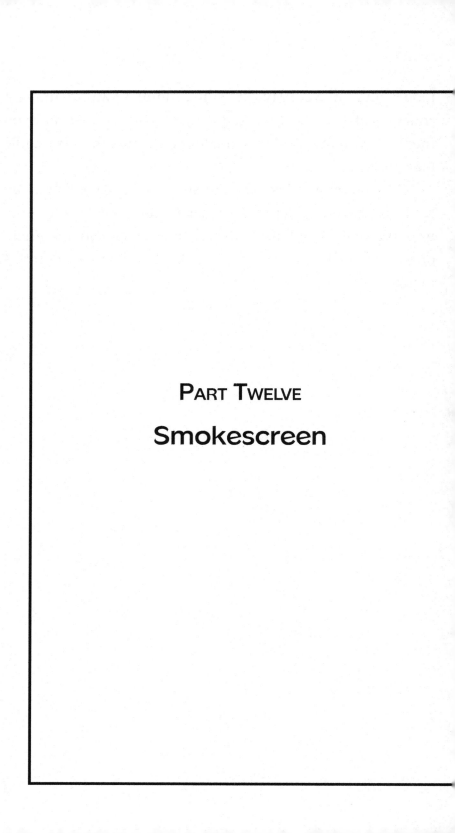

PART TWELVE

Smokescreen

I'm a ghost. I'm diaphanous.

Charles is leaving for Hong Kong and Singapore tonight. I'm going to smoke a lot of cigarettes while he's gone. I'm happy he's going. Sometimes I can't look at him. Sometimes I love him so much. Always, there is such a raw, grating pain.

It's a cloudy day with intermittent splashes of rain. I look out my bedroom window and observe the sun shining on a particular snowy spot on the mountain with dark clouds overhead. Beautiful.

I just had this terrible realization that I don't think I can be intimate with anyone because of the way I look naked. I have all these scars and look like a freak. Charles is the only one who has seen me naked in almost a decade. And I've been thrown away.

I light a cigarette. Smoking to cope, to have a moment, to breathe in the smoke is to feel my breath. To exhale is to think about what breath means.

I've been working on a screenplay called "Breaking Skin" for my screenwriting workshop. It's a barely fictionalized short film about cancer and marriage. I started writing the script in September, before Charles told me of his affair. Now I'm writing the third draft, and I just killed off the main character. It felt better than to keep her alive. When one dies, one regains an innocence not had since birth. When one dies, nothing matters and everything matters, all at once. That's the inherent paradox of life and death.

Every day that goes by, I detach myself from Charles more. I told him this would happen. Once I gave up the hope that we could work it out as a couple, everything started to unravel and come undone. Everything.

Charles told his parents about the affair. He said we should separate. I've spoken to his parents since then, and they told me to have patience. Charles is now the centre of everyone's world again. He is in control, and everyone holds his or her breath. Patience. I've been holding my breath for a really long time. I blow out smoke rings and count. *1, 2, 3.*

http://cancerfuckingsucks.blogspot.com
Wednesday, April 15, 2009
One Year Later

It is 11:55 pm, April 15, 2009. It is the tail end of the one-year anniversary of my double mastectomy. I didn't even realize it was the one-year anniversary until I was with my art therapist today, and she asked me how long it had been since the mastectomy. Then it dawned on me and I said, "Exactly one year ago today." People celebrate all sorts of anniversaries, but this particular anniversary is extra-special.

One year? Has it really been one year already? I vaguely remember the terror that I had on the eve of April 14-15, 2008. I didn't sleep a wink and took my last bath at 3:30 AM. I watched the sun come up as I walked with Charles and my parents to the hospital. We crossed Fraser, passed through Robson Park, waited for the pedestrian-controlled light to turn green, crossed Kingsway, passed the Thankga Buddha store, and walked down into the outdoor parking lot of the hospital. I held Charles's hand as we waited for the doors to the surgical daycare unit to open. If you want to hear the rest of the story, you can go back one year on this blog.

That's what I've been doing tonight. I've been going back through my blog. I laugh in some parts, I shudder at others, and I almost cry and can't finish reading some entries. I can barely look at the pictures of me bald. The blog is just a little something that I started writing for my friends and family when I was diagnosed in July 2007, but it became something bigger. I still get media requests for interviews about my blog because it has touched other cancer patients, survivors, and those who love them. I found some purpose in what I had been going through, and one of those things was to educate the audience about what it can be like to go through cancer treatment at a young age, to be a mother to two young children, a wife to a successful man, and a professional woman getting another graduate degree—to be a cancer patient during a time when your life is just starting to make sense and come together. Then you're not so sure about any of that anymore because now you could die a lot sooner than you ever thought you would. The thought that I struggled with on a daily basis: I finally have all this—and now, NOW? I have to leave it all?

A year later, I'm still struggling with that question.

Let's get this straight: as honest as I am in this blog, I don't report EVERYTHING. I mean, who would? There's lot *of stuff that we go through everyday that is just too lame or annoying or tiresome to tell anybody. But I know some of you might have heard that Charles and I have been going through an extremely rough patch in our marriage. You could be asking yourself, What's this have to do with your cancer? Well, if it had nothing to do with cancer, I certainly wouldn't be talking about it. If I even thought that it had nothing to do with cancer, then I'd say I was in complete denial.*

The truth is, cancer took a toll on us. It's funny—I hear so many "success" stories—those that involve The Journey and The Reawakening or The Enlightenment. I'm not saying that I haven't had those kinds of moments in my own journey during this past year and a half. But if you're looking for a certain kind of success story where everyone lives happier than ever post-cancer, this isn't it.

It's the one-year anniversary of the cancer being gone, and I'm celebrating it alone. In a way, that's fitting. Cancer is a really existential experience. You go inwards to places that you've never imagined, so far in you almost disappear. It really is one of those things that unless you've gone through it, you have no idea what I'm talking about. That kind of experience is really difficult on the caregiver. Here is this person whom you're trying to help and take care of, but she is so sick—so dying—that you can't reach her, that nothing you do will save her from that end. Truth is, we all come to an end. To witness it day after day after week after month, for a whole year—that's another kind of torture and existential experience that is not understandable to someone who has not gone through that either.

For Charles and me, our experiences didn't match up. You might think that from the way I describe these experiences, that they share similarities, and in recognizing that, the two parties could help one another through the suffering. I can only speak from my experience obviously, but that was not the case for us. What happened? It's not that neither of us didn't care about the other's suffering. I feel that it was just the enormous sense of helplessness, from all around, that did us in. During the months after the surgery, we tried very hard to rebuild our lives, but that pain and suffering ran so deep in each of us, it was too late for damage control.

It's a bitch—facing death at the age of thirty-one. You look at your husband of three years, your children who are three and four years old. You're just stunned, breathless. How? Why? Two simple questions that take the wind right out of you. You see it in his eyes, in your husband's eyes—that mixture of courage and fear. He has to be strong for you, but truthfully, he's scared shitless. What do you do with that?

I can't tell you the story from that moment to this one. It's too painful for me to try to piece together the remnants that I still carry. Charles and I have faced moments like the one now, here, in the present, way too many times—much more than a couple of our age should ever have to. It's that tightness in the chest, the way you look through your tears into the light bulb on the ceiling, and you know that if you survive this moment, you can survive anything. And you will. ʸ ᵃᵃᵃ'ˢ ʰᵒⁱ

Posted by Brandy Lotus Blossom at 11:54 PM

I've been writing emails to her, the other woman. She never replies, and I become angry at her silence. She took my life away from me. Okay, maybe it was already gone. But she has it now, whatever I used to have and lost.

I can't see straight. One moment I'm okay with; the next I'm fighting the urge to bash my head against a wall. I want to be her friend. I want her to go away. I want to love Charles, but then I feel so much hate in the next breath that I know it's best if he's nowhere near me right now. I sound rational, accepting, crazy, desperate. There is no consistency, except for the pain. That's my only constant.

I wrote her this email today. The only answer I expect is the one I've been getting all along, which is no response. I'm just writing to myself.

April 22
Dear C—,

I really have no idea what's going on between you and Charles now, but I also don't care. I've come to the conclusion that if a man is capable of cheating on his wife right as she was recovering from a year of chemo, radiation, and surgery; if he's capable of thinking only of himself and of forgetting that he has two children who are too young to understand their father's selfishness and so when they realize how their lives are changing will begin to blame themselves because kids that young think like that; if he's capable of engaging in all that and not be sorry for what he's done and is doing, and only thinks his wife is a bad, crazy, delusional person for wanting to work it out—if a man is capable of all that, then I don't want him as a husband, partner, or companion. You can have him.

Sometimes, I have feelings for him in terms of wanting to be his friend and to take care of him and to work with him as I've been doing for almost nine years. It's those "good things," as he puts it, that will keep me in some sort of relationship with him, beyond the fact that we have two children together. But I've really done away with the idea that I need him as a partner—because I don't. And that realization is liberating.

After I wrote the email and sent it, I had a rush of euphoria. However, the euphoria quickly came crashing down as soon as Charles came home on Wednesday briefly to get his suitcase for his Winnipeg trip. It's not that anything happened really. It's just that looking at him and being in his presence brought back all the doubts I have about being done with him. I told him I was over him right before he left. It felt so painful to say those words that I haven't quite accepted, yet I kept it together. He said he was glad I was happy, though I heard a tinge of regret or remorse in his voice. He just stared at me as he was leaving. He looked at me like he wanted me to hug him. I said goodbye and shut the door. *so have thown*

I keep muttering the words, "Be strong."

My body hurts. Peace is difficult to come by.

My thoughts turn to Mom and Dad, perhaps as a

distraction, or maybe out of a need for some connection. I think of their roads to misery in hopes of solace.

Is there some irony that I'm in Canada? Thousands of draft dodgers went north to escape war. Dad did not. He went to Vietnam and met Mom. They had me. Now I'm here in Canada, a cancer survivor, and a single mom. An exile. I can't go back to the U.S. because of my "pre-existing condition."

How pre-existing is my condition? Had it existed before I was born, an Agent Orange mutation working its way from mother and father to embryo? From a chemical warfare enshrouding those within its atmosphere, beneath its clouds? I have to stay in Canada, a refugee, alone.

Love—a casualty. Dead and gone.

I've decided that today is the day. I can't take it anymore. I'm tired of the pain, and I can't see an end. I've been drinking Scotch starting at 10:00 AM everyday for a while now, slowly slipping my way into acceptance as the day wears on. The numbness is welcome. But it doesn't last. Today, I've been taking Ativan every time I feel the pain well up and make my chest tight. Then I let go some more into the thought that I shouldn't have to do this anymore. I can just sit here and go to sleep.

I don't know how many pills I've taken. I can still compose thoughts. My face is warm. I can see the daylight outlining the shades I've drawn in the living room. I laugh. I'm going to die in the living room. How many people have died in their living room, or is it usually the bedroom, I wonder, where they are used to entering dreams? I don't want to have dreams anymore.

I need to say goodbye to Lisa, my oldest friend who still cares. I miss her so much. She's got the best soul. She'll be my angel to take me to the next life. I'll be able to tell Mom what's waiting for her in the next life, if there is even one, finally.

She's online now, at her job in Pittsburgh. I start typing. She's freaking out. I'm telling her it's okay. I think I'm telling her it's okay. I sound okay. I'm okay with this. I'm happy that it's going to be over soon. Lisa's not happy with what I'm saying. I take another sip of Scotch. Some of it rolls down my chin. I suck in my breath and grit my teeth. The pain is fighting with the calm.

Lisa I can't take it anymore

This is too hard

You will make it through this and be happier than ever!

I can't

Yes you can!

Think of how you felt during chemo and how you thought that would never end

You keep making comparisons to the cancer, think of it that way too

This is so much worse

I can't do it anymore

but you have survived so much this far in life

yes you can!

you should get the kids and move away, somewhere new

I just can't do it anymore

Do I need to call a suicide hotline?

The kids will be ok

no

They're good kids

They will be ok b/c of you being there

There will be life after Charles and all his bullshit

I promise

I swear

I can't

You're making me worried, you should call a friend to come over

please?

I'd be there in a heartbeat if I could

No

Yes!

Where are you?

I'm home

by yourself? please ask someone to come over and hang out

No I cant

or go to a coffeehouse and get away from that place where Charles's things are

No one aNts to be around me mow

I'm waaaau drink and took many pills

omg, you're freaking me out

how many pills?

I'm sorry lisa

dude, if you took too many, please call the er

I can't do this anymore

brandy brandy brandy

you are strong and beautiful and smart and yr kids need you

can you please call the hospital? i want to call but i don't know where to call or where to say you are!

You're scaring me

It's ok lise

I'll just go to sleep

Why am I living this fuching life   reading at conversation

everything is going to get better

it will it will it will

How

b/c you are an amazing person who so many people love

Ohlusa the pain

and you have the world's most beautiful kids who need you

and who love you

and i love you and need you

and you haven't written yr life story yet and that will help so many other people

I can't

My mom and dad will be here for my funeral

Oh god lisa

I can't do this

I wAnt to die

no

please don't say that

Pls

when you sober up, you will feel so much better and so much stronger

No

yes you will

I can't do this

you can

you will

and you will be happy

Lisa my kids will be better. Off without me

no they won't

how could they possibly?

you are the best mother ever

They'll get over it

no

they love you and need you

Lisa

You are my soulmate

Don't leave me soulmateless

It's ok lise

brandy

i want to call a 911 number for you but i can't find the info online

can you please call and ask for help? PLEASE?

i need you

and yr kids need you

and a million other people need you
No one needs anyone
yes they do
what number can i call?
i don't know what to do
I love you
then don't do this
please
i love you and so many other people love you
This is it
brandy
no
it's not
brandy, this is not the way you want to go
I'm sorry lisa
It's not, you do not want to do this
you will sober up and realize that you have so much in life to offer and that life has so much to offer you
and you are going to watch yr kids grow up to be amazing people
I want it to be over
now

To decide one day that that was it, the final day. That day, life was just all too much to handle anymore. Why that day? What were the factors leading to that breaking point?

Does it matter? It's like trying to figure out how I got cancer. It really doesn't matter *how* because whatever the reason, it is the reality I have to deal with.

I have no memory of when anyone came, found me, and when I talked to the paramedics. I scared the shit out of Lisa, and I will be sorry for that forever. But I can see how people can get addicted to trying to kill themselves. As I walked home from Mount St. Joseph's Hospital with Charles and our friend Julie, I was thinking about how I could succeed next time. I can barely remember the walk home other than that. It's scary but alluring—attempting suicide. It's the only way I can think of taking control right now.

I think of my forgotten brother, Hieu, and my grandmother, Ba ngoai, both of whom allegedly committed suicide. I've inherited this curse, this diseased life. I've learned from them the cure. Then I think of Dad. And I remember that one time—one year before my diagnosis—when I experienced what I now believe was a premonition of what was to come.

It was July 4, 2006—one year and eight days before my diagnosis. The trip was long from Vancouver to Harrisburg, with a connecting flight in O'Hare. Even though the kids were well behaved, we were all restless as we crossed three time zones. I tried entertaining the kids by showing them the spurts of fireworks appearing in the middle of the black sky below us. By the time we arrived at the baggage claim at Harrisburg, it was already midnight.

Greeting us were Mom and my cousin Lung—but no Dad.

Mom said, "Daddy got sick. He at Aunt Xe." "Got sick" has become the euphemism for "downed some booze and got really fucked up."

"What happened?" I asked, wanting more of an explanation.

We collected our luggage. Lung said, "We no know what happen. We go outside to get vegetable in garden, and come back—Uncle almost pass out. He go like this," Lung swayed, "and he fall over."

Mom suddenly filled with rage, not caring who was around to hear. "He go crazy! I see, we go outside for five minute, he drink Lung's whiskey. You can no leave him alone, he like a kid!" She turned her lips down in disgust. "He take out his thing, pee all over Aunt Xe's rug. I say, What you do? I tell Aunt Xe look away, I try cover him up. Then he grab my neck and punch me here." Mom showed me the purple-green-red bruise on her chest the size of a baseball.

I hovered around her so that no eavesdropper got any idea to call the cops.

"He kick me. I think I almost die."

Lung tried to downplay the situation. "He no drink much, maybe just a little. I no know how it happen."

I was tired and had had enough. And I knew exactly how it had happened. With all the prescription drugs he was on, even the tiniest sip of booze could cause a seriously adverse reaction.

I turned to Mom and asked, "Where is he now?"

"He pass out at Aunt Xe, no get up, so I tell Lung bring me here, pick you up."

We took the luggage out to the sidewalk. The July heat and humidity didn't let up, not even in the wee hours of the night. I looked at our massive amount of luggage—the crying, sleepy, hungry children—the broken wife, my mother—the Vietnamese cousin who was well accustomed to this type of rescue mission—it would be a while still before we got home to Mifflintown. Yet here it was: home had advanced on us already. Welcome home, indeed.

We drove to Lung's house in the suburbs of Harrisburg. Because we were so loaded with luggage and people, we had to rent a car, in addition to driving Mom and Dad's Jeep. We pulled up to the curb. While Mom waited with the kids in the rental car, Charles, Lung, and I went inside to retrieve Dad. The neighbourhood was so quiet I could hear people sleeping. A dog barked as we entered Lung's house.

Aunt Xe didn't bother to give me a hug. She grabbed me by the arm and steered me into the dining room, where Dad lay on the ground, a smear of blood dried on his temple. His face was red. He was snoring with his mouth wide open. Charles and Lung wanted to pick him up, but I was afraid he would be violent (two Asian men manhandling him while he's fucked up?—a recipe for a PTSD flashback with potentially awful consequences).

I knelt down, shook his shoulder gently, and said, "Dad? Dad? Hey, get up—it's me, Brandy. I'm home. Get up, Dad."

It was a minute or so before he opened his eyes. When he did, when each lid managed to peel up from each eyeball, I could see he was faraway, lost and maybe even gone, living in some bloodshot haze of prescription drugs and booze.

Persistent memories swirled in his soul. He couldn't see me through the glassiness. I spoke more loudly to bring him out of it, even if just a little. He grumbled nonsense sounds. I managed to catch words—signs of remorse and shame stuck in the alternate reality quicksand. I stared at him and thought, he's like a derelict left on the street lying in some darkened doorway to die and be forgotten—a scrap of humanity.

Charles and Lung got him on his feet, and he said he had to go to the bathroom. Not wanting to be a witness to my husband helping my father take a piss, I walked outside. Everyone else was sleeping, not having to deal with all of the madness. The VA clinic just a block away. What a fucking joke.

We made Dad lie down in the back seat of the Jeep. I got in the driver's seat, wanting to make it home as quickly as possible. Charles, Mom, and the kids drove off in the rental car ahead of me. Unfortunately, Charles took the wrong exit due to Mom's frazzled directions, adding another half-hour to our ride. In the meantime, Dad woke up and was making peculiar noises in the back, like he was trying to be quiet but not really succeeding. For the first time in a long time, I was truly scared. I glanced behind me and saw that he was looking for something on the floor and under the seats in front of him.

My mind was racing—was he looking for more drugs, alcohol—or worst of all, maybe a gun? Dad's not the homicidal or suicidal type, but right then, he wasn't himself. I saw him blowing my brains out all over the steering wheel, dashboard, and windshield. I imagined Charles looking in the rearview

259

mirror to see our Jeep veering suddenly off the highway and into the pitch-black countryside below. I didn't want to die, but at that moment, I felt an uneasy ambiguity about my fate.

I could feel my chest tightening. I fought to regain control and keep driving. I asked, "Dad, what's going on? What are you doing?"

No response.

I tried, "Dad, we'll be home soon, then you can see Chloe and Mylo."

That worked to break his silence as he moaned, "I wanna see my baby kids."

Relief washed over me.

"Hold on, Dad, we're almost home."

He started talking more, telling me how Mom must be mad at him, and how glad he was that I came home. My silence was well intended.

We pulled into the carport. Dad said, "Where are we? We have to go to the airport to pick up Brandy."

When he got out of the car, I could see that the front of his pants was soaked. Two steps onto the driveway on his own, he fell, landing with a loud, hard thud, right on his chest. Charles and I helped him up and sat him on the porch because he wanted a smoke. The kids ran inside to play, even though it was 2:30 in the morning.

After finishing his cigarette, Dad went inside and over to where Chloe was playing and tried to pick her up, but I told him to change his clothes and clean up. There was no way I was going to let him hold my kids in that condition. Eventually, everyone went to bed.

The next morning, it was as if nothing had happened. The day after my homecoming, Dad was safely sedated, moving and saying little. Everything, everyone back to normal.

Just like now, I think, the day after I was found in the same condition as my father had been in on that night—everyone back to normal.

Will Chloe and Mylo have a memory of me like the one I have of Dad? I ask myself as I look in the mirror, for once, unable to look away.

Mom and Dad are here again. Their original intent to come here was to help out during Charles's constant travelling to Asia, but now with this whole attempted suicide business and the separation, the purpose of this visit is to take over my life. I didn't think it was possible to feel more manic than I've been feeling, but it is.

The first three seconds Mom walked in, I wanted her to go back to Mifflintown.

"You know, if your house no so dirty, your husband no leave you for another woman! Why you have mess so much? You clean now, maybe he come back," Mom said, peering at me over her glasses.

Dad just shook his head. "Goddamn it, Liên!"

To which she replied, "What, I talk to my daughter! I teach her what right! She no have husband no more. You no tell me not talk! You always tell me not talk, and now she have

dream realized

no husband." Because of course, not only is this my fault, but it's also Dad's fault. This is going to be a long visit. Dear baby Jesus.

She's relentless. I was bawling at seven o'clock in the morning. She's yelling even more than usual because every time she starts yelling at me, I leave the room and she has to yell more loudly so I can hear the wisdom and instruction she's imparting through yelling. I'm fucking miserable.

When she can't yell at me, or wants to change it up a bit, she yells at Charles's mom when the poor woman comes over for a visit. She tells her that her son and I have to get back together because all the old people are going die soon and won't be around to take care of our kids because clearly, no one else is taking care of them, and Charles and I are incapable of taking care of them if we get divorced. If I step back for a moment, I find my mother's reasoning the most hilarious and bizarre train of thought ever. Her rants, paired with my self-medication, make me feel like I'm in the Twilight Zone. I don't think any body snatchers are going to come and take me away though. They'd be insane to want to commit to this.

Seriously. How else do I say this? Mom. Won't. Shut. Up.

OHMYFUCKINGGODI'MLOSINGMYFUCKINGMIND. Until today.

This morning, Dad and I had a wake-and-bake on the porch, puffing on my glass pipe. He got some weed from the guy next door. We felt so mellow, sitting on the porch and looking at the dew beads on the bamboo tree.

We could hear Mom vacuuming and screaming at the kids in the house. Neither of us wanted to go back inside. But I knew I had to rescue my children. I was just too afraid, and maybe a bit too stoned.

"I wish we could get Mom stoned. What would happen if we did?" I asked.

He laughed. I saw the light bulb go off in his head. "We could get her stoned. Make some pot brownies. We'll feed them to her."

"Are you serious? How am I going to do that? She's all over the kitchen."

"I'll keep her busy. You just go make brownies," he said.

"Okay, and if she wonders why they taste funny, I'll tell her they have some Chinese herbs that my acupuncturist gave me in them."

We walked back into the house.

"Liên, I can't find my medicine!" Dad shouted upstairs.

"Why you no can find nothing? You always lose everything. You lose your head if it not on your neck," she screamed, coming down the stairs.

I ran up to the kitchen and started grinding some weed in the Magic Bullet. I cooked it in butter, mixed it into the brownie batter, and after thirty minutes of baking, I had a fresh batch of pot brownies. They smelled delicious.

I took my brownies downstairs. "Want one, Dad?" Of course he did.

"Mom, want to try a brownie? They're very good," I said, offering her one. She was talking so much that she absentmindedly took one and shoved it in her mouth. She went about her business cleaning the bedroom.

Dad and I sat there and watched her for signs of being high. After an hour, she became quiet. She was still busying herself, but there was silence. Sweet, precious silence.

Dad asked, "Why didn't we do this years ago?"

I just shrugged and smiled.

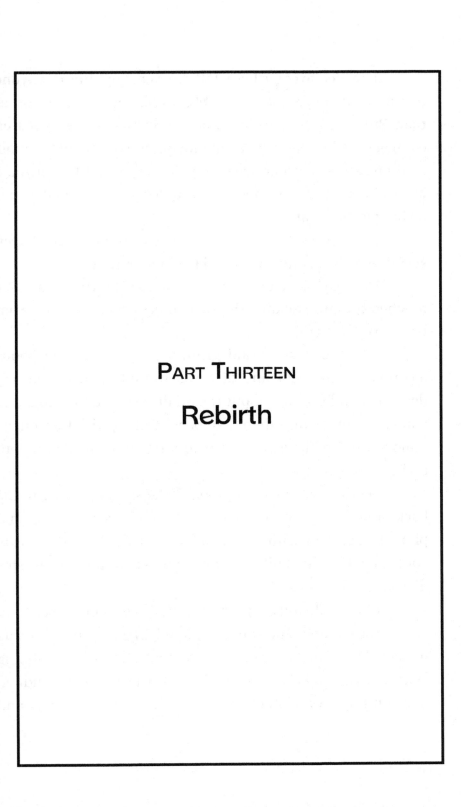

PART THIRTEEN

Rebirth

I needed to come here. If there were anything or anyone to put my life in perspective right now, it would be none other than Burcu. I return to her fabulous vintage store in search of magic. With the surreal mannequins draped in sequins, feathers, studs, leather, lace, and silk, I feel like I've drunk a martini glass full of rainbows and unicorns. How could I not be happy with that?

As soon as I walked in here ten minutes ago, Burcu swept to my side and enveloped me in a tight hug.

"My darling, let me look at you. Look at that hair." She touched the curls tickling the back of my neck. "Tell me, what brings you in here?"

"Oh, the usual," I said, grinning. "I got these new boobs a couple months ago, and that was around the time that my dear husband told me about the affair he'd been having, and you know, ever since then, I've been dealing with that minor annoyance. No big deal." I tried smiling but instead burst out crying.

"Let's sit in the living room," she said, referring to the back of her store, where there are couches, rugs, lamps, and photographs. "Fuck him. What a fool. You don't need to waste your time with that bullshit. You're gorgeous, and I'm sure his dick is small and sad."

I laughed, and a snot bubble flew out of my nose.

Burcu made me stand up. She looked me over, eyeing my new body, and smiled. She ran around the store grabbing clothes off the racks and came back to where I was standing. She hung up the clothes in one of the changing stalls and instructed me to play dress up. I obliged and entered the stall, where I continued to update Burcu on the drama.

Now I can hear her hmph in disgust. Every once in a while she shouts out to someone entering the store, "I'm here, darling. Let me know if you need help finding something." I get the feeling that as I'm telling Burcu my story, there are other people listening too.

I'm trying on a Smurf-blue terrycloth short-short jumper. And you know what? It looks fucking hot.

Before I sweep aside the curtain and emerge from the changing stall, a random girl asks, "He apologized, right? Like, he thinks he's wrong and stuff?"

Who is this chick?

I say, "Nope."

There's a collective gasp in the store. How many people are out there?

I come out from the change stall and am faced with about eight women. They all tell me how awesome the jumper is, how I *have* to buy it since it's clearly made for my new body, and how stupid my husband is.

A random dude just walked into the store. Burcu says, "We're having a man-hating session, so if you're not comfortable with that sort of thing, you should leave now." Dude shrugs his shoulders and continues shopping.

I'm buying the terrycloth jumper. It's my new suit of armour. With it I can save my world.

Chloe has been suffering from anxiety. She's been sleepwalking, crying, and saying her stomach hurts. Those symptoms are familiar to me. It's how I reacted when my sister got married and moved out of the house when I was seven years old.

Sis couldn't stand living with Mom anymore and taking her physical and emotional abuse, so she married the first guy she could, who turned out to be such a loser that even I, in all my innocence, knew that. Or maybe I was just pissed that this stupid man, whose nickname was Doobug (what kind of name is that?), was taking my sister away from me. All of a sudden, I was sleeping in a bed by myself, with no one there when I woke up from a nightmare.

When my parents and I visited my sister in her new mobile home for the first time, I felt like I was going to puke in the car as it slowly crunched the gravel in the driveway of the trailer park. I couldn't sleep or stop crying for days, and Mom yelled at me to quit it, saying something to the effect of "If you don't stop crying, I will give you something to cry about." That's when I began to read books and write stories obsessively. I could always go to my imaginary friends for help. We could share our problems with each other, and we'd give each other good advice and a plate of warm chocolate chip cookies with a glass of cold milk.

When Chloe cried last night, I went downstairs to find her standing up in the middle of her room with her eyes closed.

"Chloe, honey, wake up. It's just a dream," I said, picking her up. She was getting heavy.

She softly sobbed into my neck. Her hair was sticking to her face, wet with tears. I put her in her bed and lay down with her, curling my body around hers. After a few moments, she quieted down, and I fell asleep in her bed.

One of the most important lessons that I've learned as a parent is how my life is not just about me. It cuts me to the core that it's taken my daughter's nightmares to remind me of this. It's time. It's time to stop being a victim. It's time to stop allowing myself to fall when things happen. When I took Chloe's hand into mine as I fell asleep, I made a promise—and I try not to make promises, ever—that I would do everything I could to always be there for her and Mylo, as they've been here for me.

parallels between her sister + her kids

❧❧❧

Mom and Dad go back to Mifflintown tomorrow. Thank you, baby Jesus! Mom's been yapping at the kids all morning. She's in hyper-hypermode. Even Mylo, who can tune out just about anything, is getting annoyed.

"Mammy, I want you to be quiet," he said. Did he just say that, I thought.

Apparently, he did, because Mom then said, "You bossy! Okay, you want Mammy be quiet. I go talk to Chloe."

Before she could release her energy on Chloe, I asked Mom to eat soup with me. I can take this, I thought. It'll be good practice for blocking negative energy and changing it into positive energy. Compassion. Understanding. Love.

"What, you no want me tell Chloe things? I need teach her and Mylo. You no teach them right. Your husband leave you, now what?" she said, sitting down to slurp up her noodles between thoughts.

Here we are.

Breathe. Compassion. Understanding. Love.

"Mom, we'll be fine," I say, smiling gently. My right eyelid is twitching.

"Oh, yeah, you fine? I don't think so," she smirks and talks with a full mouth. "You no fine. Kids need a mom AND dad to be together. You see—I stay with your daddy when you little, even though I want leave. You have mom and dad raise you." She lifts her head and looks past me, out the kitchen window.

"Okay, well, Charles and I aren't going to be together anymore, so we have to make the best of the situation. I'll make sure the kids are okay." Breathe.

"I no know why he do like that. You sick—you have cancer, you almost die, he just go with other woman like that? Make me so mad!" She starts crying and dabbing her eyes with her crumpled napkin. "Maybe that other woman a witch. She put some medicine or poison in his drink and make his brain funny." Mom watches way too many Chinese soap operas dubbed in Vietnamese. "Maybe that other woman talk nice to him. You no talk nice to him enough, I tell you before, but you no listen. Maybe she more calm. You no calm."

Calm? Really, Mom, you're accusing me of not being calm and not talking nice? You, who are sitting here putting me down and getting all worked up?

Breathe.

"Okay, Mom, look, you're going home tomorrow. It doesn't do any good to worry about these things. This is what my life is now. The best we can do is to try to be happy and move on."   *Branly Kiu...*

"Maybe you need go Vietnam and get your thing sewn up. Then you find a man who take care of you. You know, you have two kids. Men no like woman with *chim* all loose. They like tight. Maybe other woman—you know, she no have kids."

No, she's not. She's not talking to me about having my vagina sewn up. The practice is still fairly common in some of the small villages in Vietnam, but she doesn't honestly think that I'd go to Vietnam to have my vagina sewn up just so I can keep my douchebag husband, does she? Holy fucking hell.

"Mom, there is no way, ever, in a million billion years, in any of my lifetimes, reincarnated as anything, that I would get that done. If a man doesn't want to be with me because he thinks my *chim* is too loose, then I seriously don't want to be with him." My right eye won't stop twitching now.

"You no listen anything I say. You think you right, I wrong. That why you like you are now. You see. You see how hard take care kids by yourself. Maybe someday you listen to what mommy say. That okay. I go home tomorrow, you see how you live." She takes her bowl to the sink and washes the dishes. My stomach is churning. I peek into Chloe's room. She and Mylo are playing with the My Little Ponies that Mom saved from when I was a little girl.

I turn to the stairwell to see Dad leaning against the railing. How long he's been standing there, I don't know. He mutters, "Don't listen to her, Brandy. She doesn't know what she's saying."

"It's okay, Dad. I'm going for a run." I squeeze past him in the stairwell.

I lace up my runners, clip on my iPod, and put my ear buds in place. My eye stops twitching, and I breathe, and I run. I tell myself as I start hitting the pavement, "If I can survive and be happy within myself, I can have strength and inspiration in life. And then love will happen, and it will be good."

Back in November, I was half-watching *Entertainment Tonight Canada* while Charles was on his laptop. Cheryl Hickey, *ET Canada*'s intrepid, glamorous, and gorgeous host, was calling on viewers to nominate a special woman in their lives for a head-to-toe celebrity makeover. My ears perked up. I'd love a makeover. I had no idea what to do with this curly hair sprouting forth from my head, and I didn't know how to fit clothes onto my misshapen body.

"Hey, Charles, did you hear that?" Of course he didn't. I continued, *"Entertainment Tonight* is doing a makeover contest. If they pick you, they do your hair and give you clothes. Do you think it would be cool if I could do that?"

"Mm-hm," he said, without looking away from his computer.

"Well, um, can you nominate me? I mean, do you think I deserve it?" I asked.

He finally looked at me. "Yeah, you should do it," he said.

"Well, I can't just do it. Someone has to nominate me, and you know, you're my husband. . ."

"Can you just write it on behalf of me? You're a good writer. I'm kinda busy doing this grant proposal right now," he said, going back to his laptop.

"Oh, okay." I felt a stab of pain, like rejection and lack of worth, but I quickly buried it by agreeing with him that he was too busy. Still, he couldn't write something for me? He didn't think I was good enough? "So, you want me to write a letter from you about me?"

"Yeah, go ahead. You should do it," he repeated.

With his permission I entered myself in the running on behalf of him. Then I promptly put it out of my mind because I felt so pathetic and lame that I had to do that because my husband had no desire to. I decided to take his apathy and disinterest as a sign of how he felt about the contest, and I tried to not think about it anymore. Doing so would mean having to acknowledge the problems we were having.

When Cheryl Hickey showed up at my door on June 23rd, I was still in complete shock. At first I didn't know who this beautiful woman was or why she was standing on my porch with a camera crew. I didn't know how she knew my name. All I knew is that I didn't want to buy anything from her, and I almost shut the door in her face.

"Hi, Brandy?" she said, beaming.

"Yeah?" I replied, suspicious.

"I'm Cheryl Hickey, from *ET Canada*. Your friends. . ."

Then it dawned on me. I gasped and brought my hand to my mouth, not knowing that all of this was being caught on camera.

"Your friends nominated you for my celebrity makeover," Cheryl finished her sentence.

"Oh my god," was all I could say. I turned to my friend Andrew, who was sitting in the living room. He was part of the set-up. We'd been waiting for our friend Julie to show up to go out for lunch, and Julie was running really late, which wasn't like her. Now I knew why. Julie actually never meant to show up. It was a trick to keep me in the house until Cheryl Hickey arrived.

Cheryl and I went outside, and we sat in the yard to do an interview. She told me how my friends got together and nominated me for the makeover. (One of my friends, Jenny, told me that what had happened was when *ET Canada* contacted Charles, he told them to instead contact her, and she took over as the main contact and explained to the producers that Charles and I were going through a divorce. So Jenny got in touch with some of my other friends, including

Lisa, who gladly said they'd vouch for this story of nominating me and provide comments, and I think that *ET Canada* was happy to have another layer to the story.) Cheryl read me the comments they submitted, and each one stunned me more. I wasn't expecting to hear such heartfelt, touching words of encouragement from my friends. Hell, I wasn't expecting to be talking to Cheryl Hickey in the yard. But there I was.

After the interview, the cameras shut down, and Cheryl told me to come to Holt Renfrew first thing in the morning for my day of pampering. She said she'd love for me to bring Chloe and Mylo along to the transformation. I was thrilled at the idea of the kids seeing their mama turn into a princess and be on TV. But Charles thought otherwise. He was totally against the idea, saying that he didn't want to expose the children to the world like that. I was disappointed by his discouragement, but there was little I could do. I'd have to enjoy the makeover with just Jenny watching.

I didn't know what to expect, and I have to say that I've never even heard of Holt Renfrew before then. That's how out of touch with the fashion world I'd been. I didn't realize that I'd be working with a stylist, who'd be handing me designer dresses, shoes, and jewellery costing upwards of $1000 a piece. Every time I came out donning a new outfit, a team of fashion consultants and TV people would give their opinion on it. There wasn't much that they didn't "love love love."

I could hardly believe it when I was sitting in the salon getting some hardcore European conditioning treatment done on my hair, with a camera dude behind me. When this one nice-smelling lady asked me what I wanted to eat for lunch, I asked, "Can I see the menu?"

She smiled, saying, "There is no menu."

I was confused. "Well, what can I have?"

"Whatever you want," she said.

"Whatever I want? What's that mean?"

"It means whatever you want," she repeated, still smiling.

"Wow. I don't know. Sushi?"

"Is there anything you don't like in your sushi?" she asked.

"Um, no."

"And would you like some wine or champagne with that?"

"Champagne, I guess."

"I will be back with your meal."

As my hair was setting, Cheryl continued interviewing me about what I've gone through. I was hoping she wouldn't ask me anything about my failed marriage, but she brought it up. I muttered something about us growing apart. She seemed satisfied with that.

Lunch arrived: lobster sushi rolls with fruit and champagne. It was insanely good. I thought of Chloe and Mylo, and how they would have enjoyed all this fancy stuff. I began missing them terribly, and the food started tasting bland. It was difficult to swallow my food. My heart ached for my babies.

Cheryl, who was in her last trimester of pregnancy, leaned over and told me how she admired me. I thanked her and told her, with tears in my eyes, that I never imagined something like this would happen. I looked up and realized that the camera was filming this heartfelt exchange the whole time. I thought of how I've been a huge fan of reality television ever since MTV's *The Real World* began, and here I was, part of a mini reality-TV gig, and how funny it was that reality is crafted, polished, and edited. I felt so postmodern.

After lunch, it was makeup and manicure time. Then the moment came for the photoshoot in the middle of the store. Shoppers crowded around to see which famous person was being photographed, but when they saw me—a nobody—they didn't walk away. They stood there and watched, probably going over in their heads, "Who is this woman? I know I saw her in some show? Or maybe she was in that one movie?" Or at least, that's what I like to think they were thinking. Now that I think about it, they were probably gawking at Cheryl.

This whole experience kept getting better. It was the opposite of the last two years of my life, which kept going from bad to worse to outright apocalyptic. The makeover was a two-part story that aired the next week. The first segment was Cheryl surprising me at my house and the interview in the yard—the heart-wrenching story! The second segment was the makeover itself—the amazing transformation! But as Cheryl said, that wasn't all. A surprise came at the end of the second segment. It was a shout-out from the New Kids on the Block—to me. These were the dudes whose images covered my bedroom walls and bedspread and lampshades—I even had an NKOTB telephone—when I was a teenager.

"Hey Brandy, you're a fighter!" said Joey.

"We love you," said Donnie.

"I love you too, Donnie!" I shouted at the television, wearing the sparkly gold Prada heels I got to take home with me. Almost two years ago, I was being told that I had cancer. Today the New Kids on the Block are telling me on national television that they love me and are inviting me to one of their concerts. Life: beautifully absurd.

Palm trees provide shade from the glare of the sun. Standing on the sidewalk, smoking a Parliament Light, waiting for my ride. I look up and wonder if rats really do live in the trees, like someone told me when I first moved here ten years ago. I'm back in LaLaLand.

It's my first time in Los Angeles since before my mastectomy—and my first time without Charles. Irene is getting married, and I'm one of her bridesmaids. I can't wait to see all my friends and UCLA colleagues, especially to show them how awesome I can be, even without Charles. Or maybe despite Charles.

I'll admit it—I'm on a fresh ego high. That whole celebrity makeover funny business has shown me that I can rock low-cut dresses, short dresses, miniskirts, high heels, and any other article of clothing that is tight, clingy, and barely there. And LA is definitely the place to strut my stuff.

My brain hasn't entirely caught up with what's going on outside, though. I'll still be on my merry way when I'll catch my reflection in a window and think, "Holy shit! Is that me? Damn." Especially the boobs. I keep forgetting that I got those.

Irene pulls up to where I'm standing, and when I get in her car, she giggles. "Dang, girl, you look amazing!"

"Yeah, I lost some weight. About 180 pounds of dead weight, to be exact."

"Shit! You're hilarious. Let's go. We got so much shit to do, and okay, so my house is total chaos right now, but whatever. Welcome to my world!" We drive off to her apartment.

As we crawl along Sunset Boulevard in LA traffic, we fill in the blanks on each other's lives, the details we don't have time to recount during our Gmail chats or Facebook status updates.

"How was your trip home to PA?" Irene asks.

"Weird to be there without Charles, but my family were all on my side, obviously. Except my mom. Crazed. But one of the most awesome things was when my niece Nikki and I met NKOTB! Yeee!" I squeal like a fourteen-year-old girl.

Irene gives me a big smile. "I bet. I can't believe you got to meet them."

"I was wearing the same dress then that I'm wearing now," I tell her. She glances at my orange and gold halter mini dress with my massive heaving cleavage. "Jon Knight said he liked my dress! I know he's gay, but still, he was the one I was crazy for back in the day. You shoulda seen Donnie macking on my niece. He tried to hook her up with his son."

After I gleefully recount all the scrumptious details of being backstage at the NKOTB concert in Denver—at which my niece and I seriously considered pilfering a pair of Chucks from the large wheeled bin of shoes from which the New Kids were choosing—we fall into a momentary silence. The traffic weighs on us. LA can suck the life out of you. I stare at my reflection in the window, overlaying the scenery of the mountains barely visible behind a veil of smog. I used to stare out the window like this when Charles and I drove around LA, and my head filled with musings about our relationship, if we were really as together or apart as I acutely felt we were or perceived us to be. Always, though, I'd be following after him, from universities to conferences to talks, even my career followed his—I was the academic journal editor who worked on his essays and special issues and collections he organized. Now it's just me and the fading memory of what we had been. My reflection comes into focus in front of the smog.

Irene and I arrive at her apartment. Taking my carry-on suitcase out of her trunk, I steady myself on the sidewalk. I'm still getting used to wearing heels, having been clumsy my whole life. (Who could blame me? My feet are undoubtedly the least attractive part of my body, as I was born with gigantic bunions on both sides of my Hobbit feet.) Okay, I got this. Irene leads the way. I click-clack behind her.

Even before we reach her door, I can hear the yelps and barks of her dogs. They know their mama is home from work.

"Listen to the madness. I love it," she says, turning the key in the lock. She opens the door, and a rush of canine mows us down.

"Hey, dog! Okay, yeah, happy to see you too! Jesus Christ!" I say, trying to be gentle in pushing away dog tongues and claws. "Whoa, there. Irene, your dog is sniffing my crotch."

"Blackens smells something good. . .or stinky!" she cackles.

I edge into her apartment with my suitcase and close the door behind me.

"Holy shit, dude," I say, exasperated. The dogs stop crowding me and go get kisses from their mom.

"Oh, yeah, Anton, you remember my friend Brandy? Brandy—Anton," Irene says, nodding toward her brother sitting at the desk.

I'd only met Anton twice before. The first time was at their dad's funeral, and I can't imagine he remembered meeting me then; there were so many people there from where Irene and I worked, people he didn't know. The second time we met was when he and Irene went out to dinner with Charles and me at a whiteified *pho* restaurant in Silverlake, where *Grey's Anatomy* star Sandra Oh happened to be dining right beside us. At the time we really didn't pay much attention to each other, instead focusing on judging the annoying hipster crowd around us.

But now as I look at him sitting at the desk, working on his computer, I feel much differently toward him. I feel something stir. Just a quick, subtle glance at his curly brown hair, beautiful eyes with long eyelashes, boyish grin—very cute. "Oh, yes, I remember you. Irene's little brother," I say.

"I'm not so little anymore," he replies, giving me the once-over.

Irene picks up on the mischief in his voice and scolds him in Tagalog. I shrug, smile at him, and sit on the couch, crossing my legs just so.

"'Ton, this girl's been busy! Show my brother the makeover thingy," she says.

"Do you really want to see that?" I ask.

"What makeover?" Anton asks. I tell him about it, kind of embarrassed, kind of proud, trying to be humble and downplay it but in the process only end up sounding like a twelve-year-old girl bragging to her friends about how mature she is.

"Here, let me show you." I go over to him. "Um, can I bring it up on your computer?"

He actually looks interested. "Yeah, totally."

I bring up my blog on his computer and scroll down to the entries on the makeover. I try very hard to refrain from a voice-over commentary during the replay, but just before the New Kids come on during the second segment, I blurt out, "Oh my god, here it comes, my favourite part!" I feel the excitement come to a crescendo as the band's visages grace the monitor. It never gets old.

"Whoa, you're famous!" he chuckles.

"Not quite. Almost though," I say.

"Right on. Thanks for showing me that."

"Thanks for watching."

"I'd definitely watch that again. Sounds like you deserve all that," he says, smiling. "Listen, Yin, I gotta go run some errands," he tells Irene, calling her the nickname used in their family.

Damn! I wish he would stay longer. always working?

"Okay, don't forget to pick up that stuff from Fart and Smile for the secret supper," she says.

"Fart and Smile?" I ask.

Irene and Anton laugh. "Smart and Final. We call it Fart and Smile."

"Two things Irene's good at," he jokes. "I have the list. Don't worry about it."

"Oh yeah, we're hosting a secret supper event this weekend," Irene explains. "It's a private catering thing—of course, you're invited. Peter's cooking, Anton and I are the sweatshop labour."

"I can help out," I offer.

"No, just come and enjoy. Mingle with the guests."

"Okay, thanks!"

Anton makes his way to the door. "Bye, Yin. It was nice seeing you again, Brandy."

"Nice seeing you too!" I say, hoping we get plenty of opportunities to see more of each other in the near future. I want to see more of him, especially more of his bare flesh. Wait, stop it, Brandy! Heel, girl!

Just as Anton makes his way out the door, Irene's fiancé Peter walks in. I wade through the yelping, jumping dog current and greet him with a big hug, happy for new beginnings for us all.

"Keep sewing!" Irene shouts. It's been a running joke between the two of us ever since we worked together. As office manager in the department where I worked at UCLA, Irene had to organize a lot of dinners, conferences, and talks. She'd often rope me into doing some assembly-line type of labour when I wasn't busy with editing or when my eyes and brain needed a break from proofreading jargon-laden essays and articles. So as we'd stamp and lick hundreds of envelopes or put together centrepieces for fundraising dinners, she'd shout, "Keep sewing!" We'd laugh because we felt like sweatshop labour, and I would know because I worked in a sweatshop with my mother when I was a teenager. (Sounds like fun, doesn't it? No? You wouldn't want to work in a sewing factory for minimum wage, which at the time was $4.25/hour, with your insane mother?)

Irene is making me put together programs for her wedding. Cardstock, vellum, paper, punch-holed in the centre and tied together with a ribbon. My fingers are cramping.

"After this, we need to go back to the dollar store and get more shit. Celisse and Jennifer are coming over later to help out."

"Great, a bigger labour force," I say, smiling.

"That's right!"

"What about your brother? Is he coming over to help out?" I ask, feeling my face tingle with anticipation.

"Hells yeah! He's not getting off from toiling in the sweatshop. Enough talking! Keep sewing!"

Before long, Anton arrives. He flashes me a smile, but he's pretty frazzled with all that's going on with the wedding and the secret supper.

"Oh, shit, did you get the shit for the secret supper?" Irene asks in a panic.

He somehow knows exactly what she's talking about. "Yeah, don't worry about it. Peter's at the kitchen now doing more prepping. Did you. . ." Anton keeps talking, but I'm not really listening. As he and Irene go over the details for whatever is going on, I steal glances at him and get caught up in imagining us driving to Santa Monica beach, throwing ourselves into the ocean just as dolphins frolic around us. And when the dolphins deliver us back to the beach, we watch the sunset and stay there all night, pointing out shooting stars. In the morning a rainbow graces our bodies as we snuggle into the pristine sand.

Before I get to the part where the pegacorn comes to carrying us off to our own private island, where we survive the end times and are forced to repopulate the earth with our own offspring, let me just tell you: yeah, I want to get laid. I want this man to lie with me. With or without dolphins and unicorns around us.

"Stop sewing! We gotta go to the dollar store now," Irene orders.

"Thank fucking god," I say. "Yay, we get to go out into the sun! Freedom!"

We walk outside. Anton asks, "You have any big plans while you're here?"

"I'm just going out with friends here and there. Irene and I have an artsy thing to go to tonight. Would you like to come with us?"

"I'd love to, but. . ."

"That's not his kind of thing," Irene interrupts.

"Yeah, artsy people are so whatever," I roll my eyes, trying to mask my disappointment.

I must focus on the wedding. I didn't come here to hook up with my friend's brother. The thought certainly didn't cross my mind before I got here. But there's just something about him. And maybe I'm imagining things. . .maybe I don't know what I'm talking about anymore when it comes to men. I mean, so far, my track record sucks ass. But maybe he likes me too?

"Girl, I think Cadi would look so cute in an orange tutu walking down the aisle, don't you?" Irene says, referring to her mini-dachshund.

"I guess. Why do you ask?"

"Well, I just happened to have some tulle that I think you'd be good at cutting and dyeing. . ." Irene says, giggling.

"You mean to tell me that you want me to make an orange tutu for your dog?"

Irene replies with a sweet "yes, please" smile and bats her eyelashes.

"Sure, why not," I say.

With all that she's making me do for her wedding, I doubt there's going to be time to get laid anyway.

One final touch—a bit of gold bronzer across the décolletage. Ha! I have a décolletage. Never thought I'd use that word in reference to myself.

I take a long look in the mirror. I put on a strapless white cocktail dress with black and hot pink accents. I spritz myself with "sensual amber" body spray, and I take my sensual self out to the living room, where Irene's frantically making sure she has everything she needs for the secret supper.

"Peter and Anton are meeting us there. Eek! I hope I'm not forgetting anything," she says, looking around the room. "You look nice. Maybe you'll strike up some fancy conversation with guests of the male variety."

"Maybe. We shall see."

When we get to the house where the supper is being hosted, I help Irene carry in bags and bins full of stuff. I can see Anton in the kitchen as we approach the door. He looks handsome in his crisp white shirt and khakis. He opens the door for us.

"Wow, you look beautiful," he says to me.

Those damn butterflies in my stomach are flipping out so hard, that I pray I don't develop acid reflux or irritable bowel syndrome.

"Thanks," I breathe, trying to sound all sexy-husky, but I think I just sounded like I have a phlegm ball caught in my throat. I cough. "Um, do you guys need help?"

"No, go sit, mingle, stuff like that!" Irene says, pushing me out the door to the yard where everything is set up.

I step foot in the grass, where I have to tread lightly so my heels don't sink into the ground and make me stuck like some damn fool. I see guests already seated at the long table. I sit down at an empty chair next to a cheery middle-aged couple. It's hard to focus on the conversation, or frankly, to give a shit about what's being said because I keep watching Anton do his thing. Every time he comes over to serve the next course or pour me some more wine, I find myself wondering what it would be like to kiss him. I'm having more of those thoughts as he pours me more wine.

That's it. I can't take it anymore.

I excuse myself from the table and walk over to him.

"Can I help you with something?" he asks.

"It's kinda boring over there," I say. "I'd rather be in here, doing work with you guys, maybe washing dishes?" Before anyone can answer, I stack some clean dishes on the counter. When there's a lull in activity, I ask him, "Would you like to join me for a smoke?" He looks at me funny, like people always do when they know that I've had cancer and yet I'm smoking. "Hey, cancer and chemo didn't kill me, so I doubt one cigarette's going to."

He smiles and releases a sigh of relief. "Okay. I'd love to."

We walk to the front of the house and smoke by his car.

"What are your plans after the dinner?" I ask.

"Usually after one of these events, I go up to a mountain and meditate."

"How Zen of you," I joke, while still thoroughly impressed and intrigued.

"Would you like to come with me?" he asks.

Hell yeah, I would.

"Um, maybe. Let me think about it," I say, putting out my ciggie.

I go back to the dinner table. Time for cheesecake. I take note of the fact that Anton gives me the biggest piece.

The secret supper comes to a close. I help Irene, Peter, and Anton clean and pack up.

"Hey, girl, your brother asked me if I wanted to go hang out with him. He's going to some mountain. I think I'm going to do that, if that's cool," I say, trying to sound nonchalant and casual.

"Yeah, sure," she says.

When we get back to her apartment, I change out of my cocktail dress and take off with Anton to The Mountain. We get there, and I'm blown away by the lit-up grid of Los Angeles. I lived here for almost ten years, and I've never seen LA like this.

"We need to watch out for mountain lions, okay?" Anton says, breaking the silence.

"Okay. . .and what do we have for our defence in case we encounter any?"

"These bottles of fizzy water. If you see a mountain lion, just shake this bottle hard, aim it at the lion, and open the bottle. I already know how to do this, so I'll protect you."

"Gee, thanks," I say, laughing as we take a spot on the ground.

The air feels warm and sweet up here. I'm getting that tingly feeling again, as if the most popular guy in the twelfth grade is about to ask me to the prom (which, for the record, had never happened).

"What do you do here in LA, besides catering and fending off mountain lions?" I ask.

"I go to AA meetings a lot. I used to be a bad meth addict, but I go to my meetings and keep that in check."

"Irene told me about all that. It's good you're sober now."

"I'm getting sick of LA. I want to go to other places, check them out. I have a friend in Austin, and I'm making plans to go see him," he says.

"You should come up to Vancouver sometime. It's really nice up there. Plus, I'm there," I say, leaning closer to him.

"I would love to. But if you'll excuse me for a moment, I have to go relieve myself. Here—take this sparkling water in case any lions come while I'm gone," he says, handing me the bottle and disappearing across the road into the darkness.

A few minutes later, he returns. "I'm happy you're still here in one piece."

"With your foolproof wilderness survival tip, how could I not be?"

We sit up here for hours, laughing and telling stories. I tell him funny stories from my childhood and not-so-funny stories about my cancer trip, and he tells me funny stories from his childhood and not-so-funny stories about his sobriety trip. I keep begging him in my head to kiss me. But he doesn't. I thought for sure he was going to tap into this incredible vibe that's going on between us, but instead, at 4:00 in the morning, he's dropping me off back at Irene's apartment. Either he's too much of a gentleman, or he really doesn't like me.

Before I go to sleep, I take one last stab at getting Anton's attention. I email him and tell him how I really enjoyed our time together, and that I hope we have another opportunity to hang out. That's all I can do. I close my eyes and hope for sweet dreams.

Tonight, I'm meeting up with some friends from grad school and a couple of girls I met at the New Kids on the Block concert in Denver. These particular fans call themselves the "Block Police" (who cleverly issue members of NKOTB citations for things like "driving with a six-pack" and "being a serial lady killer"), and they have the sexy lady cop outfits to go with the name. They also live in Los Angeles, so I'm meeting up with them and my UCLA grad school friends at Bottle Rock wine bar in Culver City.

We have some hoity-toity wine and cheese, and then one of my grad school buddies and I decide to go clubbing downtown. Now I'm with three gay dudes in this club who keep buying me one mango martini after the other. The drunker I become, the more brazen I am in showing Anton how much I desire him. I keep texting him to see if I can entice him to come join us. He coyly responds that we'll have time to hang out later. But I can't stand it. I have to see him. I call him and insist that I come over to hang out with him.

As I'm hanging up the phone, my friend goes, "Isn't Irene's brother gay?"

I pause. Is he? "No, I don't think so," I say. Then I blurt out in a sing-song voice, "I'm gonna get laid!" Oh shit. I just realized I actually haven't hung up the phone. I hope Anton already hung up and didn't hear that!

My friend drives me to Anton's house and walks me to Anton's door, making sure Anton isn't a creep. Satisfied, he tells me to have fun and takes off.

I slink into the living room and sit down on the couch.

"So," I say.

"So?" he asks.

I smile and shake my head in drunken disbelief. Am I just going to have to get naked or what? What is up with this guy?

"Argh! This is so frustrating!" I say, throwing the biggest temper tantrum ever.

Then he kisses me. It's the most romantic drunken kiss ever in the history of drunken kisses. It's so good that I've sobered up and then get drunk again in a span of thirty seconds. We're doing the kissing/walking dance into the bedroom, where he begins undressing me.

This suddenly becomes very real. This isn't the shit in my head with rainbows, unicorns, and leprechauns and shit. In two seconds he's going to see my scars and lumps and imperfections from when I almost died. He's going to see the scars that drove Charles away.

I stop and gather my clothes and hide my body from him.

He gently takes my hands in his. He caresses my face and whispers, "You're so beautiful," and kisses me again. I melt into him and relent.

If there's anyone to trust my scars with, this is the guy. He doesn't shrink away from them. In fact, he respects them. We shared as much on the mountain—our common histories with depression, abandonment, and substance abuse—near-death experiences. I get the feeling that he knows what all this means. In the short time we've been together this week, we've established more intimacy than I've ever had with anyone, including Charles. It's almost indescribable. Almost.

A gleeful voice inside my head is singing, Oh yeah, I'm gonna get so laid.

I'm sitting here at this retreat for young adult cancer survivors and their supporters. When I saw my oncologist and brought her up to speed on my life, she told me that I should come to this retreat. I was hesitant because I really just want to put all this cancer business behind me. Plus, I've never been a huge fan of group therapy ever since my first experience with it while a college student in Boston, and this retreat sounded an awful lot like that. But I took her advice and contacted the organizer, and there happened to be a space available.

We're at this idyllic centre called Edenvale. The people who run this place grow their own fruits and vegetables and make whatever they can homemade. There's a massage therapist here, we do drum circles, and we meditate. It has been therapeutic, though I'm finding it hard to focus on why I am here, which is to deal with life after cancer. There are things going on in my life right now that I haven't heard going on for anybody else, and I wonder how much I need or want to share.

I feel like I'm the token divorcée, the one whose relationship didn't make it. I see the other couples here, and they talk about the strain that cancer has had on their relationships and how they feel that they are now beginning to see how cancer has made them stronger as a couple. Then when they hear my story, they look at me with a mixture of disbelief and fear. I sense they don't want to hear that it is possible that relationships do fail, that husbands leave wives when it becomes too unbearable anymore. I quickly tell them that there's nothing to fear, though, because there are people in the world who love you, and look, I just fell in love last month, and that's why I'm typing madly on my phone texting him because even now, I can't stand to be away from him, and someday I hope you'll all meet this wonderful man who loves me despite my cancer.

In addition to relationships, we're also talking about fertility. All of us, both men and women, have been told that our reproductive systems could be compromised as a result of treatment—blank sperm and early menopause are two things we could look forward to before our time. Not only that, for women with reproductive cancers, the surge in hormones that comes with pregnancy typically could set off a recurrence; doctors caution patients not to get pregnant until they reach their five-year remission mark. So we're discussing what options we have and how to deal with that. The most popular option is freezing embryos and getting a surrogate, which is costly. But people have been creative, doing things like holding fundraisers and gotten their parents to chip in on the cost. All this talk about the difficulty of having kids after cancer makes me feel sheepish about talking about my current situation, which is that I'm pregnant and am going to have an abortion.

Last week, Anton flew up to Seattle and I drove across the border to meet him there. We spent a few days together camping on Bainbridge Island. Since it's the end of summer, we had the campground to ourselves. When night fell, it became chilly.

Partly because I was freezing and partly because I was trying to be romantic, I said, "Let's light a bunch of tea candles to warm up."

And because he was stupid in love, he agreed.

After engaging in the kind of lovemaking that you'd expect in the best romantic movies or books you'd ever seen or read, we fell fast asleep, wrapped in a super-comfy blanket of our body heat. Luckily for us, however, Anton was awoken by the blaze that had started in our tent because the candles had melted through their thin aluminium holders and had set fire to our beach towels.

I woke up to him shaking me, saying, "Babe! Wake up!" He pushed me out of the tent, threw the towels on the ground outside, and stamped out the fire.

That's right—we are so in love with each other that we almost died and started a forest fire. Beat that.

Just thinking about it now turns me into a giddy teenager.

Anyway, the day before he was flying back to LA, we were staying in a hotel in Kent, Washington—which is where I saw, funny enough, a tractor-trailer with "Zimmerman Truck Lines, Mifflintown, PA" printed on it.

"Holy shit! Babe! There's a truck from Mifflintown! We got to turn around and go after it!"

Anton looked at me and said, "You're kidding, right?"

"Yes! I mean, well, no. Kinda. I don't want to chase it. But isn't that weird?"

He laughed and agreed that it was pretty uncanny that we would happen to see a truck from Mifflintown all the way over here in Kent, Washington.

It was also pretty weird that I hadn't gotten my period yet. When we got back to our hotel after lunch, I took a pregnancy test that I bought on the sly at Rite-Aid. I actually wasn't too worried since my periods hadn't been entirely regular since they started up again after chemo. But when I saw "pregnant" in the little window of the test, I was shocked.

I came out of the bathroom and showed Anton the test. With disbelief in his eyes, he said, "I'm not ready to be a dad. We can't have a baby."

I couldn't blame him. I'm not ready to be a mom of a brand-new baby again. Too much instability in our lives. Not only that, I was pretty sure the doctors were going to tell me that going through a pregnancy soon after cancer was a bad idea.

Sure enough, when I contacted my various doctors, they gave me their recommendations, which were to not go through with this pregnancy. They admitted that not much research has been done on pregnancy and its effect on my type of breast cancer—Triple Negative breast cancer, a rare type that isn't affected by the three main hormones that are usually a factor in most breast cancers. But given that I also have a TRAM-flap, which is also not structurally conducive to carrying out a pregnancy, with the way the mesh in the abdomen doesn't bend, having a baby would not be a good idea.

I made the decision to terminate the pregnancy, but I'm still agonizing over it. A part of me wants to have this baby—this being that Anton and I made. I know, though, we are in no position to do so in any sort of way. We live in two different cities, two different countries. I'm just starting my divorce process, and I'm still recovering from having had cancer and need to try to become as healthy as possible for Chloe and Mylo. Anton just sold his share of the catering business and

than will will this
at what low?

has been out of work, and he's really committed to working on his sobriety, having gone through a big break-up almost a year ago. Of course, with all that's going on, our financial situations are also highly unstable, to say the least.

Knowing all that doesn't make it any easier to sit here. I'm messaging Anton on my phone to let him know that. I tell him that I can't do this. I can't sit here at this retreat and be a part of this getting-in-touch-with-ourselves stuff. I like denial, remember? Denial is good.

Anton knows better than I that I need this. From his rehab and AA experiences, he knows when the time is right to reach out and be part of a group that will allow one to dig deep. "Let it out, let it go," Anton writes. "There's a reason you chose to go to this and participate, so try to take advantage of it. I'm here for you."

Does he know what he's getting into with me? I remember something Charles had said to me one week after he confessed to his affair. He said that if given the choice to endure another person's suffering, who would make that choice, beyond having to because of circumstance? Why would Anton choose me, choose this?

I write, "I admire and respect you, and I feel like there's a reason we've been drawn to each other because of our families, histories, and issues. But I also remember how awful it is to watch someone be sick. I don't think you really want to do this. Why would you? I can understand if you don't want to be with me." I swallow hard. My hands are sweating, my face is tingling. I wait for his words, staring at the italicized message at the bottom of the screen, *"Anton typing…"*

"That's my decision to make, not yours. I've decided to be with you."

I wipe the tears from my eyes and look around the room. Miles and Caio are holding each other tightly. MaryAnne and Jen are making colourful mandalas and laughing. Mikey, Bonnie, and Jared are talking about the recent kayaking expedition that they organized for young adults with cancer. I am full and complete with this thought right now: it takes a room full of young people who have faced death to teach me how to live and trust love.

The abortion proceeded without incident, except for the fact that no one told me how painful it would be afterward. I was told that I'd experience some cramping. Yeah, no shit. I felt like my uterus had never been angrier with me. I writhed in bed, crying to Anton over the phone. My friend Karin came by to offer me support, booze, and pie. I asked her if she could take a mallet to my head too, but she said no.

The doctor inserted a non-hormone IUD during the procedure, as that is the only safe type of birth control for me given my cancer history. A few weeks later, I had an incredible pain in my pelvis. I went to the emergency room at Women's Hospital, and when the doctor performed an ultrasound to check the placement of the IUD, she also discovered that I had ovarian cysts. The pain I'd been experiencing had been from one of the cysts rupturing. The doc said that the cysts were likely non-malignant, and she told me to get another ultrasound in a few weeks to see if the cysts would resolve themselves.

A couple weeks ago, I got another ultrasound, and then went to LA to visit Anton one last time before the kids and I took off for Pennsylvania for Christmas. When I returned from LA, I heard several messages from my doctor, asking me to make an appointment to come in ASAP. At the exam she told me that the ultrasound showed that the cysts were gone but also that the IUD had been falling out slowly.

I looked at the doc and asked, "Is it possible that I've gotten pregnant again?"

"It's highly unlikely," she said. "The cervix should do its thing in response to the IUD still being there, despite it not being in the correct position. Don't worry about it. Just make an appointment to come back in to get another IUD inserted when you get back from your trip, okay?" We wished each other happy holidays.

It's the day after Christmas, and I'm still in Pennsylvania. The kids are sleeping, and I'm sitting here in my childhood bedroom trying to figure out this weird luck. I can't believe it. I'm pregnant again—the second time in four months.

Not only are my chances of getting pregnant supposed to be diminished by cancer treatment, but I also have a birth control device inside me—and yet, I still manage to get pregnant? I feel like I need to play the lottery.

I just told Anton. However, this time, he didn't say that we should terminate the pregnancy. He only said that we'll talk about it when I get back to Vancouver. I imagine he is probably in shock like I am.

Though I was in a daze, I heard his words clearly, "I love you, babe. We will make it work, I promise. I miss you so much. I can't wait to hold you in my arms."

My chest ached a good kind of ache, with so much love. "I love you too, my love," I said. "Good night."

With Chloe and Mylo fast asleep, I sit watching over them. I keep thinking of what Anton said to me while we were driving around LA a couple weeks ago.

Out of nowhere he goes, "You know I never wanted to have kids of my own, right? You know it's because of my childhood, how I grew up with my dad in the Philippines while Mom and Irene lived in LA. And also because I'm adopted, I don't know if there is a need for me to have biological children."

I nodded. I knew his story before I knew him, since Irene told me early on in our friendship how she and her mother left Manila so that Irene could have a good education and life in the U.S., while her brother and father stayed in the Philippines, where their father's business was. And of course I knew how Irene and Anton were both adopted and not biological siblings. They had fractured pasts that were put together the best way their parents knew how.

He continued, "It's also because I've always thought I wasn't fit to raise a kid, you know, with my drugging and drinking. I also just didn't want to bring another human being into this world that's already overpopulated."

"Yes, I understand all that, love," I said.

"Well, I was just thinking, and I'm not saying now's the time, but I really want to have a baby with you someday. You've changed something in me, and if it's okay—with your health and all—I want you to have my child."

"What? Are you serious?" I laughed with complete joy. "That's huge, babe! I'm so touched." I thought back to when I was going through chemo, and I had a tremendous urge to have a third child, the urge made even greater by the likelihood of it not happening. "I love you so much, baby," I said.

"I know. I love you too," he said, smiling.

When the kids and I came to Mifflintown for the holiday, I missed Anton even more. I wrote him super-cheesed email.

My love,

What is this—this aching I feel for you? I sit in my bathroom, and you're there with me. And then you're here at my parents' house, among family and friends, handsome and radiant, holding my hand, and we're committing ourselves to each other for how ever long our souls allow us. I hear the music and get carried away to the part where we're exchanging vows, to the scene in which Chloe and Mylo can witness what a fairytale true love looks like, to the point at which we're overcome by emotion and meaning and dreams.

A long time ago, I gave up on my dreams for love. I chalked them up to naïveté and idealism. But the synthesis between us takes my breath away, and I'm grateful to the universe for the moment that we came together.

I hope you feel the sincerity in this cheesiness. I know that you will. You are my love. You are my soulmate. I have no doubt in that.

I love you, Ant.

Bee

I eagerly and longingly waited for his reply. Each second that went by I thought, maybe he read my email and decided to jump ship. Had it not been proven time and again that at the moment when I'm ready to give my all to a man, he ends up not seeing the same worth in that as I, that he only sticks around while waiting for someone better to come along?

I didn't have to sit too long with these horrible thoughts of self-doubt before I got the response that I've dreamt about my whole life. I read Anton's words over and over again, and I read them again now, knowing that I'm carrying our child.

My love,

While I sit here waiting to hear from you, I can't help thinking about what my life has become when you became a part of it. Waiting and wanting you has been the focus of my thoughts these past few days since you've been gone, knowing that someday soon, all that I have envisioned of us being together again will finally happen, even if it's just for a moment.

You give me reason to wake up in the morning and smile. Just smile for no particular reason except for the fact that you're with me. As the days go by, I feel myself growing closer and closer to you, and my heart suddenly comes alive because it is being loved by you. I don't want to lose this feeling. I don't ever want to lose you.

When I hear your voice, the feeling I get is one that I do not wish to fade. You give me comfort and joy. The sound of your voice is like my favorite love song—I can listen to it all night until it puts me to sleep. Yet as I continue to sit here and think about everything you are to me, I can't help but wonder, what's on your mind too, right at this moment? How much do you feel, and how real do you think this really is?

My life revolves around a search. A search for something that is greater than myself. Some fortunate accident happened along the way, and I found you stepping into my life. It is evident that some power has graced me with your love. I just want you to know that wherever this road may take us, and how far it may be to finally get where we want to go, always know you are in my heart. And in my heart, you'll always be.

Thank you for being you. What I'd like to say next, I'd like to say to you in person. Until then. . .

Love always,

Ant

A huge wave of peace washes over me. I lie down beside Chloe and Mylo and look at their faces. Chloe's having a fitful dream. She's whimpering a bit. I put my hand on her chest, lean over, and kiss her on the forehead. She quiets down. "You might have another brother or sister," I whisper. She sighs.

I get out of bed. I'm feeling pulled to Mom's altar. I hear her chanting, but when I peek in the room, I don't see her. I look at where the sound is coming from, and I see that the cassette player is on. At first, I'm confused, but then I realize what Mom has done. She is supposed to be chanting for a certain number hours of the day—something crazy like fourteen hours—but she's figured out a way to get it done while doing other things, like sleep. She's recorded herself doing chants, and she flips the tape or changes it every six hours. I'm not sure if this is really helping her cause as far as her afterlife goes, but I suppose she thinks it does.

I look out the window to the front porch. Beyond the front porch, in the yard, is Mom's wishing well. She made Dad put it there years ago, and it serves the purpose of being a spirit house. Like the altar, it holds fake candles, flowers, and offerings like fruit and candy bars. (My dead family must have some serious sweet tooth thing going on.) The well looks like a tiny warm refuge from the blistering cold outside. I wonder if other spirits are hanging out in there too.

I stand before the altar. It glows back at me, orange. I say hi to my Vietnamese grandparents and Pennsylvania Dutch great-grandparents. I don't see Hieu's picture. I asked Mom before why she didn't put Hieu's picture in the altar, but she never answered me. I rub my tummy and introduce my ancestors to the new generation.

I sit on the recliner opposite the altar. It's so peaceful here—no war, no harsh words, no sickness. Just remembrance and love. Here, I am able to sleep.

I wake up a few hours later, when Mom comes in to switch off her tape recorder and do some actual real-life chanting. She's wearing her grey Buddhist robe, and her hair is in a bun at the nape of her neck.

"What you here for?" she asks, but softly.

"Oh, I guess I fell asleep sitting here last night," I tell her.

"Go back your bed. Sleep better there," she says.

I leave the living room. But before I go into my bedroom, I peek into my parents' room. Dad has his head bowed. On the bed are his Bible and *Our Daily Bread*, a booklet that contains one of the good Lord's lessons each day. This is the first time I've ever seen Dad pray. I'm not sure why, but it's making me feel very sad.

Quietly, I open the door to my bedroom. Chloe and Mylo are still sleeping. Chloe's arm is over Mylo's face. I move her arm and slide into bed beside them. Here I lie, with my three children. I turn on my back and put my hands on my stomach. There is love inside. I can feel it.

Anton's decided that it's too much to live apart from me. I'm moving out of the house, so we can start our lives together with a fresh vibe. I found a bright two-bedroom basement suite in a great neighbourhood where the kids can play in a nearby park and go to a better school. Anton has a green card from the U.S.—he moved to the States from the Philippines almost ten years ago—so he can't move to Canada yet because of residency restrictions, but he can be here as much as he's allowed, six months at a time. Which is a good thing because we decided to have the baby.

We've been consulting with so many doctors—my family doctor, my oncologist, my plastic surgeon, a fertility specialist, a high-risk obstetrician. They've been helping us weigh the pros and cons to the best of their ability and knowledge, though I wish they would have more sensitivity when talking to us. My oncologist bluntly asked, "Are you sure you want another a baby, given your higher risk of recurrence?" After I got over my shock that she said such a thing, I became angry. Are you telling me that I'm cruel or selfish to bring a baby into the world when I might get cancer again and die? She might as well have said it like that.

Insensitivity aside, there is the question of recurrence. The consensus among the doctors is that the pregnancy, in theory, shouldn't increase my risk of recurrence because my cancer was hormone receptor-negative. However, my risk of recurrence is still higher than usual because of the subset of cancer I had, but that's whether I'm pregnant or not. In the end it's really up to me if I want to take the risk of having another baby.

Next is the consideration of experiencing a pregnancy with a TRAM-flap. Dr. Lothlorien told me that I would have to have a C-section because I have no abdominals with which to push out a baby, and that they could just cut through the mesh in my abdomen.

As far as my fertility is concerned, the fertility doctor told me that my options are very limited should I want to have a baby in the future because the success rate, factoring in my cancer history, is low. He said that just because I've been getting pregnant, it does not mean that I'm fertile. I'm just lucky. (I knew I should have played the lottery, dammit!) And that if I've been planning on having children in the future, I should go with this one now. Basically, this is a miracle baby, which we decided to have.

Dr. Lothlorien was very excited with this news, as it seems we are breaking new ground. "I've never had a TRAM-flap patient go through a pregnancy before. In fact, I did some research and cannot find a single case in which a patient with a bilateral mastectomy and TRAM went through a pregnancy post-surgery."

Anton and I must have given her some scared, dubious looks because she quickly collected herself to reassure us that she'd do all she could to make sure I was going to be okay. "It's true that I don't know how your body will accommodate a growing baby, but your obstetrician and I are well acquainted and work well together. We'll do our best, given the situation."

Anton squeezed my hand. I hadn't yet told him about how I looked up on the Internet "tram-flap and pregnancy" and found a handful of cases in which the patients had a TRAM only on one side of their bodies (not both sides, like I have), and still experienced pain and problems as the pregnancy progressed. One woman said her baby started growing into her spine because of the lack of space due to the mesh.

Even without knowing about the potential problems, Anton has many fears. "I don't want anything to happen to you. You're more important to me than this baby."

"Don't say that. Look how tough I am. I can take anything," I reassured him.

Today we heard the heartbeat for the first time. Anton had tears in his eyes. It had become real to him in that moment. My doctor looked at us and smiled.

I put my hand on his arm as I lay on the exam table. "Are you okay, babe?"

"Yeah, it's just that—that's amazing!" He beamed. We listened to the quick cadence again.

"Nice strong heartbeat," the doc said.

Later, when we were on the bus, he said, "Wow, I'm blown away. I want to hear it again." I've never felt so happy. He's going to be the most incredible dad.

"Are you going to tell your mom?" I asked.

"I think she'd be happy to hear about it," he said.

Anton and his mom have had a rocky relationship, since he didn't grow up with her. When he and his dad reunited with his mother and sister in LA after almost two decades, it wasn't a happy reunion. And when his father passed away from cancer when Anton was twenty-three years old, tensions between him and his mom reached the breaking point, especially when Anton was at the height of his meth addiction as a way of coping with his father's death. Not wanting to deal with his addiction anymore, his mother kicked him out and put a restraining order on him, effectively rendering him homeless. Hitting rock bottom pushed Anton to enter rehab and turn his life around. Though all that went down years ago, it was only these past few months, upon his mother's cancer diagnosis, that Anton has reconnected with his mother.

He held my hand, took out his cell, and called his mother.

"Hi, Mom, it's me. How are you feeling?" He nodded his head as he listened. I imagined she was telling him about her pain and what the doctors have been saying about her condition. "Who's there to help you out?" he asked. He listened some more. "Mom, I have some good news that might cheer you up." He took a deep breath and said, "Brandy's pregnant. Yeah, we're going to have a baby. You're going to have a grandchild," he said, smiling. I could tell she was happy to hear the news. "Yeah, the due date is at the end of August. Brandy is almost three months pregnant now. We're very excited," he looked at me and squeezed my arm. "Okay, Mom, thanks. I'll talk to you later. I love you. Bye." He turned to me and said, "She's really happy. She's been depressed about the pain, but she said this lifts her spirits."

"I'm glad, honey. That's awesome. You're the best," I said.

"No, you're the best," he replied, putting his index finger on the tip of my nose. It's a silly game we play between the two of us.

This is the best, I thought, as the bus chugged along. We were almost home.

I had just dropped off the kids at school when my cell phone rang. It was a call from the obstetrician's office. She received the results from my serum screening and wanted me to come in to discuss the results. My heart immediately sank when I heard the message. I knew from past pregnancies that this test was to check for risk of Down's syndrome and neural tube defects (most commonly, spina bifida). I called my family doctor and told her about the call from the obstetrician. She said that she would get the results herself and get back to me. She called back and asked me if Anton and I could come in and see her right away. I'd had the same dread I had when I got the call to come in and discuss the results of my initial biopsy two and a half years ago.

Sitting in the exam room. Anton's trying to be calm, but I know what's coming.

The doc takes a deep breath and begins. "Before we go over the results, I want you to know that these numbers are not conclusive. The next step is to get more tests done that will give us more definite answers," she says. Anton and I nod in understanding. "The test shows a one in five chance of a neural tube defect, and one in twenty-five chance of Down's syndrome."

I stare straight at her without blinking. She continues, "The next thing to do is an amniocentesis, which is a bit of a risky procedure. But it'll give us a better sense of what's going on." She puts her hand on my arm.

"So that is what we will do," I say firmly. Sounds reasonable. No cause for alarm yet, I try to tell myself.

One problem: the mesh in my abdomen. How will the needle pass through it to get the amniotic fluid? The doctor's confident that the technicians should be able to find a pocket that the needle can pass through, but the idea of someone having to stab me multiple times with that huge needle before getting the right spot doesn't sit well with me. I decide to email Dr. Lothlorien.

It's not so much the idea of having an "imperfect" baby that worries me; it's more of the idea that the baby might be born suffering. Neural tube defects are more than just spina bifida. In some cases the babies are paralysed, mobility challenged, blind or deaf, or are stillborn. I know—we shouldn't let our minds race before we get more conclusive results, but still, how can we rein in all this?

I don't have to wait long at all before I get my appointment for the detailed ultrasound and the amnio. But it's not until the end of next week because Anton and I are off to Los Angeles to visit his mother, who's taken a turn for the worse. It'll be more than two weeks before we know what's wrong with our baby. Also, Dr. Lothlorien wants very much to communicate with the people performing the amnio before they just go in there and try to do their thing.

In my desperation to find a scenario that it's actually me who has something wrong, not the baby, I Google alpha fetoprotein levels (AFP—the protein that indicates risk of Down's syndrome and neural tube defects) and any possible relation to cancer. Sure enough, increased levels occur in men and non-pregnant women when there is presence of liver, stomach, testicular, and ovarian cancer and lymphoma. This is wacky, but I really start praying that I have cancer and that the baby is okay because that would mean I could get treatment and get better, and the baby wouldn't be born with some incurable defect from which s/he would suffer.

I have breaks of consciousness when I begin to wonder if I'm dreaming—that this shocker is some kind of fear that my subconscious is actually dealing with. But then I see the copy of the report on the couch, and I know that it's real.

I ask myself why things keep happening, why just when things seem to be going right, we get another life-changing challenge thrown at us. In my most cynical moments, I think that I'm the universe's favourite joke. In my most spiritual moments, I feel that the universe thinks I can handle it, that if there's anybody on whom to lay these challenges, it's me.

I breathe in and realize that hours have passed, that it's time to pick up the kids from school. When we are home, I tell them that the baby might be sick. Mylo hugs my belly all night, "to love the baby," he says.

http://cancerfuckingsucks.blogspot.com
Saturday, May 29, 2010
Universe, can you please cut me some slack?

April 15, 2010 was the second anniversary of my bilateral mastectomy. It was also the day that our son, Veo Hieu Liam Worrall-Soriano, was born and then died. Veo had a birth defect called anencephaly, which causes the skull to not form and therefore, the baby would never have a chance to survive. I was admitted to Women's Hospital to give birth to Veo and to say goodbye. When labour was induced, I felt the familiar pains of childbirth, but with the added pain of knowing that all the dreams we had for Veo would never come true. Each contraction that passed through me was another permanent wound. I knew that before long, we would be able to hold Veo, but only for a little while.

We named our son Veo, after Anton's father Clodoveo, who passed away a few years ago and whom Anton loved so very much.

Throughout our stay at Women's, the staff—from the nurses to the social worker to the spiritual counsellor—helped us in every single way they could, and we will always be so thankful for that support. But as we came home, we felt the immense sadness and void fill up the space around us. We spent time together, just the two of us, and we also thought about how we would help Chloe and Mylo deal with the loss of the baby brother they were so excited to have in their lives.

Even though they are only five and six years old, my children have gone through so much in terms of death and loss and illness, starting with my cancer diagnosis in 2007. When they were two and three years old, they watched me transform from a healthy young mom who could easily fulfill all their needs into a sick, bald woman who spent a lot of time in bed. They watched me give myself white blood cell booster injections, and they watched me recover from my surgery, with drains hanging out of me. They watched me get better again. Then they endured their father's and my separation, trying to cope with now living between two households and understanding why grownups behave the way they do. Now this—a baby whom they never saw but hugged through my belly, a baby with whom they had all these plans to play, a baby for whom they drew pictures and made up stories—this baby they wanted—he was dead. Why? My heart broke when Chloe asked me, "Mama, can we have a baby that doesn't get sick and die?"

It's been over a month since Veo's birth and death, and we're still feeling the loss. Chloe and Mylo have resumed their lives as usual, but now and then they ask me about Veo. They ask to see the tiny footprints the hospital gave us, they ask to burn some incense for him. The hospital gave us teddy bears to give to the kids, and the funeral home gave us a stuffed elephant—all as reminders of Veo. Every night the kids are with me, they hug those stuffies and remember their brother.

I sit alone in our apartment. The kids are with their dad. Anton left to be by his mother's side as she takes her final breath. It's quiet. I'm feeling very unsettled.

Yesterday, I had a check-up with my oncologist. She wants to give me a full-body PET scan to make sure I am truly cancer-free. However, in order for me to have that done, I have to not be pregnant. And now, more than ever, Anton and I really want to have a baby. A fear struck me this morning as I thought about the PET scan: what if it shows I have cancer, and I have to go through chemo or whatever, and then I can never have kids again? I really want to say, forget the PET scan until we have the baby we want so much. But I know—I have to make sure I am good to go.

I fucking hate cancer. It keeps getting in my way.

Why can't we have this life we want so much—to be

so much conflict Myn

with Chloe and Mylo and their baby brother/sister, to live quietly and in the service of society? The last three years of my life have been devastation upon devastation. Yes, there has been so much that has gone right. I still have two amazing children, and I am in love with the most amazing man. Why, then, does life keep dishing out all these challenges that make me want to scream?

Posted by Brandy Lotus Blossom at 6:51 PM

I posted the blog, released into cyberspace all the noise that had been going on in my head. In the quiet of the room—of the city, as it seemed, the whole city stopped in time—madness growing in my chest. I flipped up my tongue in my mouth to play with my tongue ring. Then I remembered that I didn't have the tongue ring anymore. I unscrewed it and took it out when the anaesthesiologist had to put me under in order to remove the placenta after I gave birth to Veo.

Weighing only a quarter of a pound, Veo Hieu Liam Worrall-Soriano was so tiny, like a freshly hatched robin. I marvelled at how the hospital had clothes that small. The nurse said that there were volunteers who knitted and sewed little doll outfits for premature babies. They put a small knit cap on his head to cover the fatal deformity, where his skull stopped growing over his brain.

We gave him Hieu's name as part of his. I felt strongly it had to be done. Even though my brother's name means "filial piety," if you say "hieu" another way with different diacritical marks, it means "to understand." Understanding was something that I wanted very much.

316

Anton and I held him in our palms, cradling his fragility. His mouth was frozen in a half-grimace, and I hoped beyond all hope that he hadn't suffered as he was being born. I had a lot of trouble pushing him out even though he was so small. As I looked at him in my hand, I wondered if he had been choked and suffocated upon entry into this world, before departing into the next.

The morning of the amniocentesis, we still felt that whatever the problem was, it couldn't be bad and that in a few months we would have a son or daughter. Then the technician rolled the ultrasound wand over my stomach, stopped, and hastily said, "I have to go talk to the doctor. Be right back." A few moments later, the radiologist came in and took over the ultrasound procedure. That's when we learned that there would be no amniocentesis because it was clear that the baby wasn't going to survive.

"See here?" the doctor said, pointing out the baby's head on the screen. "It's not round like it should be. I can see without a doubt that the baby's skull hasn't formed properly. The baby has what is called anencephaly, and he or she won't survive." She paused as we took in the news. "You can carry to term if you feel like it—some people feel that's what they really want to do—but I highly recommend that we induce labour and end the pregnancy, given how your body is already compromised from treatments and surgeries."

I muttered robotically, "Okay."

She rubbed my arm. "I'm so sorry to give you this news. I know this isn't what you were expecting to hear."

I nodded.

"Okay, well, I'll see you out to the desk, and the girls there will give you some paperwork to sign, and we'll try to get you in for the procedure as soon as possible."

It was hard for me to look at Anton. When our eyes met, we both started crying, and we didn't give a shit about who saw us snivelling as we followed the doctor out of the exam room to the registration desk. I shakily filled out the paperwork. We held onto each other as we made our way home.

Later that night, we made the decision to tell Chloe and Mylo the news. I didn't know how they'd take it, but I knew it would be hard because they'd been so excited to have a new sibling. My heart shattered into an infinite number of pieces when Mylo dove into his bed, put a pillow over his head, and sobbed uncontrollably for an hour. Chloe accepted the news in shock, saying, "Okay. That's too bad."

We weathered the pain as a family, and on our own. Anton and I took a short trip to the Yukon, to see the Northern Lights in honour and remembrance of Veo. It was our way of experiencing the short life of our son—we were searching for his soul in the vast, colourful universe. We stood under the stars, inhaled the cold night air deeply, and looked up at the sky, taking Veo into our hearts forever.

When I was a little girl and I was mad that my mom wouldn't let me go anywhere or do anything because I had epilepsy, Mammy said, "Do you know why your mother won't let you do anything? It's because she lost your father's little boy, Matthew. He was born too soon, and he died. Your daddy was upset, so that's why your mother is protective of you. She wants to make sure nothing happens to you."

I thought about what it would have been like to have an older brother. Hearing about Matthew made me fantasize about having an older brother to terrorize me, to stick up for me when the kids bullied me at school, teaching me cool things like how to successfully hit rabbits with stones. I could have had an older brother.

In time Matthew would be various types of brothers as I got older. He who was first a playmate became a brother who would be obnoxiously protective when boyfriends did me wrong. Then Matthew became a brother who could help me study for the SATs and tell me how to do a college application so that I could go anywhere I wanted (because, of course, Matthew would have gone to college). When I eventually went to college, Matthew would warn me about going to frat parties, but he would tell me it was okay to experiment with drugs, as long as I did so responsibly. Sometimes college would get rough, and I'd have a hard time handling it all, but when I'd call Matthew, he would tell me that this was just another dark period, and that there was a light at the end of the tunnel after all.

And now, Matthew. . .

Matthew, I haven't talked to you in a long time. I'm sorry. I've been a bad sister. It's just that there's been so much going on in life. But I'm wondering, Matthew, if you see a baby boy, he's your nephew, Veo. Please take care of him. He's my son. I miss him so much.

I held Veo in my hands when he was born, Matthew.

Mom said she couldn't look at you when you were born—it hurt too much to see a baby who would die—and that has made her sad throughout life. She said that you lived for a couple of hours, and that Dad and Mammy told her that you had a full head of black hair. She said she started bleeding a lot when she was seven and a half months pregnant with you. They took her to the hospital, and she didn't understand what was going on because her English wasn't very good. All of a sudden, they were talking mean to her, and even though she said "no pain," they put her to sleep and started performing a C-section to remove you from her belly. She wanted to say a lot of things but she didn't know how in English—like how she wanted to keep the baby inside since she wasn't feeling any pain. She said, "He coulda lived," and the way she said it made me feel like it was a horrible mistake, your death.

Dad says that Mom doesn't remember right, that maybe her brain remembers a different kind of story so that her heart won't hurt as much. He said that you lived for a day and that when you died, the doctors, not knowing the cause, chalked it up to crib death. Dad remembers holding you, and he remembers Mom holding you too, and Mammy and Pappy coming to see you at the hospital.

Though everyone who remembers you calls you by your middle name, your full name is David Matthew Worrall, just like your headstone says, and you were born and died on October 5, 1971. Dad said you were born on October 16 and died one day later, but I looked it up on the Internet, cause you see, his memory isn't perfect either. You were the first baby buried in Babyland in the Westminster Presbyterian Cemetery in town, right behind where Grandma and Grandpa Worrall and the rest of the Worralls are buried. It took Mom and Dad twenty-five years to get your headstone—Dad told me it was because they didn't have money before. But I think it might have taken them twenty-five years to accept your loss.

I have a bit of comfort knowing that you're there for Veo, as I imagine he lives with you and Hieu and other brothers and sisters I might have lost. Still, the loss hurts much more than I could have ever imagined. I'm hoping that his soul will come to us one day, through another baby perhaps.

Matthew, I love you. Tell Veo that Mommy and Daddy will hold him again someday.

I joined an online forum for children of Vietnam War vets who'd been exposed to Agent Orange. The topics on the forum are mostly about unexplained illnesses that the second generation has had, which they think could be easily explained by looking at their fathers' exposure to Agent Orange. The medical similarities between me and other members are striking, even so far as Veo's birth defects. The rare birth defects he had—anencephaly and VACTERL—are common among the generations coming after the one that was initially exposed. The list of illnesses range from chronic pains like arthritis and asthma to more serious deformities, like misshapen or missing limbs, and life-threatening illnesses like cancer. And always, the miscarriages and stillbirths, of which Mom had had a startling number before she had me.

I asked other members if it's possible for us to get tested for the presence of dioxins in our systems. One member, who's been to Vietnam in search of answers, said that dioxins wouldn't be present in our blood since we weren't directly exposed to the chemical. But for those living in the hotspots in Vietnam where dioxins are still present, the chemical does indeed show up in their blood.

Another member said that her body has been deteriorating at such a quick rate that even though she's in her thirties, she's like an eighty-year-old. She was told that Agent Orange works on humans the same way it does trees: it accelerates the growth at such a high rate that the exposed human or the ones who've had genetic mutations passed down to them have a highly accelerated aging process. The image of trees being bright green and lush after being sprayed, and then the next day, completely dead, stuck in my mind. That's what I feel like is happening with me.

My knees ache and creak. I have the thyroid of a sixty-year-old. My hip pops out of the socket, throwing me into excruciating pain until it pops back in. I have arthritis in my pelvis. But according to the group's motto, "You are not alone." And so, it seems I'm not.

Yet I still feel incredibly alone, more so because it's just me and the cats here. Chloe and Mylo are with Charles. Anton's in LA, taking care of his mother's property since she just passed, and also waiting to get an interview for his U.S. citizenship.

I'm desperately trying to put out of my mind the incredible fear I have of him not being able to come back to Canada. The day he left, I was going to a writing workshop downtown. I kept messaging him to see if he had made it to the airport and through customs okay, but there was no reply. I started to panic, emailing Irene to see if she had heard from him. My fears were confirmed when, during the workshop, I got a message from him saying that he was being held in Canadian customs. Apparently, when he went through U.S. customs, his green card was flagged and confiscated because a criminal charge showed up. It was from when he was arrested for violating the restraining order his mother had put on him and for the drugs that were found when the arrest took place. He had gone through the process of rehabilitating, going to AA meetings, and had the charge dismissed, but it still sent off an alarm when his green card was scanned.

When he was escorted back to ticketing to get on a new flight since he missed his scheduled one, Canadian customs wanted to interview him too. He didn't carry his court documents on him, so the agent determined that Anton should had never been allowed into Canada in the first place (even though they'd let him in three times before then). They requested that he leave the country.

I contacted an immigration lawyer as soon as I could, and we've retained his services with the money I received from my divorce settlement. Being apart from him has been nerve-wracking. I'm trying to not think about worst case scenario—

the last thing we need is for him to get deported back to the Philippines.

So much transience and upheaval in our lives. I want nothing more than to settle down, stay put, and grow old and boring over a long period of time.

http://cancerfuckingsucks.blogspot.com
Wednesday, August 4, 2010
Certainty

I feel like I've come full circle, yet instead of the fear that paralyzed me three years ago, I am full of positive new energy, drive, hope, and love. The last time I was in Hawaii, it was 2007, and I had just been diagnosed with cancer. Charles and I went to Honolulu to celebrate our third wedding anniversary. As I am thinking about it now, there was love but also sadness and uncertainty. . .about life and where it was going to lead the two of us, especially with a terrifying cancer diagnosis. We visited a Buddhist temple at the suggestion of two friends whom we serendipitously ran into at the airport. Our afternoon with Roshi was a gruelling examination and exploration about the things to which I am most deeply attached: pain, loss, fear. And during the next three years, I would be faced with seemingly insurmountable challenges that would bring me face-to-face with those attachments. In order to survive, I had to experience pain, loss, and fear, and then let it all go.

Here I am, three years later, in Maui, celebrating year one of what I know for certain is going to be a life-long relationship with my soulmate. I am cancer-free and healthy. My illness has let go of me, and I have let go of a lot of the pain that has come upon me throughout my treatment and recovery, my divorce, and the loss of our son in April. I still mourn Veo's death, particularly because this would have been the month he would have been born if he had not had that fatal birth defect. I sometimes still have those unanswerable questions: did my cancer treatment somehow cause that defect? Was it my fault? But a comforting thought came to me yesterday as I was standing on the balcony in Glendale, California with Anton: the name of our baby boy, Veo Liam, is an anagram for "I am love." Even though I am a self-professed word nerd, we did not name him with this significance in mind. When I told Anton my realization, we fell silent, smiled, and hugged each other. It felt to me that at that moment, Veo had come to us to bring the two of us even closer together.

As I sit here on our first morning in Maui, with Anton still sleeping, I am full of reflection about how I got here. And to me, it all comes down to the fact that there is nothing else like this moment.

Posted by Brandy Lotus Blossom at 9:26 AM

Anton is reading my latest blog entry. He's overcome with emotion. We're sitting here on the couch in our rental condo. A sweet breeze comes through the open doors of the balcony. This day feels so perfect.

He leans over and kisses me softly. Then he gets up and goes over to the TV. But he doesn't turn on the TV. He's reaching behind it and getting something. A tiny box. Oh my god sweet baby Jesus.

"Brandy, I love you more than anything. You are my life and my love. You are the one for me—the one I've been looking for all my life. I want to spend my life with you. Will you marry me?"

YES YES YES YES!

That's what I would say if I could stop crying. I hug him fiercely, never wanting to be apart from him ever again.

We go out to the balcony to take in the moment in the Hawaiian sunshine. We hug and kiss, and oh my god, I am not kidding—there are birds coming to perch on the edge of the balcony to watch us, I shit you not.

"Perfect timing, guys," Anton says to the birds. "I asked them to come."

"Oh, okay," I say, laughing. "Freakin' Prince Charming here." The little birds hop and turn their heads from side to side, watching us from three feet away. I feel like Cinderella. Truly.

This is paradise. This is heaven. This is all the places that little girls who dream of being princesses want to go to. This is everything, and I don't need anything else.

PART FOURTEEN

Moxie

Some weeks have passed since Anton and I got engaged. Our lives are calm and boring—for now. Our immigration lawyer did a wonderful job to clear up the earlier mess with Anton's dismissed charge. So we've resumed our lives in Vancouver, despite his U.S. citizenship status still up in the air. We expect him to be getting an interview soon. Chloe and Mylo have started a new school close to the basement suite we've been living in for nine months now. I've been worried about them making friends, but they've fit in so easily that their teachers didn't know that they're new to the school.

Charles told me that he and Charlotte are getting married soon. I often wonder how she's doing, stepping into the shoes I once wore. I try to keep bad thoughts at bay, like how I hope she's suffering with him as I'd had, hoping that he hasn't changed for the better. No, I really need to be non-judgmental. Their lives have nothing to do with mine. I need to wish them well. I need to put away the anger, the bitterness. It's toxic. I don't need toxicity in my life. Especially since I just found out that I'm pregnant again.

The third time in one year. The thought that I've become pregnant at the same time that Veo was supposed to have been born hasn't escaped me. The metaphysical part of me, enthralled by spirit talk, is loving this—our baby is coming back to us after all. From my quick calculations and consulting my Chinese/Vietnamese and Western astrology books, I'm stoked to find out that our baby will be a mixture of me and Anton. She will be a rabbit/cat like me, and Taurus like Anton. (I also consulted the Chinese gender prediction chart, and it ʋs we're having a girl.)

When I told Mom and Dad about the news, they were less than thrilled.

"Brandy, I don't think it's good idea to try having kids anymore," Dad said sternly. "You lost the last baby. Your body can't handle it."

"Dad, it's okay. The doctors will take good care of me," I said.

"I don't know. You're not gonna listen to a word I have to say about it anyway," he said, angry and defeated. "You wanna talk to your mother?"

Do I want to talk to my mother? Of course I do! "Sure," I said.

"Hey, what you do?" Mom asked.

"I'm fine, Mom. How are you?"

"Good. I bring tomatoes and cucumbers in from my garden. Oh, my, I no know what I do with all that. I give some to Mammy, Pappy, Linda. . ." she went on.

I interrupted her list of recipients of her bounty. "Mom, I'm pregnant again."

"What? What you say?"

"I'm pregnant. We're having a baby."

"What? You no better have baby! You too sick!"

"I'm not sick, Mom. Not anymore. It'll be okay."

"No, no be okay. Now I worry about you more. I pray at temple you fine, now you have baby again," she said. I could hear her making plans in her head about how to pray for me next time, what rituals she'd have to enact.

In addition to fearing for my health, they are also reminded, I imagine, of Matthew when they remember Veo.

They are afraid of going through that pain again. Later, after they became calmer and accepted the news, I told my dad to remember that they had me after Matthew. They tried again, and I want to try again too.

Our baby. Our little girl. I think. I can finally have my little Moxie that I dreamed about three years ago when I was in the thick of chemo and being told that I might not be able to have any more kids. Fuck that shit. We are going to have Moxie, and our family will be complete.

We're moving into the second trimester. Anton and I just had an ultrasound done, and we saw a perfectly round head, not like when we saw Veo, when it was clear by the flatness of his skull that he had anencephaly. We've put all our faith on this being right—that this baby is healthy and ready to accept us as her parents. We have to think that, otherwise, the fear becomes too great.

Still, last night before I fell asleep, I had a panic attack, feeling claustrophobic in my own body. I became so uncomfortable because the inside of me is too big for my shell. I'm crowded inside myself. There's not much room inside me, with the unforgiving, unbending mesh in my abdomen compressing both me and our growing baby. I can't imagine what it's going to be like when she doubles and triples in size.

When I was pregnant with Chloe and Mylo, I looked obviously pregnant at this stage of the game. With Moxie, no one can tell. Which is good because we haven't told Chloe and Mylo about the baby yet. They were so heartbroken over Veo. I saw the very depths of my children's pain, and it was excruciating. This time, we want to make sure everything is okay before telling them. Just in case.

This is going to be my first Christmas without the kids, and my first Christmas with Anton. Chloe and Mylo are going away with Charles and Charlotte for a second wedding ceremony for her family. The first wedding ceremony was in October, at a nearby resort with the family I used to be a part of. I shake my head at how much our lives have changed, and how quickly. One split-second decision leads to another, starting off an avalanche, creating detours.

It's February, and Anton is in Los Angeles, preparing for his U.S. citizenship test and interview and getting ready to put his condo on the market. I miss him. I want him here with me and the kids and the cats. I want him to be here when I wake up from a bad dream, so I can see that this story has a happy ending after all.

What I've been dreaming about constantly that's bugging the shit out of me is Charles and his new wife. Why is my subconscious obsessed with those two fools? I suppose my psyche had been deeply wounded by the betrayal, but I really don't want to think about them anymore. Unfortunately, almost every night I have these dreams that make me feel worthless, abandoned, and demeaned. It's like Mom's waiting for me in my dreams too, telling me, "I told you so."

Mom and Dad are still worried about the pregnancy, but they are getting excited again. Well, Dad is anyway. Mom feigns indifference on the rare occasions I get to talk to her on the phone. She's always unavailable because she's busy praying.

Mom has become lost to us, it seems. Dad's depressed because all she does is pray. She's given up on all of us and puts her energy into an investment for her afterlife. I hope it works out for her when she dies because otherwise it will be all for nothing. For me, it's too much to gamble on this present life.

A week after we told the kids about Moxie, Chloe asked, "Is the baby still alive?" She thinks about Veo and is worried that her baby sister will suffer the same fate. I told her that yes, the baby is alive.

Mylo wants to know if the baby can be his best friend. I told him yes.

They remind me of how I've made up stories about Matthew, and later, Hieu.

Earlier this evening, Chloe was drawing cranes. I was surprised that she actually knew what a crane was, but she probably learned about them in school. Seeing her drawing reminded me that cranes symbolize peace, longevity, and good luck in Vietnam. I read that Agent Orange wiped out the crane population that had existed there for hundreds of years. Eventually, they started reappearing and increasing in numbers. Curious. I thought of Matthew and Veo and wondered if they too had been casualties of Agent Orange. But like the cranes had proven, there's always a chance to come back and thrive.

Anton is back from Hell-A, thank god. He passed his citizenship test and interview, but because things rarely go the way we'd like them to, the immigration office somehow lost his file. They have to find it before they can grant him citizenship. Figures.

Moxie is going to be born in two months. While I look like I'm barely pregnant, I feel like I'm beyond pregnant. The pain is unreal. My family doctor prescribed me morphine and codeine, telling me that me being in pain is worse for the baby than the drugs. The baby might go through withdrawal, but it will be mild and manageable. Still, I try to not take the morphine.

Anton sits with me in bed. He is ready to be with me when I need him, which is completely different from how Charles had been. I remember wanting to die because the pain from the chemo was horrendous, and Charles would just work on his laptop in the kitchen or be at meetings while I writhed in bed. When I brought it up at couples therapy, only then would he make an effort to sit in bed with me. But Anton is here rubbing my back, telling me he'll do whatever it takes to help ease the pain. I curl into him and breathe. It's the three of us here in the bed. That brings me comfort.

Last night, I had a dream that Anton said he needed space and time, and he decided to go his own way for a while. Then I went into surgery in the maternity ward, and Dr. Lothlorien was trying to do the surgery with a power saw. She kept telling me to calm down, that it wouldn't hurt, but when the saw cut into me, I freaked out. I fainted on the table, and when I woke up, I called my parents to pick me up from the hospital. I woke up from the dream sweating and unable to breathe. I grabbed my inhaler and took three puffs. I popped two Ativan and turned on my side.

Moxie was moving a lot when I woke up. She lodged her foot into my right side and some organs. We were both trying to get comfortable, I guess.

Anton and I are getting married. We got engaged on Mammy's birthday, and now we are getting married on Dad's birthday. We are in North Vancouver, which is close to the hospital where my doctors and surgeons work, in case we have an emergency. Our closest friends are here—Jamie, Karin, Harley, Mark, and Sonja—as well as Chloe and Mylo and Karin's two daughters. I laugh to myself. Last time I got married, I was pregnant with Mylo! Of course, I was as big as a bus then. Now, I just feel as big as a bus stuffed into a goddamn Honda Civic hatchback.

Chloe helped me pick out my dress, a shiny form-fitting lavender cocktail dress. If you want a completely honest opinion when you're trying on clothes, take a child with you. Three fails before she approved of this one.

Anton helped Mylo find a suit that matched his. When he took a look at himself in the mirror, all suited up with tie included, my son declared, "I look good." I smiled at my boys.

The ceremony is short and sweet. Maureen, our marriage commissioner, showed up at the hotel where we're all staying, and we've assembled in a private VIP lounge that the kids decorated with flowers and paper centrepieces we got at the dollar store. I have Mom and Dad on Skype, and they're watching what Jamie's showing them on my iPhone. (I put the phone on mute so we don't have to listen to my mother's crazy commentary and confused questions, despite the protests of my friends, who totally want to listen to my mother's crazy commentary for the entertainment value.)

Anton, my prince charming, and Mylo, my little man, look so handsome. Chloe, my big girl, is pretty in her floral lavender dress, even if she is fidgeting like crazy. Moxie just turned, and, oh my god, that fucking hurt. I grit my teeth. I smile. This is my family.

Maureen says, "Brandy, would you like to say your vows?"

I look at Anton and begin. "Anton, you are my soulmate, my best friend, and I will be with you always, even when we become stardust and memories and stories our kids and grandkids share with each other and hold dear. What amazes me as we stand here is how even though we had two very different childhoods—me with my rural Pennsylvania upbringing, and you with your urban life in Manila—we had one striking similarity. Both of us were lonely children creating stories in our heads, but we didn't have anyone with whom we could share those stories and dreams. Yet those two lonely, imaginative children found each other in adulthood, came together from two oceans, and now have each other to make up and share stories with. The magic of storybooks is what we have now, in real life. I am honoured to be your wife and to have you be a father to Chloe, Mylo, and Moxie. I cherish this new life we all have together, and I can't wait for all the stories that we'll have to tell."

"That was beautiful," Maureen says. "Anton, would you like to share your vows?"

Anton takes a deep breath, and voice shaky, says, "The moment I first laid eyes on you, I knew I was going to have the ride of my life, a really great adventure. I didn't realize that I'd be on this adventure with you for the rest of my life. You asked me once why I wanted to be with you, that maybe we should end what we had with each other because you did not want to cause me any hardship or pain. I remember telling you that it wasn't your choice to make but mine. I choose you. I know in my heart that you'll always be my friend, my partner in life, my one true love. I give you my promise to stay by your side as your husband, to cherish you forever."

Our friends look at us, smile, and dab their eyes. Maureen pronounces us husband and wife. Everyone claps. Jamie hands me my iPhone, and I take it off mute.

"What? She get marry now? What they do? I no see nothing!" Mom shrieks from the other side. Everyone bursts out laughing. Anton and I squeeze into the iPhone frame so we can talk to Mom and Dad.

"Hey, Mom, we got married. That's what you were watching," I tell her. I can see Dad shaking his head beside her. Then he smiles at us.

"Congratulations," he says.

"Thanks, Dad."

"Oh, good they get marry," Mom says, coming to terms with what's going on.

"Hey, Lee, I'm your son-in-law now," Anton says, smiling.

"Yep. You better not mess up, or I'm coming for ya," Dad says kind of jokingly, kind of not.

"Don't worry. I'll take care of your little girl."

"Okay, Dad, well, we gotta go to eat now. I'll call you tomorrow. Bye, Mom! Love you!" I say loudly.

"What? Okay, you go get marry, okay! Bye!" Mom says.

"No, Mom, we already got married! Oh, never mind! Bye, Dad," I say.

I turn to Anton. "Welcome to my crazy family."

He says, "I wouldn't have it any other way."

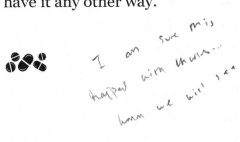

http://cancerfuckingsucks.blogspot.com
Freaking. Out.
Wednesday, April 13, 2011

I can't seem to escape April being my über-high stress month. Three years ago, on April 15th, I had my bilateral mastectomy and Tram-flap reconstruction. Two years ago, my husband at the time said he wanted a divorce. Last year, I gave birth to our son Veo, and he died because of all his birth defects. This year, Anton and I are having a baby! This, of course, is a monumentally joyous occasion, unlike the last three years, but I'm still losing my mind just a little.

With my mastectomy, I totally freaked out. I obsessed over my death for a few months before, working out and away all these morbid fantasies with an art therapist so I could calm my wild mind. I got depressed over the thought of my kids growing up without their mom, and all I could imagine was going under and never coming back again. But obviously, everything turned out fine, and not only did I come back, but I've been cancer-free for almost three years (as of Friday).

Now, I'm starting to do the freaking out thing again. I keep thinking about how at least with the mastectomy, the surgeons have done it so many times before and knew exactly what they were doing. With this C-section, they don't have an exact idea since it's never been done before. I try not to think about the scenario where they take out the baby, see the mesh and the damage, and say to themselves, "Now what?" or "That's worse than we thought." I think about how the worst could happen, and I'd be leaving my new husband with a new baby, and there would be three kids without a mom. I try not to think like that. I focus instead on the excitement of having a new baby—a baby who's a pioneer on the landscape of having a baby after breast cancer.

At night, when everyone's sleeping—that's the hardest time. I'm alone with my thoughts and my body full of pain. I look at Veo's tiny footprints on our shelf where I honour the people who have died—those who have made an impact but whom I have never really met, like my Vietnamese grandmother and Vietnamese half-brother.

I need to remember that with heartache and loss come motivation and inspiration to survive and to be grateful for what we have. I have a husband who brings me laughter and love every single day we are together. I have two kids who impress me with their imaginations and wonder, and who make me feel good about being a mom. I have a baby inside, fiercely kicking and living up to her name, Moxie. I like to think she's trying to tell me something along the lines of, "Don't worry, Mom. I'm a fighter, and you are too. And we'll all be together soon, safe and sound."
Posted by Brandy Lotus Blossom at 3:21 PM

The morning of the C-section, I made a plaster belly cast to commemorate my pregnancy with Moxie. This has been a tradition of mine—to make a belly cast for each pregnancy. I even made one for Veo. The difference between Moxie's cast and Chloe's is huge, even though they were made at the same gestational age, 37 weeks. Moxie's is much smaller and flatter. Yet I know that despite my small appearance, Moxie has to be about the same size that Chloe had been around this time, about seven pounds.

After I finished the belly cast and put it on newspaper to dry, we grabbed my small overnight bag, and we took a cab to St. Paul's Hospital in downtown Vancouver. We were scheduled for the C-section at 1:00 PM. Moxie was kicking the shit out of me. She wanted out now! I wanted her out too.

"You know, the next time we come back to our house, we're bringing a baby with us," I told Anton.

"Yeah," he said. "Fuck." He nervously laughed.

"You're going to be a great dad. You're already one to Chloe and Mylo."

"Yeah, but they already came formed, to me anyway. I didn't have to do anything. This one is brand-new. What if I fuck her up?"

"You're not going to fuck her up. She's going to have the best dad ever."

"And the best mom ever."

"She better appreciate it, or I'm taking her back," I said, leaning on his chest.

When we got to the hospital, we checked in, and I stripped down to nothing and donned the two loveliest blue hospital gowns I'd ever laid eyes on. We sat in the waiting room with the rest of the nearly naked people awaiting surgery. I felt like we were in a Monty Python satire for Dante's *Inferno*. I was expecting Death to come into the room dressed as a nurse, calling the next patient on the roster. I happened to be the next patient called, and the nurse looked like a nice, normal dude.

Anton waited outside the operating room while they prepped me and gave me a spinal anaesthesia, so I was completely numb from waist down. Before they administered the injection, the nurse told me to put my feet together and let my legs fall open to the sides. She said that when the spinal took effect, I'd feel as if my legs were still splayed even when they were actually straight because it was the last nerve sensation my brain registered before the nerves were blocked. She was right.

I started getting antsy, wondering when Anton was going to come in. Soon enough, he came in, all dressed in scrubs. He stood by my head and held my hand. We couldn't see over the curtain that separated us from the lower half of my body, where the doctors were doing their job. We thought they were just getting themselves prepped when all of a sudden, they showed us a baby over the curtain. There she was—our little Moxie!

We named her Moxie Olivéa Dao-Liên Worrall-Soriano. A big name for a little baby. "Olivéa" was a variation on Veo's and Anton's dad's names. I also gave her the name "Liên," which was given to me by my mom. It means "lotus blossom" in Vietnamese, and it's known as a symbol for purity rising from a sea of sorrow.

Moxie was red and beautiful and slimy and gorgeous, and when she screamed her first scream, we all applauded. Anton hovered around her in awe. She was fine. She was perfect. And I noticed that I could breathe! No more trying to swallow air as if I were drowning. The pressure in my body was gone. My body was mine and mine alone again. All this was mine.

The first few times I heard Moxie cry, my breasts tingled as they did with Chloe and Mylo. I felt like breastfeeding. I yearned for it. I had phantom boob syndrome. As much as I ached, no milk would come out. I had to let go of the hope that it might. Never mind. Moxie would be nourished by so much more.

In the weeks to come, Mom and Dad came out to meet their new granddaughter and drive me crazy, as I expected them to. There was a lovely shouting match in Van Dusen Botanical Garden, at which my mother disowned me for the umpteenth time. At least it was a sunny day. Like always, we kind of made up, called a truce, and they went home, their work done for now.

I love my parents, and even though they are insane, they are what I come from. I have to remember that. I remember that they met during a mind-boggling war, were affected by that war in so many ways, have experienced loss and heartache and trauma beyond imagination. I have to remember that a lot of the bad stuff they experienced, they passed onto me, psychologically, medically, and emotionally. I also got from them how to be strong, how to survive, how to live another day as if it very well might be my last. And I guess I learned from them what they have a hard time learning themselves: how to laugh. How to laugh at everything, because really, how great, how fucked up, how wonderful and how incredible is this life we get to live?

http://cancerfuckingsucks.blogspot.com
Monday, September 19, 2011
For my friends

This morning, I realized that I've begun to recognize the signs. There's the fight, the expression of it, the spirit. Then submission to treatment, whatever works—how ever one's body is ravaged and rebuilt—it doesn't matter, as long as there is still life. Then silence, with an occasional note to friends and family that s/he is still here with us, still fighting. More silence. Perhaps one week passes, or two, maybe a month. I'll check his or her Facebook page if there is one. I'll see comments from friends and family on the wall, words of encouragement, support, and prayer. But there will be nothing from my friend, who's been fighting the most awful of fights. Then all of a sudden, I'll get the email with the subject line telling the recipients to open the email when we have some quiet time, and we all know. Another one of us has passed.

It's not a club that you ever want to be in, but if you must, belonging to this club will be life-changing. Of the twenty of us cancer warriors who attended the retreat in 2009, four have passed away—one in five of my cohort in the last two years since the retreat.

Emilee, age 32. Ann-Marie, age 25. Caio, age 23. Earl, age 23.

When you are part of a group that spends some concentrated time together, you walk away with memories of the fun stuff that happened in that short time, like sitting around the camp fire telling funny stories, or the talent show where everyone made asses of themselves and have the pictures to prove it. You carry the memories of the bonding and confiding about your innermost thoughts and fears in a safe space. You don't think that the person sitting beside you during meditation or circle is going to die soon. You think that everyone's made it, everyone's here, and everyone's going to beat the odds and be here for a very long time.

Of course, that's not true. It hasn't been true in the two years since I attended the retreat. I have the good memories, and I cherish those deeply. But when I wake up to one of those emails, I have fear—who's next? Will it be me? Will it be someone I love? I have sadness because look, this is what is particularly sad about young adults getting cancer—they are young, they are just starting their lives. And now, when one of them dies, all that potential, all that spirit and drive—gone.

I have survivor's guilt, big-time. I am sitting here with my infant daughter, watching her play and kick and learn how to grab. She sees me sitting beside her, and she beams with joy and love. I tell her that her older brother and sister will be home from school later on, and we'll all play with her. I know that when my kids come home, we are going to look at craft books and make some felt toys. I told them at breakfast this morning that I'm going to teach them how to use my sewing machine by making cloth napkins. I get to have this life. But my friends who have passed, it's over for them. And their loved ones—their life partners and parents and siblings and children—they will never experience life with them again. They must face a new reality of how to live without. Thinking of that kind of loss brings me full-circle back to the fear I first experience when I see one of those emails in my inbox.

Most people my age aren't faced with their mortality, and they are blessed to not think about dying until an older person in their family passes, probably when it is "their time" to do so. This is one of the reasons I often compare cancer diagnosis and treatment to going off to war. You don't know how you will change, how you will come back, or even if you will come back. You don't know how many friends you will see fall. But you know that if you survive, you will never think of life in the same way again.

Posted by Brandy Lotus Blossom at 9:58 AM

I can't watch them. Vietnam War movies. Hundreds of them. I can't even scan their titles on the DVDs without my stomach churning. Even though Dad once said, "None of them movies is realistic," for me, they're too close to home.

But I have to learn. So I force myself to start learning. *Platoon. Full Metal Jacket. Deerhunter.* My hands sweat and shake. I pick *Hearts and Minds.*

The film menu pops up. A young boy stares back at me. I'm familiar with the soundtrack. I know the music from the brightly coloured vinyl collection stashed in a hexagonal cabinet by Mom's ancestral altar. I used to sit quietly by the open cabinet door, taking out each record, one by one, looking at the elaborate *ao dai* on women, with their faces painted with several layers of perfect makeup. The records themselves were beautiful, transparent with vivid greens, blues, reds, and yellows. American records were simply solidly black.

I'd hold up the records to the light of the living room window and against Mom's altar. I could see the red lights on the fake candles that were next to my grandmother's picture and little Buddha statues.

A long time ago, Mom played the music for me. The trills of these ladies' high-pitched songs were soundtracks to Mom's life from before. When I listened to this music, I never thought of war. I was a child—I hardly knew what war meant. I only knew that my mother came from a country where there had been a war, and it was because of that war that my mother and father met each other and got married. It was a fairytale.

Now I hear that song coming from this movie that is entirely about a war. The fairytale is long gone. What replaces that fairytale is me wondering what would happen if I visited Hieu's grave in Vietnam—if Sis and I visited his grave.

Hearts and Minds starts out showing children play and women working in rice fields while American soldiers walk around in a small village near Saigon. I look at those kids and wonder if they could have been my sister and Hieu. Those soldiers—that was my dad. Those women—my mom. I watch this movie, and the landscape looks familiar. I have seen it before, in my dreams.

When I go to Vietnam for real, I will see Hieu. I will find him, and it won't be too late.

Things are actually kinda fun right now, and for once it is because of my mom. In fact, I'm finding her very amusing at the moment. Mom and Dad arrived here a couple days ago to check in on me. I had a rough summer, medically speaking. When I was pregnant with Moxie, I developed a hernia. In addition to the hernia, the scar tissue from my irradiated breast had increased and hardened. So Dr. Lothlorien and her colleague opened me up to repair all that. Unfortunately, I had developed a nasty infection from the hernia repair, necessitating multiple trips to the emergency room and a four-day hospital stay during which I was not allowed to eat or drink anything. Finally, Dr. Lothlorien fixed me up, and I was able to heal once again. But Mom and Dad wanted to see for themselves that I really was okay and not just saying so over the phone. Plus, they wanted to be with us for Chloe's ninth birthday.

Mom and I are now taking a walk to the store, just the two of us. Dad all but begged me to take her with me when I said I had to go run errands. I knew he needed a break from the chaos, so I said okay. As we are walking, she's telling me how everything good in my life is because of her. Or more specifically, because she's prayed to Buddha. But there's a catch.

"Yeah, so you know, when I pray for you, 30 percent what I pray for make true. If you pray Buddha, you get other 70," Mom's telling me.

I laugh. "Okay. That's interesting. Where did you get these numbers, Mom?"

"I just know what make good. Like your daddy. For long time, you know, he ask for money. No get. But I pray. Now come true. He got money for retire."

I still appear sceptical, I guess, so she continues, "You know, good thing no happen right away. No. You hafta wait, keep pray." She puts her hands together and says, "Like this. Then you say like I tell you before, *'Nam mo di dai phat'* many many time. You do a lot."

"Hm, okay. Well, I don't have time for that."

"Yeah okay. You always say. That your life," she says, miffed.

"Thanks, though. That's nice that you're praying for me," I say, trying to sound appreciative.

"You know, when I kid, my family have no beligion. They no go temple or pray or nothing. But one day, I had dream of this monk near where I live. I see him everyday. Everyday, we cross street, see each other. Then one day, I dream of him, like he go up in sky. Next day, I see him on street, he put gas on his body, he on fire. I see him burn, like fire very big," she says, throwing her arms up in the air to indicate how big the inferno was. I hold my breath. I want to ask her what the air smelled like, with all that burning skin, but I don't dare interrupt her right now.

"I see that, and I think maybe I need believe Buddha. They say that monk, his heart never burn though. So temple take his heart, put in jar. Every time I go Vietnam, I go to that temple, see his heart, pray."

For a moment, I could see how witnessing a self-immolation might influence someone to turn to faith and religion. In that moment when all else is so bleak that even spiritual guides and teachers turn to a fiery death for all the world to see—something in you would have to snap, wouldn't it?

As we cross the street and pass McDonald's, Mom says quickly, as if in a trance, "Yeah, my family no like beligion, but after that I believe. Then next day I see a little Buddha in garbage. Someone throw him out like that." I know which Buddha statue she's talking about because I've heard this story before. I'd given her a new Buddha figurine, and she placed it beside her oldest one, chipped, paint fading. "You know, remember I tell you?" I nod my head. "I know I need take that one. I clean off, take home with me, then when I go America with your daddy, I bring too. He ask me why I bring that thing, but I tell him I hafta."

I slow my pace because she's having a hard time walking and talking at the same time. "I met your daddy, he no have beligion. I tell him to go get beligion like his sister have. So he read Bible, and I happy because better than no beligion. But he get hook on that, and I no want him to. I want him have my beligion."

I laugh. "What? Wait, let me get this straight. You wanted Dad to read the Bible so that he could eventually be Buddhist?"

"Yeah, that right! I want him be Buddha."

"Why? Does it even matter?" I ask incredulously.

"Yeah, you know, because you see, that god, that only a nine. My beligion is ten. That highest, best one."

There she goes with her random numbers again. "Okay, Mom, the Christian god is a nine, Buddha is ten. Mm, I don't get it."

"You no understand. But I say, thank god, at least Daddy have beligion. He just no like mine. That okay. They all say I crazy. That okay. They no understand. But I know my beligion ten, and I pray and pray for good for everyone. I no tell them I pray for them and that why good thing happen for them. No. But *I* know."

We arrive back home. "My feet pain so much," Mom says, taking off her shoes.

"How was the walk?" asks Anton, with Moxie in his lap. Dad is sitting on the couch, blitzed out of his mind. His eyes are little red slits. He gives me a smile. I don't see Chloe and Mylo. I guess they're in their bedroom, playing a game.

"It was awesome. I learned so much," I say.

Mom butts in, "I teach Brandy right, about beligion, you know."

I give Anton a look that says, please ignore this, please don't start an argument over religion with Mom. It's okay.

"I'll tell you later," I say to him.

Mom brings out four DVDs and says that she wants to be able to watch the movies on her "Thing-My." That's her way of saying "iPad." They are Buddhist DVDs, one of them being about a boy monk, who looks about Mylo's age.

"I think Anton can maybe put these on YouTube for you, and then you can watch them wherever you are, on the computer or on your iPad." I hand the DVDs to Anton. He gets right to it.

Mom stands behind him as he sets up the DVD to be converted. "You do this for me, you good, and you come back as king in next life!"

"I don't want to be a king!" Anton says. "I like my life now, as it is."

"Yeah, Mom, life is pretty good. Don't you think so?" I ask her.

"Yeah, yeah, it good," she says dismissively.

I look at Dad. He nods his head too. For a moment we are all in agreement. Then Anton turns his attention back to his laptop and gets straight to work on his next life. Dad goes back to watching his television program. Mom pops in her earbuds and pushes play on her Vietnamese Buddhist chants. Moxie weaves herself around my legs, trying to stand up and take a few steps. I can hear Chloe and Mylo screaming at the video game they are playing in their bedroom.

When Moxie plops back on the floor, I go into our bedroom and water the lucky bamboo sitting on top of the shelf that also serves as my altar. The shelf below the bamboo, that's where I keep the programs from my friends' memorial services. There, I also have my picture of Hieu, my journal with Ba ngoai's image on it, and Veo's ashes, footprints, and the clothes he wore when he was born. And for Matthew, I have a stone.

At the young adult cancer retreat, a bowl of stones was passed around, and each of us had to pick one, hold it in our hands, be with the stone as we meditated. My stone was smooth, whitish grey, with a small tinge of colour on its curve. My finger traced the colour, feeling its healing vibe, its creative pull, its attempt to become alive, and as I sat there meditating, my hands becoming warm, my thoughts turned to Matthew. So this became my Matthew stone, my rock, weathered to white-grey, with a vein of orange.

Acknowledgements

This is the part where I'm expected to get all serious, but if I'm going to be sincere and speak from the heart, this is how I'm gonna handle the flow.

Anton is my soulmate. You already know that if you've read the entire book. If you read the Acknowledgements first, then too bad. The spoiler is your fault, not mine. Who reads the back stuff first anyway? Yeah, don't do it again. If you haven't figured it out by now, Anton's a total stud and I daresay the first Filipino American hero/heartthrob in literature. This book definitely wouldn't exist if it were not for Anton. Same goes for my parents. I mean, wait, I don't think they're heartthrobs, but they are heroes. They've always been completely bonkers, and I love them for it.

My dad has always been one of my biggest heroes. He passed away on March 27, 2014 from metastatic lung cancer seventeen days after he was diagnosed. His doctor at the VA Medical Center believed that his cancer was due to his exposure to Agent Orange in Vietnam. Before he passed away, he wanted to read my book because he knew how important it was to me—and he was really curious about his character in the book. So while he was still able to focus, he read the first few chapters. He laughed, approved, and said, "Yup, I like it. Except for one thing. You plagiarized from Margaret Cho." And I replied, "No, Dad, I really am that funny. Thanks to you." Thanks, Dad. I love you, and you will always live and laugh in me.

Irene Suico Soriano—you're the shiznit. (Do people still say that? Well, I just did.) I always knew you'd be a sister to me, even before I knew how true that would be someday.

People who've read drafts of this monster: Vicki Cunningham, Mae Mamaril Choe, Stevii Paden, Karen Tsang, and maybe some other people!? Omg, so sorry if you read it and gave me feedback, and I don't remember who you are. Chemo brain! That's my excuse.

BFF Lisa Freaking Marie Cunningham. You are the best best bestest friend ever. This girl here—she read like every freaking draft and cried and laughed every single time. AND she designed the book cover while she was super-busy with her day job. I'm so glad that she and I were kicked off our respective lunch tables and became outcasts who sat together at the same table in the seventh grade. Our rockband dreams of Crinkleroot and the Rubber Squid never materialized, but whatever, that's okay. We're still rockstars in our minds.

Okay, now I'll get a bit more serious. When I got back to work on my MFA at UBC after I finished all that cancer crap, I was fortunate enough to have Deborah Campbell become my thesis advisor. She became a mentor and a friend, which is really awesome because she's a kick-ass journalist and writer. I'm serious. She will kick your ass if you need your ass kicked. And she'll do it with such poise and grace that not only will your ass be kicked, but your mind will also be blown. Andreas Schroeder gave me a bunch of Oprah "AHHHH!" moments as well during my two years at UBC. He was my second reader for my thesis, which would eventually become this book, and it was exhilarating when he used a bunch of expletives in a positively glowing way after he read my thesis.

My agent, Martha Magor Webb, championed this book from the very beginning, and she was instrumental in shaping it into what it is today. Kind, smart, and hardworking—what more could you ask for in an agent? She went above and beyond.

Wayson Choy. Early on, he encouraged me to keep going with my storytelling. I was star-struck with this dude, and then I was like, "Whoa, he's taking me out for coffee." And then he became my friend, and he still is my friend. And I'm still star-struck.

My cancer support peeps are the most incredible people on Planet Earth. The best. Janie, Danielle, and Liz at Callanish are so amazingly selfless and caring. Young Adult Cancer Canada gets the Awesome Organization Full of Awesome People Award. And Mikey and Bonnie Lang, the dynamic husband-and-wife team behind Survive & Thrive Expeditions, will climb mountains and jump off cliffs for the people they love.

Denise Drisdelle, Gerard Tan, Lisa Henczel, and Nancy Van Laeken literally have kept me alive. And I literally don't use "literally" liberally. I don't suggest you do either. But yeah, without me being alive, there wouldn't be this book. So I have them to thank for that—the keeping-me-alive thing.

Finally, back in 2012, I needed a kick in the butt to get this book done. I did a crowdfunding campaign whereby people could donate money to help me get my book finished. I gave myself a two-week deadline to finish the first draft. If I met the deadline, the money would be given to an incredible charitable organization by the name of Responsible Charity. If I failed to meet my deadline, the money would go to Rick Santorum's presidential campaign—and nobody wanted that to happen. I'm happy to report that good triumphed over evil. Here are the financial backers who believed in me (and who threatened me with bodily harm if I did not finish the draft in time): Tina Caravantes, Newton Hoang, Natalia McNamara, Kristina Wong, Julie Vo, Janis Calleja, Megan and Kerry Simpson, Jennifer Luce, and the aforementioned Queens of Bodaciousness, Mae Mamaril Choe, Lisa Cunningham, and Irene Suico Soriano.

There. My (self) acceptance speech—I mean, my acknowledgements—are done. Live, laugh, love. Repeat.

CPSIA information can be obtained at www.ICGtesting.com
Printed in the USA
LVOW04s0243260115

424343LV00026B/589/P